Paragraph

A Journal of Modern Literary Theory

Volume 30, Number 3, November 2007

Blanchot's Epoch

Edited by Leslie Hill and Michael Holland

Contents

Introduction LESLIE HILL AND MICHAEL HOLLAND	1
Maurice Blanchot, 1907–2003 JEAN-LUC NANCY	3
Responses and Interventions (1946–98) MAURICE BLANCHOT	5
The Time of his Life MICHAEL HOLLAND	46
R/M, 1953 CHRISTOPHE BIDENT	67
From the Star to the Disaster KEVIN HART	84
Blanchot in *The International Review* CHRISTOPHER FYNSK	104
A Green Blanchot: Impossible? TIMOTHY CLARK	121
'Not In Our Name': Blanchot, Politics, the Neuter LESLIE HILL	141
Notes on Contributors	160
Index: *Paragraph* 30 (2007)	162

Introduction

Leslie Hill and Michael Holland

The work of Maurice Blanchot (1907–2003) spans almost the whole of the twentieth century. As a writer of fiction, literary critic, thinker, and political commentator, Blanchot fulfilled and exhausted some of the century's most pressing challenges. The twentieth century, then, may be thought to have been Blanchot's epoch, upon which he imprinted his unmistakeable signature and which left its indelible imprint on his work.

Where does Blanchot leave the twentieth century, its thought, its literature, its engagement with the political? Blanchot himself was keenly aware that no epoch is ever properly contemporary with itself. The word epoch not only refers to a period in history, a delimited time or sequence of events, but also means a parenthesis, a pause, a moment where time is suspended. So if Blanchot speaks of his epoch from a place firmly embedded in the struggles and transformations of that epoch, he also writes from a place that exceeds the confines of that epoch, in which history in the received sense gives way to a time that is never present, always to come, yet at any point in time, always over.

In what ways, then, does Blanchot's writing ask to be read at the beginning of this new century, this new millennium? In this centenary year, as an increasing number of books, articles, conferences and doctoral dissertations are given over to consideration of his work, this special issue of *Paragraph* brings together contributors from France, Britain, and the United States, each of whom approaches a different aspect of Blanchot's incisive presence throughout the twentieth century, each of whom seeks to address the significance of Blanchot's writing for the times to come. We are particularly glad to publish for the first time in English Jean-Luc Nancy's centenary tribute to Blanchot, a text which undertakes the challenging task of measuring the extent of Blanchot's singular importance as both thinker and writer.

Contrary to what is sometimes claimed and more often silently assumed, Blanchot after 1945 remained profoundly engaged, often in unexpected ways, in his epoch. As testimony to this singular presence of Blanchot within his epoch, this issue brings together in English for the first time a selection of his responses and interventions between 1946 and 1998. As these texts make clear in diverse but always forceful ways, the solitude and anonymity which for Blanchot were the writer's inescapable lot were also the source of a particular form of openness and availability on his part to both public and private exchange, as either a respondent or a correspondent, and at times formed the basis for decisive involvement in contemporary political and social events.

Maurice Blanchot, 1907–2003[1]

JEAN-LUC NANCY

The Infinite Conversation:[2] with this title, belonging to one of his most imposing books, it might be possible to attempt to sum up emblematically the thinking of Maurice Blanchot: in truth, less a thinking than a stance or a gesture — that of a certain trust. Above all else, Blanchot trusts in the possibility of *conversation* [*entretien*]. What is maintained in the conversation (with another, with oneself, with the proper pursuit of the conversation) is the perpetually renewed relation between speech and the *infinity* of sense that constitutes its truth. *Writing* (literature) names this relation. It does not transcribe a testimony, it does not invent a fiction, it does not deliver a message: it traces the infinite journey of sense in so far as it absents itself. This self-absenting of sense is not negative, it is sense's chance and what is at stake in it as such. To 'write' means relentlessly to approach the limit of speech, that limit which speech alone touches and in touching it un-limits us (us speaking beings).

Blanchot was able to recognise in this the event of modernity: the evaporation of all transcendent other worlds and, by that token, of any secure division between 'literature' and experience or truth. He made it possible, within writing, to begin the task of giving a voice to that which of itself remains mute. To give a voice in this way is to 'keep watch over absent sense'.[3] This is an attentive, careful, and affectionate kind of vigilance whose concern is for that reserve of absence by which truth is given: the experience inside us of the infinite outside us.

This experience is possible and necessary once the sacred books with their hermeneutics of existence are no longer. Literature — or writing — begins with the closing of such books. But it does not form any profane theology. It rejects all theology just as it does all atheism: all installation of any single Sense. 'Absence' in this case is merely a movement: an absenting. It is the constant passing of all speech into the infinite. 'The prodigious absent, absent from me and from everything, absent also for me. . .' to which *Thomas the Obscure* refers is not a being nor an instance, but the continual slippage of me beyond me, by which there comes, even as it still lies in wait, the 'pure feeling of his existence'.

This existence is not life as immediate affection and self-perpetuation, nor is it its death. The 'dying' ['*mourir*'] of which Blanchot speaks — which is in no way to be confused with the cessation of life, and which is, quite on the contrary, the living, or 'living-on', or 'sur-viving' invoked by Derrida when he was at his closest to Blanchot[4] — forms the movement of the ceaseless approach to absenting as true sense, destroying in it all trace of nihilism.

Such is the movement that, being written, can 'give to nothing, in its form of nothing, the form of something'.

Translated by Leslie Hill

NOTES

1 Text written at the invitation of the Haut Comité des célébrations nationales of the French Ministry of Culture to mark the centenary of Maurice Blanchot's birth. (Translator's note.)
2 *L'Entretien infini* (Paris, Gallimard, 1969). *Entretien*, which also has overtones of care, support, and time taken, is commonly used to refer to a discussion, interview, or a relatively formal conversation. As such, however, it is less a turning together towards some external point (as the word *conversation* implies), than a holding (*tenir*) between (*entre*), an affirming of the distance or gap between terms that allows the relationship between them to be maintained without either term being fused with the other. (Translator's note.)
3 *The Writing of the Disaster*, translated by Ann Smock (Lincoln and London, University of Nebraska Press, 1986), 42. (Translator's note.)
4 See Jacques Derrida, 'Living On', translated by James Hulbert, in Harold Bloom et al., *Deconstruction and Criticism* (London, Routledge, 1979), 75–176. Derrida's essay is by way of a reading of Blanchot's story, *L'Arrêt de mort* (*Death Sentence*). (Translator's note.)

Responses and Interventions (1946–98)

Maurice Blanchot

1 *Days of Hope* by André Malraux.

'*L'Espoir* d'André Malraux', in *L'Espagne libre*, collection 'Actualité' (Paris, Calmann-Lévy, 1946), 106–11. Blanchot's contribution to the first and only issue of a review founded by Georges Bataille, which was to be edited jointly by him, Blanchot and Jean Prévost.

It is perhaps opportune to wonder why Malraux's novel about Spain is called 'Days of Hope'.[1] The novel, we may recall, ends with the victorious battle of Guadalajara. Manifestly however, hope here is not for the victory, sooner or later, of the revolutionary forces over Franco. If it is not unconcerned by that victory, if it calls for it even, and not as an impossible and profligate dream but as an event already assured by history, the book is in no way restricted to the outcome it foresees. The Republicans' failure did not make the title of Malraux's novel seem ridiculous. *Man's Estate*,[2] which is in many ways a gloomier book and which concludes with the tragic collapse of the Chinese revolution, is also a book on which hope has left its mark. It is through disaster and the terrible closing scenes of torture and death, and against a devastating background of desolation and misery, that hope is born. And though this hope bears the mark of the fate which crushes it, it is reborn and rises above it, and in the end it follows its own course, it is unchangeable, always threatened and always triumphant.

We may assume that, in Malraux's work, the theme of hope — like the other themes no doubt — almost always has a double meaning, one of which is political. There is no way in which revolution can be defeated. It suffers serious setbacks, and the mistakes of its leaders sometimes lead to catastrophes made all the harsher in that those who pay the price of them are the masses whom revolution is meant to liberate. But whatever the ups and downs of the movement, it cannot be brought to a halt. As it is linked to a whole, to the entire volume of history considered as a real totality, it never really comes to rest. It is in that sense first of all that revolution is permanent. And even leaving aside such purely theoretical considerations, and confining our attention to the simple, basic ideas of internationalism, which are necessarily familiar to Malraux's characters, it is clear why the defeat of the Shanghai uprising cannot be definitive. What does May do when, having lost the man she was close to, she sees the hope for liberation which was also her main grounds for hope disappear with him? She leaves for Moscow. 'Even now', she says, 'even though we are defeated politically and our hospitals are closed, underground forces are regrouping in every province'. And the men who are dead awaken in others the idea of living the way they lived: they help them become conscious of the meaning of their revolt. As *The Conquerors*[3] puts it: 'the coolies are in the process of discovering that they exist, simply that they exist'.

For Malraux, however, the political foundations of this hope are in no way messianic. If the reality of revolution does not depend exclusively on particular circumstances that will not recur again, or particular acts of will; if it is stronger than all errors, and more durable than what fortune brings, it is clear that its strength and its weakness are linked to factors which are affected by organised intervention, and in particular the tactics adopted by those who lead it. In that respect too, this hope is inherently political: good politics confirms it, bad politics renders it illusory. The fact that revolution is never defeated is a certainty which allows more or less the same sort of hope as that other saying: humanity cannot die. That is not enough to justify an optimistic outlook on the future, especially when the desired goal will not tolerate being put off indefinitely until tomorrow.

One of the subjects of *Days of Hope* is undoubtedly the political organisation of hope. Everyone knows those chapter-headings with such a powerful ring to them: 'The Lyrical Illusion', 'The Exercise of Apocalypse'. Any defensive impulse or revolutionary uprising has its origin in powerful collective sentiments such as hate, enthusiasm or fraternity. The people become aware that they no longer exist under the category of the material and social demands which unite them, but in a state of fundamental emotion relating to their existence as a community: they live their class consciousness, and live it in a way that is uplifting. That is Apocalypse. But the struggle cannot be content with the forces that enthusiasm provides. It is a matter of technique, of tactics and of method. It depends upon the power and the solidity of its leaders; it is above all a question of means. One of the dramatic features of Malraux's novels is that in them, we see impulse, courage, willing, in short every collective value raised to the highest degree, pitted against tanks, planes and the implacable reality of a highly experienced army. The outcome of such a struggle is in no doubt. Apocalypse must change and become organised, 'on pain of death'.

Hope now becomes a matter of organisation. Political action, particularly when its goal is the material transformation of society, can of course not take place haphazardly, in a confusion of random individual initiatives. It does not set itself unrealisable goals, it is a search for what is viable and possible. Particularly if it takes the form of a war, it can no longer give priority to anything except the demands of that war, and all that counts is the greatest possible effectiveness. Garcia expresses these imperatives in the clearest possible form: 'Action can only be thought of in terms of action. Political thinking is exclusively a matter of comparing one concrete thing with another concrete thing, one possibility with another possibility. Either our people or Franco — one organisation or another organisation — not an organisation versus a desire, a dream or an apocalypse'.

Up to that point, everything seems simple. It is clear that nowadays, a war can only be a technical one and that it is no longer possible to wage war while talking only about sentiments. Hope presupposes a political project, politics requires discipline and in the end, discipline expresses itself by means of an army, comparable to any other army ('There are no just armies', Garcia also says). All that remains therefore is to recognize the twists and turns which popular action must go through in order to endure and triumph: how militants become excellent officers, how some learn to give orders, others to obey, how each becomes aware that it is not enough to know how to fight, you also have to learn combat. The problem appears simply to be one of experience and apprenticeship. In reality, it turns out that the practical nature of this problem gives rise to an unresolvable conflict, and in Spain, this conflict acquires absolute and hence dramatic status. Indeed, it becomes clear that the organisation of hope puts hope itself in danger. For some, and in Spain that means for highly combative elements within the proletariat, hope has the paradoxical characteristic of not necessarily bearing any relation to the future: it is not a project but an affirmation; it does not relate to something to be done, but to a way of being. What it expresses is existence itself in its nobility, its fraternity and its total liberty, and not a transformation of the material conditions of that existence. 'If we are crushed, here and in Madrid', says an anarchist named 'the Negus', 'men will have lived with their hearts for one day. Do you see what I mean? In spite of the hatred. They're free. Something they've never been before. But I'm not talking about political freedom, see, I'm talking about something else!' And the same character also says: 'No "dialectics"; no bureaucrats instead of delegates; no army so as to have done with the army, no inequality so as to have done with inequality, no cutting deals with the bourgeoisie. Live the way life should be lived, right now, or die. If it doesn't work, beat it! There's no return ticket'.

This conflict is in certain respects unresolvable. On the surface, things eventually sort themselves out. Action dispels individual dreams. Solidarity obeys orders and disciplines itself, because after all it isn't solidarity for nothing, it wants to succeed, and that being the case, success also has its laws. Malraux's novel traces out impressively — so that the guiding presence of the novelist is never felt — through what series of combined actions, deliberate compromises and mutual sacrifices to a common cause the most varied and opposing groups in the revolutionary action succeed not only in reaching agreement, but in forming an efficient and coherent whole. The victory at Guadalajara which ends the book may well be a short-lived one; it nevertheless constitutes a fully-fledged outcome in so far as it is the victory of organised forces that have been effectively led, which is to say of one equally well-organised side over another. Hope has clearly become something achievable. But at what cost? The ideal expressed by the anarchist has been sacrificed. Those whose aim was to take part in the war without recourse to any other values except absolute ones, and who would, for example, only participate as freedom fighters because it was for freedom that they were fighting, are dead, or more than dead: disappointed. Here is what Malraux says of the Negus: 'For the last month, he has stopped believing in the Revolution. The Apocalypse is over'. It is questionable whether the word hope still means anything to him. And in general, since the aim was to organize the Apocalypse, failure lies in the fact that the Apocalypse has vanished, and rather than rendering the lyrical illusion durable, organization has dispelled it. In the closing pages of the novel, Garcia, whose attitude has always been that of a political realist, comes out with a most ominous thought: 'You'd think,' he remarks, 'that combat, Apocalypse, hope were like bait used by war to trap men'. And he adds: 'Now war has begun', just as he will say a little further on: 'the age of parties has begun'.

If the conflict on which hope is constructed is examined more closely, it can be seen to take very diverse forms. It is perhaps rather simplistic to see in it a conflict between facts and values, politics and morality. Because Communism is just as much a world of values as anarcho-syndicalism ('Dimitroff versus Durrutti', says the Communist Manuel, 'is one morality versus another, it is not a conspiracy versus a morality'); and furthermore, anarchists aren't crazy, with no experience and no political importance ('Let's not go round looking as if we think anarchists are a bunch of nutcases. Spanish syndicalism has been doing important work for years. Never compromising with anyone'). But the fact is that one side's aim is to transfer into politics what forms the basis of their existence — or what they feel does so: an unyielding demand, a command which brooks no delay, something absolute and — to use a convenient word — absurd. While the other side, on the contrary, assert very firmly the specific truth of political action, a truth linked not to the feeling of existing, but to a set of scientific laws, the observation of economic facts, the establishment of a given concrete situation, etc. Is it important to model politics on one's life, to live it with generosity and nobility, or again as something absolutely profound and impossible which will be the very symbol of liberty? In fact, replies Communism, that doesn't make much sense, if what is noble and generous is precisely to model your life on politics, and not just any politics, but the methodical working-out of the movement of history whereby the impossible is eliminated from the world, and liberty becomes the form of all social activity.

Perhaps what makes Malraux's novel such a rich one is the fact that in its main development — since if, in addition to the twists and turns of the struggle against Franco, this book contains a precise subject, it is the training, the months of apprenticeship undergone by Manuel, who is initially a Communist, then learns to be one — in its broad outline, the novel tends to be an endorsement of political realism, and yet at no moment does the opposing view of the world appear belittled or even less true than the one which it opposes. The fact is, it is not possible to be rid of a human undertaking on the grounds that it is contradictory. It can be contested from a particular point of view, that of political or military efficacy for example; it can be argued that it causes chaos, plays into the hands of the enemy or even that it is a misguided attempt at transferring onto revolution, in other words onto an action, a tragedy which can only totally be experienced outside of that action. That said, however, this view of the world remains, and the contradiction which is revealed in it is powerless against it. The anarchist is not just an individualist who meddles in revolutionary matters in pursuit of a private Apocalypse. His individualism is essentially fraternity. Rather than confining him within himself, it is devotion to others or vengeance aimed at others: in any case, be it hatred or friendship, it constantly presupposes relations between men. The freedom he calls for and wants to live at all costs (and precisely, without any thought for the cost), is thus not the solitary freedom of the unattached individual either; rather, it is total freedom lived with others, won for others, asserted and driven to its utmost in an intense burst of existence. In this way, he is necessarily driven to action, since what is at stake is not his own fate, but the freedom of other men with whom the only possible relations are not political, economic or material in nature, but human, which is to say: based on friendship. This action in the name of fraternity and liberty can only derive its meaning and its conditions from liberty and fraternity: like the values it upholds, it tends to be absolute. It is without limit. It is, whatever form it takes, either fraternity or death. 'The Negus', Garcia explains to a Communist party official, 'once said that his men are always ready for death. With the best of them, that's true. Note that I say: with *the best*. They are drunk on a fraternity they know can't last for ever. And they're ready to die after a few days of elation — or vengeance, as the case may be — when men will have lived according to their dreams. Note that he said to us: with their hearts... The fact is though that for them, that death justifies everything'.

Manuel is a Communist. At the beginning of the book, he is not a perfect Communist, but gradually the tasks he is given make him become aware of his responsibility. He learns to become a leader. He commands a regiment. He knows how to require discipline. He punishes severely, if necessary. And he participates victoriously both in the battle of Madrid and at Guadalajara. He thus accepts all of the duties that political and military action dictates. But what makes his story the most significant one in the book is the fact that he accepts them without ceasing to be aware of the sacrifices they impose, and perhaps also without ceasing to be faithful to an attitude which ought to make him reject them. He too wants to avoid any loss of fraternity. He too wants to remain human. He was obliged to condemn to death some deserters who had been led astray by spies, and he watched them crawl at his feet without being able to intervene in their favour. The conflict inside him is no less intense than the one going on outside between the different elements in the revolutionary struggle. 'Look', he says, 'I haven't taken a single step on the road to greater efficiency and better command that hasn't taken me further away from men. Each day, I'm a little less human'. And he adds this, which is quite serious: 'To be close to the party is worth nothing if it means being separated from those for whom the party works. Whatever the efforts of the party, perhaps that link only stays alive thanks to the efforts of each one of us...'. Nevertheless, these sentiments cannot undermine the need to act. He suffers from the conflict, but he puts up with it. The only original side to his attitude is that he does not reject such problems as superfluous or anachronistic or inopportune, but rather wears them down by learning from them how to develop. He has kept a strong sense of his own personal destiny: he wants to fulfil a certain idea of himself. The party, the war, the struggle, all that is essential, but the man who, in the party, through war and struggle, is in search of himself, of his own extreme, that too is essential.

The last page shows us Manuel trying to project ahead of him the life he will have later on. This life appears unknown to him, and it displays the terrifying potential of the unknown. 'Manuel heard for the first time the voice of what is more solemn than the blood of men, more disturbing than their presence on earth — the infinite possibility of their destiny.' Hence, the hope which appeared to us at first to be linked to the political implementation of a grand revolutionary design; which then, in the process of being implemented, took the form of a conflict; and then hovered between tension and reconciliation, between the divided hope of finding yourself again through action by sacrificing yourself and sacrificing action, and the mature, calm hope of sacrificing neither action nor oneself — that hope now reveals the horizon on which it must be contemplated if it is not to become a new prison. Is man's fate limitless? Perhaps this infinite possibility should not be understood as the promise that limits can be exceeded, obstacles denied and finally our finite condition shaken off. It is the power to choose one's destiny that is infinite: the possibilities for choice have their conditions, choice itself does not. Revolutionary action concentrates on the conditions of choice, and seeks to modify them by bringing into being, in the world, permanent values that exist once and for all. Ultimately, it tends to make choice unnecessary. But choice continues to be choice, even if it is useless, even if it is impossible. And hope always has the same name: liberty.

Translated by Michael Holland

NOTES

1 André Malraux, *L'Espoir* (Paris, Gallimard, 1937); *Days of Hope*, translated by Stuart Gilbert and Alastair Macdonald (Harmondsworth, Penguin, 1996).
2 André Malraux, *La Condition humaine* (Paris, Gallimard, 1933); *Man's Estate*, translated by Alastair Macdonald (Harmondsworth, Penguin, 1972).
3 André Malraux, *Les Conquérants* (Paris, Grasset, 1928); *The Conquerors*, translated by Stephen Becker (London, Journeyman, 1983).

Intellectuals Are Always Guilty

'Les Intellectuels sont toujours coupables', *Combat*, 26 July 1946, 2. Blanchot's reply to a survey of intellectual attitudes to responsibility carried out by the newspaper over the summer of 1946.

It is strange to ask if the writer is responsible: he is responsible before the laws he recognizes, before those he does not recognize, before others that he is alone in recognizing, and also before that absence of law which his work [*oeuvre*], where imposture necessarily predominates, deludes him into considering essential.

Translated by Michael Holland

Is Something Happening?

'Se passe-t-il quelque chose?', *L'Express*, 10 May 1957, 25. In this piece, Blanchot launched a new literary award, the *Prix de mai*.

The question of literary prizes is an annoying one. This relic of school speech-days, this habit of getting together, on the part of people without authority nor mandate, to assert that such and such a book, rather than some other, deserves glory, and even to confer glory upon it, this choice which represents nothing so much as the desire of the reading public not to have to choose and to be able to speak about books without ever having to read them, the plots and intrigues that arise as a result, the interests of publishers (here at least there is something solid), the restless movement of curiosity, contentment, and discontent, a mixture of anecdote and untested opinion, which is part and parcel of literary society, the irresistible need, whenever a new literary prize is set up, only to select books that are likely to be popular and thereby acquire an authority of which it is claimed that, once one possesses it, good use will be made of it, albeit that on every occasion what first comes to mind is self-promotion, as though the point is not to celebrate a book, but the prize itself—and alongside this the growing discredit into which all prizes have fallen, hand in hand with their success and with the erosion of their influence, and together with the bizarre confidence that one is always ready to have in oneself, the always recurring temptation to try to take advantage of this absurd situation in order to steer it back towards a more promising outcome: one could continue forever listing the consequences each one of us has to face as a result of the habit of literary prizes, a habit which is widespread in the world, but, in France, is already something of an obsession.

The writers associated with the Prix de mai have therefore few illusions and, as far as I can see, few pretentions. In no sense do they wish to confer success or fame on a neglected book which might deserve it. They will never claim they have selected the best novel of the year, they will not even claim they have selected a fine, well-written book by a hitherto unknown author. They do not think they are in a position to salute masterpieces, nor even to believe any exist, though they are full of consideration for successful works which are barely in need of their judgement and even less of their meagre approval.

What then is their intention? This is very precise. What they have in common is the shared thought that there is still something to be expected from the novel. This much is simple, naïve perhaps. But what is it that they expect? Certainly not more novels—there is no shortage of them already—but precisely books that are slightly different or slightly irregular, which are not yet novels, but give shape to new possibilities, or put a face on what does not yet exist.

Perhaps we are all making a mistake. But the fact that the novel has reached a limit, not only for literary technical reasons, but more serious ones too, this makes what goes under the name of the art of the novel entirely uncertain, makes it important therefore and worthy of attention.

We are all aware that here something is happening. For ten years already, and going back a little further, to Proust and to Sartre's *Nausea*, some works—not many, admittedly, but this small number, if one thinks about it, is already large—all testify to this.

On the meaning of these books, often very different from one another, and on the movement that is affirmed in them, different opinions are possible. The main thing, first of all, is to pay attention to the fact that they do exist, and not to submerge them in the welter of novels that are published all the time, nor to be content with granting them curiosity value, nor simply displaying the kind of futile, superficial interest that confuses matters by trying to keep track of everything.

The writers associated with the Prix de mai have no other priority than that of sharing their concern for these new possibilities. Each individual thinks a little differently from all the others, necessarily so; each one reads differently from the others, and at times reads other books. From the sharing of their certainties and uncertainties, agreements and disagreements, is it possible that a decision might result which, for them at least, clarifies matters? In the main, will their selection succeed in having some meaning and tracing a pathway for the new novel? Or else will it not simply indicate, when people meet up together as a panel of judges, the impossibility of resisting the pressure, the neglect, the pleasure of surprising people by reaching surprising verdicts? Last of all, will majority opinion not always prove too ponderous to be able to recognise the exception or, what is even more to the point, to give up trying to recognise it when it it is nowhere to be found: after all, why should the novel be able to reinvent itself every year?

To all these questions it would be misleading if I replied with excessive confidence. Perhaps our selections will be poor ones. Perhaps we will have nothing to select. I do not know. We shall see.

Translated by Leslie Hill

'At the very moment when the question you have sent me...'

'Au moment où la question que vous me communiquez...', *La Brèche*, 2 (May 1962), 6. Reply to a survey carried out by this Surrealist review under the title 'The World on its Head'. Respondents were asked to consider the following questions: 'The increasing possibilities for interplanetary travel seem to entail, in the eyes of most people, the possibility of applying to extra-terrestrial "worlds" the inevitably anthropocentric *system of references* which more or less functions here. Does this conclusion seem to you more or less to "go without saying"? In particular, does it allow speculation as to the mental reactions and intellectual judgements which would be those of future "cosmonauts"? Were such a journey (there and back) actually to take place, would it or would it not be likely to provoke an uncontrollable crisis of understanding, in which the very notion of culture would become derisory?'

At the very moment when the question you have sent me was entering your minds, it turns out that, in a quite different context,

I was writing a few lines which may perhaps serve as a reply. I repeat them, therefore, out of respect for the coincidence which has allowed me to go out to meet you, unwittingly and seemingly on a presentiment. Here they are: 'Man alone is absolutely foreign to me, he alone is the unknown, he alone the other, and in that he is a *presence*: such is man. (A presence which rests neither on being nor on having; a presence which could be described as immediate, were mediate and immediate not inappropriate words here.) Every time we shift the burden of strangeness onto a non-human entity, or when we transfer onto the universe the movement of the unknown, we rid ourselves of the burden of man. From time to time, we feebly imagine a fearful encounter, in a sky full of planets and stars, between ourselves and a being both different and superior, and we ask ourselves: what would happen? We have no trouble replying, for this being has been there for ever: it is man, he whose *presence* provides us with our sole measure of what strangeness is'.[1]

I shall add just two remarks: everything would need — will need! — to be known to me before my relation with the Unknown that is man, unimaginable man, can appear in its true authenticity and as the sole burden of the Outside. Then this, which is the beginning of an answer to your last question: it is not some planetary trek that will bring about a crisis of understanding, it is the crisis of 'understanding' which opens up, among other possibilities, that of travel.

Translated by Michael Holland

NOTES

1 The first two sentences of this fragment are identical to part of 'Tenir parole', *NNRF*, 110 (February 1962), 290–8 (291), which is collected in *L'Entretien infini* (Paris, Gallimard, 1969), 84–93 (85); 'Keeping to Words', *The Infinite Conversation*, translated by Susan Hanson (Minneapolis and London, University of Minnesota Press, 1993), 59–65 (59–60). The remainder is inserted into the text in its 1969 version (translation modified). (Translator's note.)

A Letter to Raymond Bellour

Lettre à Raymond Bellour, *Cahiers de l'Herne*, 8, Henri Michaux (1966), 88.

Dear Raymond Bellour,

As you know, I am happy to participate in the volume of tributes, and you know why that is: there are few writers I feel closer to than Michaux. But it goes without saying that my participation must not be taken as a sign that I approve of an enterprise like *L'Herne*,[1] or of the opinions of its editors. To be more precise, the fact that Céline was a writer in the grip of delirium does not make him uncongenial to me, but this delirium found expression in antisemitism; delirium here is no excuse; all anti-semitism is basically a delirium, and even if it is delirious, anti-semitism remains *the capital offence*.

NOTES

1 Numbers 3 and 5 of *Les Cahiers de l'Herne* (1963, 1965), both edited by Dominique de Roux, were devoted to Louis-Ferdinand Céline (1894–1961). (Translator's note.)

Three letters to Christian Limousin

Trois lettres à Christian Limousin, *Gramma*, 3/4 (1976), 5–7.

13 February 1975

Dear Christian Limousin,

I have given some thought to your project,[1] which Alain Coulange informed me of. I think it should be planned in a spirit of complete freedom in relation to me; your efforts must not appear to be guaranteed or certified or prepared in collusion with an author. That is what the inclusion of unpublished material would appear to indicate. We would be stuck in the usual rather snobbish, rather complacent genre. In any case, what difference is there between what is published and what is not? Everything, in a way, can revert to being unpublished, it all depends on how forcefully it is contemplated, on the extent to which knowledge is carried away or becomes unstuck, on what innovation can come from citation when it becomes incitation. On that subject, here is a small fragment which is, precisely, original and unpublished: 'If citation, in its disintegrating power, destroys in advance the text from which it is not only uprooted, but which it exalts until it is nothing but an uprooting, the fragment without text or context is radically uncitable'.[2] It is that impossibility that renders everything uncertain.

Kind regards.

Maurice Blanchot

4 May 1975

Dear Christian Limousin.

Absence is something I have no choice about rather than something I have decided. I would not wish it to surprise or disappoint anyone. Publishing is always more difficult. To publish using my name is impossible. Please do not see this as a mark of indifference, or worse, suspicion.

If your wish is that writings should testify to a presence, this idea comes to mind once again: why not extract from what is already published but perhaps remains unread, sections of text which you will then fragment, exposing them by means of this fragmentation to another light, and through the juxtaposition of these different fragments, compose a figure, an absence of figure which will, let us hope, be unexpected?

But this suggestion must leave you free. That freedom is what matters to me most.

With my best wishes.

Maurice Blanchot

28 July [1975]

Dear Christian Limousin,

Your letter reached me after a delay. I shall reply briefly. Even if I wrote them, I cannot recognize that I am *myself* the author of the texts you refer to. They are indeed very close to me, I consider myself responsible for them, but they were published anonymously and so belong to everyone. All I can say is that I was involved in the publication of *Comité*, but as one obscure figure among others, and as it were without a name. It is for you as readers to decide, and to say for example, in breach of the principle of anonymity: 'these texts could have been written by M.B., but it is we who take the decision as readers to attribute them to him'.

I would add that the 'Declaration on the Right to Insubordination' was written in a strictly collective manner, and as we said to the judge, we all wrote it. This collective responsibility must be preserved.

As for 'Essential Perversion', it is a text which is signed. There are no difficulties there.

Kind regards.

Maurice Blanchot
Translated by Michael Holland

NOTES

1. *Gramma* was edited by Alain Coulange, Christian Limousin and the late Patrick Rousseau. Two special numbers, 'Lire Blanchot, I' and 'Lire Blanchot, II' (3/4 and 5) appeared in 1976. As well as the collective 'Declaration on the Right to Insubordination in the Algerian War' (1960), and 'La Perversion essentielle' [Essential perversion] (*Le 14 juillet*, 3, 18 June 1959, 18–20), the first number included a selection of originally anonymous pieces taken from the sole number of *Comité*, the organ of the 'Comité d'action étudiants-écrivains' with which Blanchot was involved during the events of May 1968 (for all these texts see Maurice Blanchot, *Ecrits politiques* (Paris, Léo Scheer, 2003)). The letters were preceded by a brief statement justifying their publication on the grounds that 'they make clear Maurice Blanchot's relation to the current number, and to what it is possible today to write in the direction of his work'.
2. This fragment is included without variants in *L'Ecriture du désastre* (Paris, Gallimard, 1980), 64; *The Writing of the Disaster*, translated by Ann Smock (Lincoln and London, University of Nebraska Press, 1986), 37. (Translation modified.)

Two letters to Maurice Nadeau

'Deux lettres de Maurice Blanchot (avril 1977)', *La Quinzaine littéraire*, 741, 16–30 June 1998, 5.

17 April [1977]

Dear Maurice Nadeau,

I am still very poorly, and can only write you a few clumsy words, which concern the item about *Gramma* that has appeared in the *Quinzaine*.[1] It goes without saying that I am writing to you as a friend, and that I am certainly not asking for a rectification — on the contrary, a writer must be exposed to the four winds and allow to be said what it is felt should be said.

But to a friend, for a friend, it's a different matter. The authors of the article, out of ignorance, have misunderstood the situation. I shall mention just one or two facts. The first is symbolic: it is not just the disagreement, but the hostility verging on hatred which kept me well away from Brasillach, who represented what was the essence of fascism and anti-semitism. During the occupation, it was *Je Suis Partout*, whose editor Brasillach was (I am not accusing him personally, I can't be certain), which denounced me to the Gestapo, almost costing me my life. The second fact is that I always steered clear of the 'Action Française', because of everything that it stood for. The third fact is that

I took steps (with the help of Thierry Maulnier, a very different person then from what he has become) to close down *L'Insurgé*[2] the moment it allowed an article with a hint of anti-semitism in it to appear.

I shall not defend the texts that I saw fit to publish at that time. There can be no doubt that I have changed. As far as I can tell, I changed under the influence of writing (at the time, I was writing *Thomas the Obscure* and *Aminadab*),[3] and also through my knowledge of events (at the time I was working on a paper whose proprietor was a Jew,[4] and we were visited by many German Jewish émigrés). I have always considerd Nazism and anti-semitism to be pure evil, against which we were ill defended. When the collapse came, I was present at the sitting of the Assemblée Nationale when, in a base and servile gesture, it handed its powers over to Pétain (what Herriot himself said was abject).[5] At that moment, I realized that Europe and perhaps the world were surrendering to the worst. My decision was immediate. Come what may, our duty was to keep alive centres of resistance in France, intellectual ones if nothing else. That is why I refused to leave for London, though I was invited to do so. That was how I met Georges Bataille, and also became involved in clandestine activity which I have never spoken about, and shall not speak about here. But the feeling of horror never left me.

What therefore seems unjust to me about the commentary in the *Quinzaine* is the phrase 'provides a *fully informed* account of all the facts' [*en présente* en connaissance de cause toutes *les données*]. It is the opposite that should be said. But I repeat: *I am not asking for any rectification.* I am writing to a friend in order to confide to him what seems to me to be the truth, so that he may bear witness, should he see fit, when I am gone.

Yours, dear Maurice Nadeau, both faithfully and affectionately.

Maurice Blanchot

21 April 1977

Dear Maurice Nadeau,

In case my hastily written letter was not explicit enough, allow me to insist that you keep it silently to yourself, and not make it public in any form. It is addressed to friendship alone.

Affectionately,

Maurice Blanchot
Translated by Michael Holland

NOTES

1 *Gramma* 5 ('Lire Blanchot, II') (1975) contained a selection of Blanchot's pre-war political texts, with an accompanying article by Mike Holland and Patrick Rousseau, 'Topographie-parcours d'une (contre-) révolution' (8–41). Maurice Nadeau's review *La Quinzaine littéraire* (254, 16–30 April 1977, 5) published a brief anonymous comment on the number, one sentence of which prompted Blanchot's letter. (Translator's note.)
2 Blanchot, Maulnier and others founded *L'Insurgé* in 1937. It appeared weekly from January to October of that year. (Translator's note.)
3 *Thomas l'obscur* (Paris, Gallimard, 1941); *Aminadab* (Paris, Gallimard, 1942); *Aminadab*, translated by Jeff Fort (Lincoln and London, University of Nebraska Press, 2002). (Translator's note.)
4 From 1933 to 1940, Blanchot wrote for Paul Lévy's weekly *Aux Ecoutes*, eventually becoming its editor-in-chief, and very briefly, in 1940, its principal editor. (Translator's note.)
5 On 10 July 1940, the French Assemblée Nationale voted to transfer executive power entirely to Marshal Philippe Pétain, thus formally abolishing the Third Republic. The Radical Socialist Edouard Herriot abstained in the vote. (Translator's note.)

Refuse the established order

'Refuser l'ordre établi', *Le Nouvel Observateur*, special issue, May 1981. This was Blanchot's response to a questionnaire on committed literature. The magazine asked as follows:

1. Can a writer today still believe in the virtues of committed literature?
2. What in your opinion is the best this kind of literature has produced?
3. If necessary, would you be willing to put your pen in the service of a cause? If so, what?

How to respond to your questionnaire when the writer is always in search of a question that is not asked of him in advance and which obliges him, whenever he believes he can be content with a question, slowly and patiently to put himself into question, faced with the lost question which is no longer the same and makes him turn aside from himself? Committed literature: it is like travelling back thirty years, to the time when Sartre, by polemical defiance more than by theoretical conviction (a defiance addressed to the classical writer he believed himself still to be), gave the expression a resonance that made it incontrovertible, that is, put it beyond controversy. Speaking generally, almost all writers, I mean those on the left, were annoyed and opposed to it, whether one thinks of André Breton, Georges Bataille or Roland Barthes (if I may be allowed to put words in the mouths of the dead, however much they live on within us). To confine myself to the history with which I am myself familiar, Sartre himself was most surprised when one of the key decisions in the whole post-war era and which had the greatest impact on events (prior to May 68), by which I mean the 'Declaration of the 121' on the right to insubordination in the Algerian war, appeared to be the work of writers who might be described as uncommitted but who had no choice but to subscribe, not without risk, to the need to refuse, just as the government was tending towards a hateful form of oppression. With characteristic authority, he quickly made the cause his own, but I believe it prompted him (this is what he told me) to question the overly simple statements with which he wanted to shake up (and rightly so) literary good conscience.

What is there to add? There is perhaps such a thing as the power of culture, but it is ambiguous and always runs the risk, if it forfeits its ambiguity, of placing itself in the service of another power which enslaves it. Writing is, at the limit, that which cannot be effected, which is always therefore in search of non-power, refusing mastery, order, and most of all any established order, preferring silence to the language of absolute truth, thereby contesting everything and contesting without cease.

If I had to cite a text that might suggest what a literature of commitment would be like, I would look for it in distant times when literature did not exist. The earliest, and the one closest to us, is the Biblical story of Exodus. There we have everything: the journey out of slavery, the wandering in the wilderness, the waiting for writing, that is, the legislative writing of which one always falls short, so that the only tablets received are broken ones, which cannot in any case constitute a complete answer, except in their fracture, or fragmentation even; finally, the necessity of dying without completing the work, without reaching the Promised Land which as such is inaccessible, yet is always hoped for and is thus already given. If in the Passover ceremony it is traditional to reserve a cup of wine for whoever will precede and announce the messianic advent of the world of the just, one can understand why the vocation of the (committed) writer is not to see himself in the role of prophet or messiah, but to keep the place of whoever will come, to preserve that empty place against usurpers, and to maintain the immemorial memory that reminds us we too were all slaves once, and that, though we may be free, we remain and will remain slaves so long as others remain so, that there is therefore (to put it too simply) freedom only for the other and by the other: a task which is admittedly an infinite one, and risks condemning the writer to a didactic, pedagogic role and, by that token, excluding him from the demand he bears within himself and constrains him to have no place, no name, no role and no identity, that is, to be never yet a writer.

Translated by Leslie Hill

There is No Guardian Silence. A Letter to Alain Coulange

'Il n'y a pas de silence gardien', *Contre Toute Attente*, 4 (Autumn 1981), 1.

12 August 1981

Dear Alain Coulange,

Almost every day, I receive letters which ask me questions. If it is true that as a rule I keep silent [*garde le silence*], it is clear to me that silence does not keep me, but exposes me rather, and that is as it should be: there is no guardian silence.

I should like to reply to you as the writer you are: every book that we write is the last book; if others continue to come, that means it has not yet been written.

I shall say nothing about the literary situation, or the philosophical situation. What is going on there? Who could be fatuous enough or have the impropriety to answer? And is it really important?

For me, May 10th was a happy event,[1] even if happiness is not destined to last.

With all good wishes for your work.

Maurice Blanchot

Translated by Michael Holland

NOTES

1 In the second round of the French presidential elections on 10 May 1981, François Mitterrand was elected fourth President of the Fifth Republic. (Translator's note.)

Two letters to J.-B. Pontalis

'Lettres à J.-B. Pontalis', 19 November 1981 and 12 February 1982, in *Nouvelle Revue de psychanalyse*, 25, Spring 1982, special issue on the theme of 'Le trouble de penser' ('Trouble with thinking'), 355–6, to which Blanchot had been invited to contribute.

19 November 1981

Dear J.-B. Pontalis,

Please do not believe that my delay in replying to you was due to a refusal to 'think' about what you proposed. But the theme is so huge and so primordial that it presupposes at one and the same time both that it might be possible to say how things stand with trouble-free thinking even before engaging with it, and that any thinking that does engage with it is inevitably troubled in that very process.

Tocqueville's expression[1] takes us back to the idea that tyranny releases us from the trouble with thinking because it removes from us the concern with thinking (no thinking without trouble). Already for the Greeks, the age of tyranny, in the sense that they understood the word, was the golden age. But, alas (?), we have lost that simplicity and know that tyranny, whether it is good or bad, needs an ideology both to impose itself and to impose it, and decrees all kinds of prohibitions against thought or, on the contrary, claims that under its tutelage there can no longer be any trouble with thinking. (Whence the fact that any disobedience or transgression justifies psychiatric detention.) Yet, there was a time when the term 'ideologue' was well received and was not an insult, as it later became under the influence of Marx and precisely when it is used by anti-Marxists unaware of the implications of the term.

I wonder also whether the use of the word thinking and in particular of the verbal substantive, thinking [*le penser*], is not a legacy of Heidegger who on the one hand contrasts thinking and the experience of thought with philosophy and, on the other, leading us as he does so towards the word *eigen*, and towards the event that would bring to our being that which is 'most proper' to it (*Ereignis*), offers the equivalent of what in French is mistranslated as authenticity, which is perhaps also the equivalent of trouble-free thinking.

To which one will always be tempted to reply: why 'proper' rather than 'improper' or, as Derrida suggests, a-propriation? Is the project of a thinking without lack and without trouble not merely a project marked by a lack of thinking, in the same way that the special positing of a language without ambiguity ruins all language, including scientific language?

Here are just some of my thoughts, naively expressed.

Yours, if you are willing, most cordially,

M. B.

12 February 1982

Dear J.-B. Pontalis,

Forgive me for having missed the deadline and for not alerting you earlier and more clearly. The fact is, matters were not clear to me either. I perhaps still had the hope, as time went on, of overcoming the trouble that comes from the vague question of the 'trouble with thinking'. As though there might be a kind of pure thinking without trouble, without the need for some prior expression that had always already troubled it by clarifying or determining it. To acknowledge in thinking the part that belongs to terror is to forget that one cannot limit that part, which is a generous, but unstable and precarious omission, which makes it possible to formalise this fear, and see in it merely a phase in the conflict between the requirement for expressive plenitude and the lack or the loss that any already fashioned expression (tradition) has in store for it, though it is in fact already at work in the distancing or wrenching apart without which language would not exist at all. When Georges Bataille, shortly before his death, clearly put it that 'fear is what sustains me, fear of what is at stake in the totality of thinking', he felt the need to add, in a movement so firm that what was struggling to express itself in him was already effacing itself: 'fear... yes, fear, which alone is touched by the unlimited nature of thought... fear, yes, but fear of what? — The answer fills the universe, fills the universe and me —... obviously the fear of *Nothingness...*'

This fear is something we witnessed, fear — that cannot be shared — was given to us that we might share it, and that we might master it in the very rejection of all mastery. But it implies the discretion that culminates in silence, even as it turns us aside from it.

Let me add (and here matters, unfortunately, are more straightforward) that the 'historical' events — taking place in Poland — are sometimes so difficult to bear that one is prompted to interrupt everything, which is perhaps only an idle alibi to avoid thinking about the 'trouble with thinking'.

I know that you will understand me even in these inadequate justifications.

Most cordially, yours,

M. B.

Translated by Leslie Hill

NOTES

1 The title of the issue ('le trouble de penser') was drawn from a famous quotation, placed at the head of the volume, from Alexis de Tocqueville (*Democracy in America*, translated and edited by Harvey C. Mansfield and Delba Winthrop (Chicago, University of Chicago Press, 2000), 663), in which de Tocqueville remarks on the fact that even benign, despotic regimes find it impossible to cure their citizens of the 'trouble of thinking and the pain of living'. This context explains Blanchot's allusion, in the second letter, to contemporary events in Communist Poland, where in December 1981 martial law was imposed by General Jaruzelski, and the popular workers' movement Solidarity banned by the regime, with many of its leaders being imprisoned. (Translator's note.)

We work in the dark

'Nous travaillons dans les ténèbres', *Le Monde*, 22 July 1983, 9. This was Blanchot's response to a questionnaire addressed by the newspaper to several contemporary authors, in which it asked: 'What is it, in your opinion, that represents glory [*la gloire*] for a writer today?'

You will be the first to realise how disconcerting your questionnaire is, given how old-fashioned it appears. And then, like any questionnaire which does not correspond to an inner necessity, it sets a trap into which, whatever happens, one always ends up falling. Either one refuses to answer, and this silence is itself a haughty and negligent response. Or else one answers seriously, and seriousness, which is always somewhat laughable when the notions concerned are not serious ones, is merely the sign that one has already accepted the obligations of the notoriety which one claims otherwise to want to avoid. Or else, the answer is an ironical one, that is, a literary cliché, the surrealist or Freudian *Witz* by which one commits oneself in joking manner, therefore always more than one thinks.

It is my turn, then, to ask you a question. Why all these questions that you yourselves describe as 'absurd' (to which everyone therefore adds their own)? I notice merely that you no longer speak of immortality, given how excessive the claim may appear, though it endures down the ages. Poor Gide, unhappy Proust, unlucky Malraux, and even dear Sartre with those childlike dreams that never left him. Should we rid ourselves of such writers without trying to understand their concerns? Gide, in 1922, revealed that what he took to be the 'most secret reason' driving him to write was the need 'to put something beyond death's reach'. Something or just himself? That would once more be the traditional wish: to write in order not to die, to trust in the survival of the work. 'Genius', whether in classical or Romantic terms, is what braves death, and what is an artwork, if not death made futile or transfigured, or, in Proust's evasive words, death rendered 'less bitter', 'less inglorious', and 'perhaps less improbable'.

Ten years earlier — at roughly the same time, therefore — Kafka, confiding in a diary that was not intended for publication, says almost the exact opposite, in words that state the contrary only by virtue of the wilfully abrupt manner in which they are translated. Let me sum them up as follows. To write, yes, but why write? In order to be able to die (happy). But how will he manage to write, if he agrees to withdraw from the world and enter into mortal solitude? Whence this other formulation: to die, in order to be able to write. Rilke, again at much the same time, also says nothing different: the poet is poet only by dint of his familiarity with the non-familiar, and he is not simply mortal, he is the most mortal of all living beings, doubly, infinitely mortal; which is a way of reminding us that the writer draws his ability to write from a premature relationship with death — and with death's 'timid eyes', as Tolstoy once put it, in a metaphor Leskov found so devastating (as the Russian poet Vadim Kozovoï recently told me).[1]

To what extent are such dreams or (apparently contradictory) requirements still present to us? How far have they become irredeemably alien? There was a time when 'artists' claimed to rival great figures in history, heroes and military leaders — like them, they wanted to enter into popular memory; like them they would continue to have an active presence, beyond all time. We have assuredly become more modest: which is also to say more immodest. To us it seems derisory to content oneself with the glory of museums in order to persevere in the slothful timelessness of idols. And why renown or reputation anyway, this call to be a pure, inactive name? Writing is admittedly a kind of work, but one that is entirely lacking in reason, that demands nothing, cannot be justified, and cannot be crowned by any recompense. Writing: a singular exigency (call it bizarre) which is more ethical than aesthetic, since it responds to a prescription without obligation or sanction.

It is again to our old master Henry James that it would perhaps be right to appeal to express the strangeness of this requirement, in which neither glory, nor renown, nor popularity can have a part.

'We work in the dark — we do what we can — we give what we have. Our doubt is our passion and our passion is our task. The rest is the madness of art.'[2] (The madness of writing.)

Is this a confession? Arrogant or pathetic? This is for each to judge.

Translated by Leslie Hill

NOTES

1 The correspondence between Blanchot and Kozovoï is published in the journal *Po&sie*, 112–3 (2005), 3–121. (Translator's note.)
2 Henry James, 'The Middle Years', in *The Figure in the Carpet and Other Stories* (Harmondsworth, Penguin, 1986), 258. (Translator's note.)

Encounters

'Les Rencontres', *Le Nouvel Observateur*, 1045, numéro hors-série, November 1984, 84.

Can the *Nouvel Observateur* be twenty years old? Sometimes it seems to me younger, sometimes older, especially as I recall once working for *France-Observateur*, which takes me back to earlier periods. For that reason, I think I shall answer your question better by going back in time. For me, what mattered were the encounters, where chance is transformed into necessity. Encounters with people, encounters with places. This is what my biography amounts to. The encounter with Emmanuel Levinas (Strasbourg, 1925). Husserl, Heidegger, the discovery of Judaism. The encounters with Georges Bataille and René Char (1940). The call to irregularity. The limit-experience. Opposition to the Occupier and to the Vichy regime. A clandestine existence. Eze-Village (1947–1957). Ten years of solitary writing. The encounter with Robert Antelme and his friends (1958). The Algerian War, the Declaration of the 121, the attempt at founding an International Review.

With the same people and with everyone,
May 1968.
M. B.

                             Translated by Michael Holland

'The question is certainly a traditional one.'

'Pourquoi écrivez-vous? 400 écrivains répondent', *Libération*, numéro hors-série, March 1985, 64. Blanchot's reply to the question sent by *Libération* to 400 writers: 'Why do you write?'

The question is certainly a traditional one. My reply will be unoriginal. I shall borrow it from doctor Martin Luther when, in Worms,[1] he declared his refusal to recant. *'Here I stand, I cannot do otherwise. God help me.'* Which I shall modestly translate: *'In the space of writing, whether writing or not writing, here I stand, stooped, I cannot do otherwise and I expect no succour from benevolent powers'.*

                             Translated by Michael Holland

NOTES

1 Luther uttered these famous (and perhaps apocryphal) words at the Diet of Worms, before the Emperor Charles V, on 16 April 1521. (Translator's note.)

Peace, peace to the far and to the near

'Paix, paix au lointain et au proche', *De la Bible à nos jours: 3000 ans d'art*, exhibition catalogue, Grand Palais-Paris, Salon des indépendants, 6 June–28 July 1985, Société des artistes indépendants, Paris, 1985, 51–4.

In our tradition as it becomes exhausted while yet maintaining itself, it seems to me that there have always been two chosen peoples, two 'miracles' or two enigmas: two small populations, almost imperceptible on the map and yet rich with a message that has educated the centuries. One, however, has never suffered as a result of being this model nation, the exemplary representative of something that sustains our nostalgia. It has never been a subject of complaint against the Greeks that they passed down to us the logos, philosophy, beauty and a certain idea of democracy. The Greeks: a chosen people par excellence. But for the

Jews the same election or a higher and more ancient election is held to be an arrogant claim, a particularity that isolates, even if what was passed down or taught to the Jews is valid for all, and is the affirmation or promise of the Unique that is valid for all.

God is supposed only to have revealed himself to one people. Many thinkers, as well as some Christians, or even certain Jews, have always found this hard to digest. 'Why did the Creator not communicate to all the peoples of the Universe the secret of his Unity...?' But perhaps the idea of election has been misunderstood. 'Henceforth, if you hear my voice, and keep my covenant, you shall be a "segulah", dearer to me than all others, for all the earth is mine.' A 'segulah', it seems (and here I am repeating a knowledge that is not my own), is not so much the affirmation, the distinction of 'election', but 'a charm', a 'precious treasure' and perhaps a 'mediation' (but I find this last sense unconvincing). The point is to make it clear that the Jewish people was not chosen among others because from the outset it was the one most worthy of a lofty choice, but that this choice imposed a burden, a heavy additional burden, an excess of responsibility, and a blessing that could be suspended whenever the covenant was broken, because nothing is ever given once and for all (but nothing, either, is definitively withdrawn).

The fact remains that the Jewish people are a people apart, not because of ethnic or racial particularity, but because they were constituted as a people by the revelation on Mount Sinai — and up till then were a crowd, an amorphous mass, subject nonetheless to the ordeal and apprenticeship of the wilderness. Admittedly, the revelation was heard or received by one man alone, but the expectation of it was shared by all and consecrated them as a people, a people of priests (sacerdotal office was nevertheless reserved for a minority), a prophetic people: 'When I had not yet formed you in the womb, I knew you, and when you had not yet emerged from the womb, I had appointed (i.e., separated, sacrificed) you; a prophet to the nations I made you'. Election is not a privilege. If the revelation of the Thora chooses itself a people to act as its bearer, it was not in order to give them the impression that, as a result of this choice, they were somehow better, but to make known that their privilege consisted in not being privileged: 'The absolute rule for your generations: both yourself and all strangers will be equal before the Eternal.' This unique revelation was also a revelation of the unique. Never were the Greeks, these bearers of the logos, aware that there should be equality of speech and of law with the Barbarians. The situation is little short of astonishing.

The Hebrews were singled out from amongst all the nations (which is what Egypt represents) in order to acknowledge, in this withdrawal or this setting aside, the opening to all and to all the nations, and before the Eternal the equality of all (but not the abstract, repetitive equality which excludes responsibility and fraternity). It is as though what was revealed to the Jews was that they were other in order to be released from the Same, and in order to become responsive to alterity in the extraordinary concern for the other. For at the very moment when the Eternal, by an ambiguous election, sets the Jewish people apart with a view to their singular vocation, and proclaims, in a manner that seems untimely, that 'all the earth is mine', he renews the demand for universality from which Jewish singularity must not allow itself to be deflected, but to which it opens itself — in order to keep it open: an infinite task.

Do we need to be reminded (yes, I do, no doubt) that such was from the very beginning the task of Abraham? Leaving Ur — this great closed civilisation — in order to respond to the call, he departed, without knowing where he was going (his only knowledge was Chaldean), through the wilderness, through this ordeal of the unknown with the uncertain promise of the future, going towards…, towards himself, towards the overcoming of himself, towards the other name, Abraham, that would be given to him in order to signify his vocation as someone whose task was to guide others and whose own being lay on the threshold ('Now the Eternal appeared to him in the plains of Mamre and he was sitting at the entrance of the tent when the day was hot').

Guide, passage, crossing: this is at once the definition of the Hebrew and his vocation, but also the double manner in which the particular is in relation without relation with infinitely distant infinity: that which it is not appropriate to represent even metaphorically. This is a relation of voice or speech, a speaking that does not mediate in the way of the logos and does not abolish distance, but which cannot be heard other than by the absolute interval of separation, infinitely maintained. At the same time, God is not only the God of philosophers, withdrawn and preserved by his absence, for he accepts he must particularize himself in some way in order to allow himself to be addressed as the God of Abraham, Isaac, and Jacob (as Pascal was still aware). He does not historicize himself, admittedly, but passes and crosses through history, teaching Israel that Israel is not removed from history, and that it is Israel's task to appear in history in order to judge it and pass through history by way of its very separation.

The universal vocation of a people set apart and chosen so that this very particularity may have the value of a prophecy is not something likely to pass without conflict, or at least without a dialogue, in which Jewish thought, which is so welcoming (though it is often accused of the opposite), now not only welcomes Greek philosophy, giving it a meaning that will perpetuate it beyond itself, now maintains itself through all the complexities of history as a Tradition having both a universality and a requirement of specificity and which today can enlighten us — at the very moment when, finding in both a kind of oppression and a lure or a myth, we are suspicious of the one and the other (reason as idol and as myth: such arguably is the suspicion that founds modernity, including the threat it represents to itself today).

All the terms with which one may be content in order to evoke or invoke this double finality of Judaism: immanence, transcendence, eternity, history, universality, particularity, eternal Zion, and temporal Zion, are important because, in their very threadbare quality, what stands out is the need for a renewal that will exceed and upset all established discourse. It is not enough to challenge philosophy, but to awaken in it a question or a meaning it has perhaps not been able to sustain, even in spite of the labours of so many exceptional thinkers. How, for instance, to think the closeness of the Eternal in the Bible, what is sometimes called his fellowship, without ruining what is no less essential: the absolute distance, the withdrawal from all presence, the voice of absence that resounds in the distance of historical understanding? How can the Infinite, which is not pure and simple transcendence or definitively superlative supereminence, but a 'growing surplus of Infinity', be exposed to the constraint of finitude without breaching finitude itself, with a dangerously fusional experience that will exclude or dissolve the holy value of separation? An extraordinary thinker (I mean this in the literal sense, without laudatory connotations) will be necessary, in this time of ours, to reacquaint us with the fact that the meaning of the beyond, of transcendence, may be gathered up in an *ethics* which would not simply be some forgotten or neglected discipline, but one that imposes upon us a philosophical reversal, an upheaval affecting all our theoretical and practical assumptions (even if these are not scorned, but returned to their proper place). In this way, the absolute distance of God will not be signified as a movement in sensuousness (as religious experience), but '*turns into my responsibility*' which thus becomes infinite, so to speak, by making itself into an always insufficient obligation towards the other. It is not that God's alterity may find a substitute or an analogue in the alterity of the other to whom, released or expelled from myself, I am called upon to respond with limitless responsibility. Other, admittedly, 'but otherwise other, other with an alterity prior to the otherness of the other', transcendence to the point of absence and excluded from Being, making possible its denial or disappearance.

It may perhaps be permitted to evoke here — clumsily — Moses' strange demands, first of all asking the Eternal to tell him about his 'goodness', at once his actions and our obligations (that is, the decisions of God in the government of the world, since through them there is indirect knowledge of God). The wish is granted. Such questions can therefore be asked. But when Moses, going further in order to extend his understanding of the divine, presents the irrepressible request, in every respect a dangerous one: 'Show me, now, your glory!', he has to contend with the eternal refusal: 'you will see my back but my face shall not be seen'. And if God with infinite precaution agrees to let himself be seen from the rear — that is, as having always already passed by, that is, as a trace which guarantees no presence, it is not in order to attenuate the prohibition, it is rather to privilege invisibility and forestall the perils of direct knowledge of the divine. Judaism, by the gift of the written and oral Thora, in which a unique intrigue with the Most High is inscribed, is the testimony, always worth repeating, which warns against the temptations of Presence and the futile brilliance of Manifestation.

Messianic *impatience* is perhaps the danger of dangers. Ethics is bound to a doctrine of patience within urgency itself, for the questioning of the other does not allow time, and demands of me a response that is beyond me, subtracts me from myself and, in this subtraction, opens me up to what is greater than me and greater than any me.[1]

The demand of justice for always greater justice: in me, outside of me and in justice itself, thus also in the knowledge and exercise of justice. All of which presupposes what may be called the tragic imbroglio of *the other* and others; whence the intervention of the social and the political, under guarantee of the law, in the service of all that is far (first of all) and of all that is near — whence perhaps the repetition of the word peace, that this last word may be enriched by this echoing of itself in an incomparable repetition.

The long road of justice is a hard one. Like the journeying of Abraham, who departed alone, travelling towards all — from particularity to universality — under threat from the night and with all the hopes of the day.

P.S. — In this text, while naming no commentator by name, I am nevertheless indebted to many. And, to one, I am indebted for almost everything, both in my life and in my thinking.

Translated by Leslie Hill

NOTES

1 One should not however conclude — it would be another sign of impatience — that concern for the other may be taken as a fruitful way of responding to the concerns of the divine (charity will *not* be rewarded in heaven), nor that ethics may be thought to take the place of the theological. If philosophy is still conserved in what transcends it, its challenge is to raise the logos to the point where the logos breaks and, in that breaking, to seek a another field than that of an increase in power, and another coherence than that of the system, and a transcending of the universal that cannot be led astray or appeased by any kind of totality.

A Letter to Blandine Jeanson

Lettre à Blandine Jeanson, in *Photographes en quête d'auteurs* (Paris, Agence VU, 1986), 49. The volume contains photographs of numerous contemporary French writers. In the end, the authors substituted for a photograph of Blanchot a photograph of his letter.

6 February 1986

Dear Blandine Jeanson,

Please do not be offended by my negative reply. I have always tried, more or less justifiably, to *appear* as little as possible, not so as to privilege my books, but to avoid the presence of an author with a claim to an existence if his own.

Naturally, this is an entirely personal requirement, which has no validity for anyone else (perhaps).

I therefore wish Jean Gattegno's project — and yours — the success that you hope for.

Maurice Blanchot
Translated by Michael Holland

Do not forget!

'N'oubliez pas!', *La Quinzaine littéraire*, 459, 16–31 March 1986, 11–12. Published on the occasion of the twentieth anniversary of the magazine's foundation by Maurice Nadeau, who was also responsible for its immediate predecessor, *Les Lettres nouvelles*.

My association with *La Quinzaine littéraire* is fitful, insufficient, and almost non-existent as far as writing goes, but assiduous as far as reading is concerned.

Paradoxically, *La Quinzaine*[1] has lasted longer than it was entitled to expect and will no doubt endure, even if for each one of us the future gets ever shorter, to the point of making time in its chronology futile.

Time, time — is something of which we have no need.

As it is hard for me, as I look back, to distinguish between *Les Lettres nouvelles* and *La Quinzaine*, I will mention some of the events that shook these publications, as they shake me still today, because they were greater than their signification.

1) The Declaration of the 121, published by *Les Lettres nouvelles* (as it was by *Les Temps modernes*), for a brief period caused both publications to be suspended, while also showing the explosive capacity and power of disclosure of what censorship tends to erase.[2] Recently commented upon by Dionys Mascolo and by Marguerite Duras,[3] the Declaration retains its singular potency. I will add nothing further, except that Maurice Nadeau was in the first rank of those involved.

2) May 68. I see nothing more important, politically and perhaps philosophically, in the course of the last twenty years. Here again, *Les Lettres nouvelles* (for June–July 1969) helps us not to forget, for it was in that issue that a series of texts elaborated *collectively* a year earlier by what was poorly named the Students-Writers Action Committee were published. I will recall that these texts are not attributed to any author and, on the contrary, tend in their very mode of writing to appeal to the demand for anonymity, the loss of name, the refusal of individuality, as though in this whole period the experience of a community, which was not exemplary, but without example, blazed the trail for what Jean-Luc Nancy did not so much name as point to under the heading of 'inoperative community'.[4]

May 68. Let me also reproduce, barely modified, another anonymous text from the Committee, which sought to describe some of the features of this movement which was neither individual nor collective, but brought closer the other's distance in his or her proximity, making each of us a companion to whoever or whatever did not accompany us: 'Revolution... destroying all without there being anything destructive in this, destroying, rather than the past, the very *present* in which revolution was taking place, and not seeking to provide a future, extremely indifferent to any possible future (its success or failure), as if the time it sought to open up was already beyond these standard determinations.'

3) I will now say something quite different, and yet which was experienced or noticed in this very same movement. If the famous slogan 'We are all German Jews' has remained in historical memory, it has veiled the irreconcilable differences between those who, in the courtyard of the Sorbonne, defended the Palestinians (because they seemed to be the weakest), and others who bore witness on behalf of Judaism, bore witness on behalf of Israel representing vulnerability itself.

But did they bear witness? Did they have the strength to bear witness, or rather did the strength of bearing witness not destroy (or simply impair) the truth of the weakness whose side they (including myself) tried to take (even when taking sides meant abolishing the very thing on whose behalf they desired to take sides)?

If, during all these years which the time of La Quinzaine allows us to evoke — years beyond duration — I may be allowed to quote, amongst so many memorable books, one book that is not a book at all, but a film, Claude Lanzmann's *Shoah* (the word means 'annihilation', but is also the given name of what cannot be annihilated), it is because it bears witness to the ultimate event that could not occur except in the absence of all witnesses, by the destruction of all witnesses, and the radical prevention of all testimony. This is what the genocide of the Jews was: not only the annihilation of all Jews, but the annihilation of that annihilation itself. Nobody was meant to know, neither those carrying out the orders, nor those giving them, nor the supreme instigator, nor finally the victims who should have disappeared in the ignorance and in the absence of their own disappearance. The 'secrecy' demanded and maintained everywhere was the secrecy of what exceeds and destroys all revelation by a human language — a destruction of the trace that is language — this 'without trace' or erasure of the human face.

Assuredly, one can cite more banal reasons. People were not meant to find out, destiny was not meant to be alarmed, it was necessary, by mediocre means, to improvise horror, and render the impossible

possible. Everything occurred so to speak under God's blind gaze. I have no doubts that Hitler himself, and those working for Hitler, did everything they could to elude this gaze.

'An SS man immediately told us:
"Top secret!"
"Top secret!"
"Sign this."'[5]

In *Shoah*, Claude Lanzmann also records these words of Richard Glazar: 'It was almost normal. Just as it was normal that for everyone upon whom the gates of Treblinka closed there was death, had to be death, *because no one was supposed, ever, to be left to bear witness.*'[6]

Perhaps today Treblinka is no more (is this true?), but there are still the gates that will close upon us, unless, while not breaking the silence, we do not transmit the intransmissible, to the furthest limits of the universe and beyond, where, as Celan reminds us, 'nobody bears witness for the witness'.

P.S. The wish of all those in the camps (Auschwitz, Belbec, Sobibor, Treblinka), the last wishes: Know what happened, do not forget, and at the same time never will you know. Whence my title: 'Do not forget'. Do not forget the very thing that will make you lose all memory.

Translated by Leslie Hill

NOTES

1 The magazine's title, literally translated, means: 'The Literary Fortnight', whence Blanchot's opening remarks on this question of time. (Translator's note.)

2 On the 'Declaration on the Right of Insubordination in the War in Algeria', of which Blanchot, alongside Dionys Mascolo and Jean Schuster, was one of the main architects and signatories, see 'The Right to Insubordination', the only interview ever given by Blanchot, translated by Michael Holland, *The Blanchot Reader*, edited by Michael Holland (Oxford, Blackwell, 1995), 196–9. The text of the Declaration, when it was published in *Les Lettres nouvelles* and in *Les Temps modernes*, prompted the seizure of both journals by the authorities, with the result that almost all that was known of the Declaration was its title, which was largely of Blanchot's devising. (Translator's note.)

3 See Dionys Mascolo, *A la recherche d'un communisme de pensée* (Paris, Fourbis, 1993), 439–46; and Marguerite Duras, *Le Monde extérieur* (Paris, P. O. L., 1993), 78–80. (Translator's note.)

4 See Jean-Luc Nancy, *The Inoperative Community*, edited by Peter Conner (Minneapolis, University of Minnesota Press, 1991). (Translator's note.)
5 Claude Lanzmann, *Shoah*, translated by A. Whitelaw and W. Byron (New York, Da Capo, 1985), 63; translation modified. (Translator's note.)
6 Claude Lanzmann, *Shoah*, 41; translation modified. (Translator's note.)

Our Responsibility

'Notre responsabilité', in Jacques Derrida et al., *Pour Nelson Mandela* (Paris, Gallimard, 1986), 213–7.

How can we speak, or write, in an appropriate fashion about the segregation of Blacks and Whites? Thus it is that what was experienced when Nazism excluded from life and the right to life an entire portion of humanity, persists beyond the disaster which seemed to render such a wretched doctrine impossible or unformulable.

And the fact is, *apartheid* acquired its legal form at precisely the moment when the colonial nations were collapsing, as they recognized that they did not have the privilege of embodying the diversity of the human spirit. For the Boers, on the contrary, everything happened as if they had a responsibility to arrest progress and verify Hegel's ill-considered statement: 'Africa has no history'.[1] If we wished to find excuses for them, we could say that they themselves have not changed, and that they have retained and even consolidated the prejudices of the former colonisers (those of the sixteenth and seventeenth centuries, a time when Montaigne was discovering that there are cultures which are different yet equal).

At first, these adventurers hoping to settle in some unknown lands had force on their side, as well as a culture based on exclusion, and a limited form of religion which is moreover a persecuted one. The centuries passed. The archaic prescriptions remained. They simply protected themselves by means of fierce codes, which were at the same time contradictory. It was more or less implicitly understood that everyone (coloured people and Whites) had their own culture, which could only develop through a reciprocal separation. This hypocritical decision yielded almost immediately to the terror of sheer numbers and the need to use 'inferiors' for menial tasks. Whites and Blacks lived side by side, and their coexistence was indispensable, while remaining dangerous. In many cases, the Blacks had to be present (in order to work), but not present (having no right to a purely personal or idle presence).

In that way, *apartheid* gave rise to legislation which was almost more intolerable than slavery. Blacks are indispensable, but they expose Whites to dangerous contamination. Accordingly, it is a serious crime for a Black to become a cultured individual on the Western model. If such a misfortune occurs, it destroys the balance of society, and may lead to Communism or its equivalent. Hence the sentence imposed on Nelson Mandela. He is too well-educated and too able to remain free. Communism, community and democracy are driven out. In the end, laws are insufficient, because they preserve certain guarantees. They must therefore be suspended. There is a state of emergency, all freedom of information is banned, the nation turns in on itself, and eventually cuts itself off from the rest of the world, except for trade: business remains the ultimate truth.

I do not recall these painful facts only so that they should not fade from memory, but so that their memory should make us more conscious of our responsibility. This barbarism, this suffering, the countless assassinations are all something we are party to, in so far as we greet them with a degree of indifference, and our days and nights are not disturbed by them. It is very striking that the man who unfortunately leads the government of this country[2] should deride what he calls our concern for good conscience — his own is clearly not affected by what is happening over there, in another world. Similarly, the inertia of the European Community disqualifies that portion of what is ideal and civilised which it claims to represent. Let us therefore be aware that we too are responsible and guilty, if we do not give voice to a call, a denunciation, a cry and again a cry.

And may we be worthy to repeat the words which Breyten Breytenbach addressed to Winnie Mandela:

> *Our heart is with you*
> *Africa will be free.*[3]

Translated by Michael Holland

NOTES

1 G.W.F. Hegel, *The Philosophy of History* (New York, Dover, 1956), 99. (Translator's note.)
2 The Prime Minister of France at the time was Jacques Chirac. (Translator's note.)
3 Breyten Breytenbach, 'Lettre à Winnie Mandela', preface to Nelson Mandela, *L'Apartheid* (Paris, Minuit, 1985); 'A Letter to Winnie Mandela. May 1985. Paris', in *End Papers* (London, Faber & Faber, 1986), 213–5.

'What is closest to me...'

'Maurice Blanchot: "Ce qui m'est le plus proche..."', *Globe*, 30 (July–August 1988), 56. Blanchot's response arrived too late to be included in the special issue which *Globe* devoted to the fortieth anniversary of the founding of the state of Israel. It was therefore published in a subsequent number, under the heading: 'For the first time, the great writer makes a public statement about Israel'.

Come what may, I am with Israel. I am with Israel when Israel is suffering. I am with Israel when Israel suffers for causing suffering. I can say nothing more. Of course, I have my political preferences. I am for Peres. I believe Begin was wrong, very wrong, to encourage colonisation. But I do not feel that I have the right to appear to preach, when that which is at stake is what is closest to me.

Translated by Michael Holland

Writing Devoted to Silence

'L'écriture consacrée au silence', *Instants*, 1 (1989), 239–41, special issue on the francophone poet Edmond Jabès (b. Cairo 1912, d. Paris 1991).

In homage to Edmond Jabès

Should we forget? Should we remember? Remember what? Remember something for which we have no name — the Shoah, the Holocaust, the Extermination, the Genocide. Some time ago, a correspondent of mine, replying amidst many questions to a number of fragments in *The Writing of the Disaster* and to a text which appeared in *L'Arche*,[1] told me this: that Benny Lévy (Sartre's associate and friend during his last years) thinks too much fidelity to the testimony of the Horror makes us liable to nihilism. He invokes God's admonishments: 'Inscribe this as a memorial in the book... that I will surely obliterate the remembrance of Amalek from beneath the heavens'. Then, in Deuteronomy, in what is perhaps merely a softer reworking of Exodus: 'You shall remember what Amalek did to you on the way, when you went out of Egypt... Amalek who did not tremble before God'. (This absence of trembling is tantamount to supreme arrogance, as though he wanted to put himself on the same plane as the Most High.) The story ends: 'You shall obliterate the remembrance of Amalek from beneath the heavens. You shall not forget!'.[2]

The two exhortations are similar yet different. In Exodus, 'God' it is (the unnamable name) who asserts: 'I will surely obliterate the remembrance of Amalek from beneath the heavens'. What is said in Deuteronomy, on the other hand, is this: that 'You (i.e., yourself) shall obliterate the remembrance of Amalek from beneath the heavens.' From one to the other, the change is remarkable. But in both cases, if what is prescribed is the need to obliterate, then so too is that of remembering: 'Inscribe this as a memorial in the book' (Exodus). In Deuteronomy: 'You shall remember what Amalek did to you' — and finally: 'You shall not forget!'

Do Forgetting and Remembering go hand in hand? You may only release yourself from remembering if you keep it in forgetting. Beyond remembering, there is still Memory. Forgetting does not obliterate the impossibility of forgetting. Everything perhaps begins with forgetting, but forgetting ruins the beginning, making one remember that forgetting only refers to the forgetting that torments us by not granting us the absence that is irresponsibility.

Let me borrow from Emmanuel Levinas (what have I not borrowed from him?) this scruple of Ben Yoma, who said to our sages: 'Will the remembrance of the exodus from Egypt still be obligatory in the Days of the Messiah?' (to which the answer is yes, even if the memory is not the same).[3] And the words of Isaiah: 'Remember former things no more, nor consider the things of old.' Are we thus released, unburdened, from what we suffered? Quite the contrary, for what Isaiah announces is the war of wars, of Gog and Magog; he enjoins us not to lament the past, for the worst is still to come and even the past is still to come (I simplify inordinately).

The Shoah: let me copy out yet again what was written at Birkenau and which escapes memory just as it does thought by way of a warning from which no thoughts and no memories are released: 'Know what happened. Do not forget. But never will you know.' Claude Lanzmann tells us: 'Do not ask *why* it happened. Here, there is no why.' If one asks oneself the question of the horror, the question how it might be possible for it to be explained, and the question of how this possibility too might be possible, then it becomes clouded (lost) in so far as something is preserved: the question itself. Neither memory nor forgetting, to which the task of transmission falls, 'because the act of transmission alone is what counts and because no intelligibility pre-exists transmission' (which is itself always uncertain, left for others, without transmission ever releasing them but on the contrary burdening them all the more). 'No why, but neither any answer to the refusal of the why.'

Nothing then to be said about remembering, about the past (which does not pass), nothing about the *trace*, nothing about the piercing point. The onus on each one of us is to remain (or go under) in the face of the event: event beyond answers, beyond questions. That is the covenant.

Jabès: 'The desert has no book.'
Jabès: 'There is no innocent memory.'
Jabès: 'Here, the end of speaking, of the book, of chance.'

Translated by Leslie Hill

NOTES

1 See Maurice Blanchot, *The Writing of the Disaster*, translated by Ann Smock (Lincoln and London, University of Nebraska Press, 1986). Blanchot is also referring to '"N'oubliez pas"', a letter to Salomon Malka, *L'Arche*, May 1988, 68–71; 'Do Not Forget', translated by Michael Holland, *The Blanchot Reader*, edited by Michael Holland (Oxford, Blackwell, 1995), 244–49. (Translator's note.)

2 Why does Amalek have the reputation of being the very embodiment of Evil, when there have been so many other persecutors of Israel? Let us not forget what Levinas and David Banon teach us. Amalek was no insignificant figure, but son or grandson to Esau, and nephew to Jacob. An extraordinary blood-line. Except that Amalek's mother, who was of royal descent, but had no crown, was a foreigner who had the profound desire to convert to Judaism. But her desire was not granted: the patriarchs who were unable to discern her vocation and saw in it the banal wish to find a husband, rejected her. Having been banished in this way, she could have gone back, with the resentment of all those who are spurned, to reign among her own people. But she humbly undertook to become a concubine and a servant to Eliphaz, son of Esau, concluding that it was 'better to be a maid servant to this nation than to be a princess to any other nation'. The reject, however, was Amalek, who embodied the bitter memory of his mother's repudiation. What followed was the misfortune of endless resentment, which was the cause of enduring and yet unjustified evil. Here, Amalek's cruelty may be seen in the fact that he attacked the Hebrews, hardly had they journeyed out of Egypt (and even before they had managed to do so), and while they were still a confused, unorganised, and vulnerable mass, ready for peace, not war.

3 Emmanuel Levinas, *In The Time of the Nations*, translated by Michael B. Smith (London, Athlone Press, 1994), 76. (Translator's note.)

'Yes, silence is necessary for writing...'

'Oui, le silence est nécessaire à l'écriture...', *Globe*, 44 (February 1990), 72. Blanchot's contribution to a dossier on 'Great Silent Figures' [*les Grands Silencieux*].

Yes, silence is necessary for writing. Why? Contrary to Wittgenstein (at least as he is superficially understood), I would say that it is precisely in what cannot be said that writing discovers its resource and its necessity. This also means that the author, considered as an 'I', must seek as far as possible to disregard himself. There is no reason for him to survive, and if he lives, in principle no one knows it, and perhaps he doesn't either.

I have been close to Emmanuel Levinas for what will soon be 65 years. He is the only friend to whom I say 'tu'. I owe him a great deal, not to say everything. It is an undeserved blessing.

Translated by Michael Holland

'I think it is better for a writer...'

'Je crois qu'il convient mieux à un écrivain...', *La Règle du jeu*, 3 (January 1991), 221–2. Blanchot's response to a 'New Enquiry into the National Question'. The only question among those sent to him which Blanchot answers is number 2: 'According to you, is there such a thing as a "good" and a "bad" nationalism?'

I think it is better for a writer to try and ask new questions, rather than answer questions that have already been formulated.

However, to the questionnaire you present me with I shall reply unequivocally:

There is no such thing as good nationalism. Nationalism always tends to assimilate [*intégrer*] everything, all values, that is how it ends up being fundamentalist [*intégriste*], that is to say, the sole value.

The international exigency: permit me to refer you to the revue *Lignes*, number 11, which contains the dossier of *The International Review* (1960–1964), in which the concerns which were ours, as French writers, Italian writers, German writers and English writers are set out. The failure of our project did not prove it was a utopia. What does not succeed remains necessary. That still remains our concern.

Translated by Michael Holland

'Allow me to reply briefly...'

'Laissez-moi vous répondre brièvement...', La Règle du jeu, 6 (January 1992), 181. Blanchot's response to an enquiry into 'Posthumous Existence', whose pretext was the so-called 'Barthes affair': a controversy surrounding Barthes's literary legacy. Blanchot does not reply directly to any of the questions sent to him.

Allow me to reply briefly: literature is the sort of power that takes account of nothing. But when is there literature?
Closest regards.

Translated by Michael Holland

'The Inquisition destroyed the Catholic religion...'

'L'Inquisition a détruit la religion Catholique...', La Règle du jeu, 10 (May 1993), 206.

The Inquisition destroyed the Catholic religion at the same time as Giordano Bruno was killed.
  To condemn someone to death for a book destroys the religion of Islam.
  What remains is the Bible, what remains is Judaism considered as respect for the other by means of writing itself.
  To write is, through passivity, to place oneself already beyond death — a death which fleetingly establishes a search for the Other, a relation without relation to others [autrui].
  I invite Rushdie[1] to my house (in the South). I invite the descendant or the successor of Khomeini to my house. I shall be between the two of you, and the Koran also.
  It will decide,
  Come.

Translated by Michael Holland

NOTES

1 On 14 February 1989, Ayatollah Khomeini, the religious leader of Iran, proclaimed a *fatwa* against Salman Rushdie, the author of *The Satanic Verses* (1988), denouncing the book as 'blasphemous against Islam' and calling for its author to be killed. (Translator's note.)

'The intolerable repression by the police...'

'L'intolérable répression policière...', Message de Maurice Blanchot en faveur du poète Faraj Bayrakdar, *La Quinzaine littéraire*, 726, 1–15, November 1997, 30.

The intolerable repression by the police seeks to prevent a name from being uttered, and to deny the right of speech to the Syrian poet Faraj Bayrakdar,[1] who has been in prison for his opinions since 1987, so that we should not be able to hear him. But his cry of suffering reaches us and touches us. In his voice there echoes the call of every political prisoner. May the chain of solidarity which has formed in support of this unknown friend go on growing, so that a legitimate demand may be satisfied: his immediate liberation.

Translated by Michael Holland

NOTES

1 The Syrian poet and journalist Faraj Bayrakdar was arrested in March 1998 by Syrian Military Intelligence, on suspicion of being a member of the Communist party. After seven years of detention without trial, during which he was tortured, he was sentenced to fifteen years imprisonment in October 1993. A campaign for his release by the Comité international contre la répression (Cicr) began in France in 1993. A press conference calling for his liberation was held on 27 September 1997 at the Maison des Ecrivains in Paris. A collection of his poems, *Ni vivant, ni mort* [*Neither Alive Nor Dead*] (Paris, Al Dante) appeared in 1998. He was released on an amnesty in November 2000. (Translator's note.)

Writing, Between Life and Death

'L'écriture, entre la vie et la mort', *Rémanences*, 8 (April 1998), 28. Blanchot's contribution to the journal's appeal to the President of the Republic for Claude Lucas to be released from prison. It is probably Blanchot's last published piece.

Claude Lucas's novel *Suerte*[1] begins with the words: '*In those days, wasn't I already dead?*' That is a sentence worth lingering over, for if we wish to reduce literature to the movement which makes all of its ambiguities accessible, it is to be found there, at the heart of the thing itself: literature, like common speech, begins with the end which alone makes understanding possible.

In order to speak, we must see death, see it behind us. When we speak, we rest against a tomb, and this emptiness of the tomb is what constitutes the truth of language, but at the same time, emptiness is a reality and death becomes being. There is being, there is a logical and inexpressible truth, and there is a world, because we can destroy things and suspend existence.

Claude Lucas's novel clears a way for itself in this in-between, in this truth which says that there is being because there is nothingness. Death is the possibility of man, it is his *chance*, and thanks to death there remains for us a future in which the world reaches completion; death is the greatest hope for mankind, its only hope of being human.

That is why existence is its only real torment; existence frightens Lucas's hero as it does other members of society, not because of the death which could put an end to it, but because it *excludes* death, because beneath death, it is still there, a presence at the heart of absence, the inexorable light against which each day dawns and closes.

But it is to Claude Lucas that we wish to speak now.

Translated by Michael Holland

NOTES

1 Claude Lucas, *Suerte* (Paris, Plon, collection 'Terre Humaine', 1996). The novel won Lucas the Prix France-Culture for 1996.

Claude Lucas committed a hold-up in 1987. He was arrested in Spain and spent six years in prison there. He was extradited to France in 1994 and tried in 1996. The six years spent in Spanish gaols could not be taken into account under French law, and he was sentenced to a further twelve years in prison. Yvan Mécif, the editor of the literary review *Rémanences*, launched an appeal in Lucas's favour, which attracted widespread support among writers and intellectuals. He was released from prison in 2000. (Translator's note.)

The Time of his Life

MICHAEL HOLLAND

Abstract:
Throughout his life, contemporaries of Blanchot either sought to relegate his writing to the past, or else espoused it uncritically in a gesture akin to what Jean-Luc Nancy once called *syncope*. Blanchot thus divided his epoch in a way that was less a polarization than a struggle for the present in which thought takes place. Consequently, readers today in search of what makes Blanchot continue to be a contemporary find that the time of his writing is shrouded in a curiously unstable quantity of oblivion. This article argues that Blanchot's refusal of biography brings about an inaugural disruption of the temporality of rational thought. From the outset, the 'I am' of reflection is accompanied in his writing by an 'I am dead' which is narrative in nature. Jacques Derrida's work is taken to exemplify the espousal of Blanchot by his contemporaries. Despite the acuity of Derrida's analyses of the fractured present of rational discourse, however, the article seeks to demonstrate that the priority of narrative in Blanchot's thought gives rise to a temporality for which philosophy can never find the measure.

Keywords: Blanchot, Nancy, Derrida, time, death, biography, narrative

— 'Mais c'est ma vie que vous voulez. Il faudrait que je n'aie plus rien à vivre pour n'avoir plus rien à dire.' — 'Pas exactement votre vie; c'est au contraire votre vie que je réserve.' — 'Alors, vous voulez plus que ma vie.'[1]

Centenaries turn writers into figures from the past. In so doing, they serve as a reminder that a writer is no longer a contemporary. But does that matter? Isn't the time in which thought and writing take place impervious to the accidents of chronology? Hasn't the writer as living subject long since been marginalized, thanks to the developments we call theory?

The convenient response to these questions, which seems to render them rhetorical, is that by turning writers into figures from the past centenaries celebrate the time-defying power of writing and thought, the timeless present with which they surround the cascade of finite 'Nows' in which an individual life seeks endlessly to be contemporary with itself. To forget that a writer is no longer a contemporary is thus, paradoxically, to confine his writing to the here and now of the reader. To be reminded that he is dead is to rediscover that relation between each 'Now' and an absolute present, without whose stabilizing transcendence conscious life would disintegrate into a scattering of oblivious episodes. Yet as their recent invention attests, centenaries became important at precisely the time when the relations between 'Now' and the present as an absolute were suddenly[2] beginning to change. They can therefore be seen as one of the ways in which modernity has resisted the changes in relation to time which it also set in motion. Consequently, if marking a writer's centenary today provides a simple way of reaffirming the timelessness of thought, it must also foreground the question of how the writer lived that timelessness 'Now'.

*

Now that he belongs *in* the past, a feature of Blanchot's career as a writer stands out: from almost as soon as his name became known, there was a persistent attempt, on the part of significant contemporaries, to deny him contemporary status and relegate both him and his writing *to* the past. In his review of Blanchot's second novel, *Aminadab* (1942), Jean-Paul Sartre managed to slip in the reminder that 'M. Blanchot was once, I believe, a disciple of Charles Maurras'.[3] The previous year, *Je suis partout* denounced his first novel *Thomas l'obscur* (1941) for being as 'Jewish' as his pre-war politics had been.[4] For *JSP* as for JPS, despite their differing viewpoints, it would seem that Blanchot belonged to the class of what one collaborationist writer, Ramon Fernandez, called 'the conspiracy of survivors and hangers-on from the old world',[5] who sought to prevent France from entering either the new world which Germany was creating, or the one that Germany's defeat would usher in.

In the 1950s, a decade when France behaved as if it seemingly had no past, Blanchot was denied contemporary status less through an association with the past than by virtue of what was seen as a retreat into either abstraction, as Gaëtan Picon argued,[6] or an unwittingly theological nostalgia in Georges Mounin's analysis.[7] Repeatedly in this decade, Blanchot's work was characterized by its remoteness from its time, and this proved to be a reputation that even his return to political activity after 1958 failed to alter. During the events of May 1968, *Tel Quel* denounced the politics of Blanchot and his associates as a throw-back to 1789, rendering them irrelevant to a revolution carried out in the spirit of 1917.[8] A few years later, the documentation of his between-the-wars political writings in the journal *Gramma*[9] linked him to a past with which the French were just beginning to come to terms. In 1983, Jeffrey Mehlman published a denunciation of the complicity of French writers with anti-Semitism, in which Blanchot was grouped with pre-war figures such as Gide, Bernanos and Giraudoux.[10] Finally in the 1990s and beyond came a campaign by those involved with the journal *Ligne de Risque* to brand Blanchot as a nihilist, a denier of the future and an agent of death.[11]

Such a persistent pattern must raise the question: what was so uncongenial about Blanchot's writing that across the deepest divides which gave his epoch both its fragility and its consistency, the consensus prevailed that there was no place for it in the present? The answer at first seems difficult to perceive. The 'invisibility' for which he was renowned,[12] the anonymity he aspired to,[13] his conviction from the start (and thus well before Barthes) that writing presupposes that the author is dead,[14] all make his relation to the present appear not just insubstantial, but positively spectral. Blanchot and his contemporaries would seem in fact to have shared a common purpose; for himself as much as for them, as a contemporary he was a posthumous figure.

This apparent collusion conceals a basic difference, however: the attitude of his contemporaries, over the whole of Blanchot's career, amounts to a clear *refusal* of that continuity between past and present which centenaries celebrate, a pre-emptive and sometimes peremptory turning of the page as far as Blanchot was concerned. On his part, things were less simple. Writing 'posthumously' was not a way of bypassing the present, but rather a means of exposing his reader, in the present, to the impersonality of writing itself. Paradoxically, however, Blanchot's refusal to allow his readers any insight into his biography in fact makes it harder than say with a writer such as Sartre to respond directly to the invitation which this self-effacement extends, and treat everything bearing the signature 'Blanchot' as writing, and nothing else. With Sartre, as with all great 'names', the fact that readers carry about with them what amounts to a neat biographical vignette means that a firm line can be drawn between life and writing in their case. However, the perverse effect of Blanchot's self-effacement has been to make it *less* straightforward to differentiate between the biographical subject and the subject of writing in his case. In order to see how that is, the relationship between biography and writing must be examined more closely.

As Ann Jefferson has recently argued, biography played a constitutive role in the emergence of the modern figure of the Author: 'The function of biographies was to endorse the magisterial status of the artist as creative origin of the work of art', and provide 'the index of a culturally sanctioned form of literary accreditation'. Biography was thus 'at once a generically distinct form of writing and an enabling construct in the mind of readers'.[15] Clearly, when the time came for the Author to 'die', this generic distinctness made the task of killing him off seem simple: for writing to escape the 'great' work and become text, it needed simply to turn distinctness into radical difference, unhitch itself from the biographical and so disable the constructive process which shackled it to the Author. But this simple view of the 'death' of the Author fails to take account of a crucial dimension of biographical writing: to be, generically, it necessarily presupposes the death of the living subject whose life it narrates. To present a life as a coherent whole, even if the whole remains partial because the subject is still alive, requires a view from beyond the whole. To live as an Author, as Sartre eventually realised, is to view yourself as already dead.[16] At the heart of the modern constitution of the Author, therefore, prior to the 'death' which post-modern writing will seek to inflict on him, lies another act of 'killing': that which is implied by any biography.

To say that modernity remained oblivious of the role of death in the constitution of the living Author is to do no more than understand it better. More problematical is the fact that, when Barthes proposed the 'death of the Author' as the move which constructs and enables the passage from Work to Text, the fact that the Author whose death is necessary for writing to become text is himself the product of a death, tended (and still tends) to remain concealed. It nevertheless raises important questions: if death has already done its work for a writer to be an Author, where is the death that will kill the Author to come from? Can a human subject die more than once? Both the concept and practice of 'text' considered as discursive plurality remain constrained by a failure to reflect on the role of death in the constitution of the figure whose death it decrees. It could even be argued that not a single segment of the vast and open corpus of what Barthes called text(s) has ever escaped the Author and his biographical origins.[17] The 'death of the Author' may well free writing from the timelessness of the work and plunge it back into the plurality of discourse, idioms and codes; but as long as it does not give its due to the death which enabled the constitution of the Author in the first place, which is to say: to the biographical gesture, then its attempt to put an end to the 'life of the Author' as a way of being for a writer will never fully succeed.

The death which authorship presupposes will, paradoxically, haunt the 'text' as a rogue surplus of life.

Perhaps it is becoming more possible to see how Blanchot's self-effacement differs from the attempt by so many contemporaries to relegate him to the past. Put simply, his refusal to *be* an Author by eschewing biography does not expel life from his writing. Rather, in order to 'kill' the Author he refuses to be, Blanchot in effect 'kills' the reader, by taking over the biographical gesture which brings the Author into being *before* the reader can carry it out. A posthumous moment thus becomes inseparable from the time of his own writing. As a consequence, the speaking subject of each sentence by Blanchot that a reader reads is silently and simultaneously the subject of a paradoxical and irrepressible narrative act which states: 'I am dead'. In refusing biography yet continuing to write and to publish, Blanchot thus interferes in the processes which construct the author much more disruptively than if he wrote anonymously or simply ceased to write. By emptying the biographical gesture, which he takes over, of everything except its anticipation of his own death, he exposes the fact that the borderline separating the life of a writer from his writing, for the reader of that writing, lies not between writing on the one hand, and life in the world on the other, but between two moments or acts of language: that found in the writing itself, that which constructs the writer's biography as a narrative.

The paradox I began with can now be elucidated somewhat: if the impossibility, for Blanchot's reader, of endowing him with a life interferes with Blanchot's wish to be read as already dead, this can be seen to arise because what at one level is *nothing but* writing (because the name Blanchot refers to a body of writing and nothing else) is haunted by a surplus of *life*. This is a quantity of life lying beyond life considered as that which is bounded by death, yet it has no place in the timeless life of the mind. As such, while remaining inseparable from the body of writing bearing the name of its author, Maurice Blanchot, this is life without name or identity, neither that of a writer nor that of a reader, something impersonal, anonymous and alien which both shadows and overshadows the speaking subject of Blanchot's writing, so that for his reader, the borderline which usually separates the life of the individual who writes (which the reader does not share) from the life of the mind (which the reader seeks to share with the writer) is replaced by an interval traversing the subject of the writing he is reading, in so far as that subject does two things—think, narrate—seemingly at once.

It is perhaps easier now to understand the gesture of those contemporaries who sought persistently to confine Blanchot to the past. For them, he was not just an outmoded figure, but an awkward anachronism, an unsettling throwback, a survivor into the present of something which should be dead. As a result, and not surprisingly, if Blanchot's name has become inextricably associated with death, this is not death as the obverse of life, but death where life should be, death *in* life. And it is in those terms that the editors of the journal *Ligne de Risque* recently denounced Blanchot as the 'Commander', the 'Enemy', the writer single-handedly responsible for the death-fixation which affects French writing and the agent of a nihilistic hatred of the future.[18] And once again, Blanchot would seem to have colluded in this process of denunciation: a thematics of *death*, then *dying*, typifies his non-fictional writing from the 1950s on and increasingly provides its focus. What is more, following his return to active politics after 1958, action itself, under his influence, appeared inseparable from the negations of mortality. Blanchot's role in the activity surrounding the *International Review* in the early sixties caused Roland Barthes to describe him as 'a great leader of negativity with a capital N';[19] and in 1968, his own text entitled 'La mort politique' asserted (no doubt to the puzzlement of some of his comrades): 'Political death keeps watch [*veille*] in us, "a light in the sepulchre" (...). We participate in it, whether we like it or not'.[20]

To sum up therefore, for many contemporaries Blanchot was a figure from the past who insisted on continuing to write, and eventually to intervene politically, in the present; a figure who, while behaving as if he were already dead, lived on as the agent and advocate of a doctrine or theory of death and dying. Seen this way, it is hard to dismiss entirely the view of his contemporaries that Blanchot was always a suspect, not to say dangerous, intruder in present-day thinking as it has developed since 1945. What his contemporaries were rejecting by seeking to relegate him to the past (what they could not *be* contemporary with) was the way he allowed the past to invade the present. Their gesture can thus be seen as an attempt to reinstate a temporal relation considered essential to thinking and writing in the present, which Blanchot's writing challenges fundamentally. And no doubt it is tempting to many, as a consequence, to see his centenary as a way of making Blanchot history once and for all — 'forget Blanchot' as Vincent Kaufman has recently urged[21] — and against the trend of such celebrations, to deny his writing both contemporary relevance and purchase on the future.

★

But all that is just one side of the story. Blanchot's survival as a writer, the persistence of which exasperated so many of his contemporaries, is something which a number of major thinkers have for their part continuously nurtured and sustained. To read Foucault or Nancy or Derrida is to encounter thinking that not only draws explicitly and substantially on Blanchot's work, but is also structured fundamentally by what may be called an espousal of Blanchot, an acquiescence in what his writing demands which goes way beyond the usual limits of tolerance which obtain in philosophy, and is as unconditional and as absolute as the rejection of his writing by other contemporaries. With Foucault, from the anecdotal level[22] to the fundamental structures of his thought,[23] there is almost a subjugation to Blanchot. With Nancy (and also Philippe Lacoue-Labarthe), a comparable level of adhesion and acquiescence can be observed.[24] No other thinker enters and leaves the work of these writers with such *droit de cité*. The unthinking rejection of Blanchot's writing by many his contemporaries is thus not matched in the likes of Foucault, Derrida or Nancy by a reasoned acceptance of it, in which critical judgement is given its due: the oblivion to which many have sought to consign Blanchot's writing has as its counterpart what amounts to a *suspension* of judgement on their part. Oblivion is therefore not opposed by those who refuse that option, but rather displaced to become integral to their thinking and their writing. In espousing Blanchot's writing and suspending judgement in the process, they thus accommodate within the ambit of their own thinking a moment of oblivion akin to what Nancy has called *la syncope*, and which he identifies as the precondition of all rational thought: 'What is called consciousness can doubtless only be apprehended as an identity when it swoons: that is *syncope*. (. . .) [I]f it *is* not the *cogito*, at the same time there is no *cogito* without it'.[25] In a way that would seem unique — notwithstanding some passing strictures on Derrida's part[26] — another thinker's methods and practice are not just accorded equal status with those of their 'host' (which as in all good philosophy would expose them to rigorous critique), but granted a precedence which leaves them immune to critique, unreflected upon, haloed with the oblivion of the *syncope* which both precedes them and gives them precedence for the thought which accommodates them.

In so far as thinking is not impaired if it relates positively both to those for whom Blanchot is better forgotten and to those who have espoused his thinking absolutely, readers of Blanchot today thus find themselves exposed to a curiously unstable quantity of oblivion. Of

course, any reader in search of what makes him a contemporary has the
option of privileging Blanchot's own writing over the responses of
those who either rejected or espoused it. Nevertheless, anyone who
seeks to give a writer contemporary significance cannot ignore what
being a contemporary meant for that writer during his writing life.
Seen in that light, Blanchot's writing, in its contemporaneity over
time, can only remain elusive for a reader today. Driven from the
present on the one hand, subsumed in the present on the other, the
name 'Blanchot' on any piece of writing takes his reader today to a
version of the present that is simultaneously the site of two distinct
temporal displacements. In each case, the reader can only ask: where is
Blanchot? and find that the only solid element of a reply is: somewhere
in the vicinity of an oblivion which simultaneously traverses time along
two axes, dividing present from past and dividing present from itself,
so that the present to which Blanchot 'belongs', and with which a
reader seeks to be contemporary, is reduced to what seems to be an
unfigurable edge, bordering on oblivion. For some reason therefore,
Blanchot's writing divided his epoch in a way which was not simply a
polarization but a struggle for the present. In the process, his place in
the present became unlocatable. The only way, in the circumstances,
to explore Blanchot's contemporaneity in its singularity is thus to take
the argument against those who would relegate him to the past as
given (while holding in suspense the question of *what* it was about
Blanchot's position in the present that produced that reflex), and focus
on the extraordinary espousal of Blanchot's thought by those thinkers
who were willing to be his contemporaries.

As a thorough study would reveal, a repeated invocation to Maurice
Blanchot accompanies all of these thinkers throughout their careers,
drawing attention to the extraordinary docility towards his thought
that characterizes all of their work. Far from paralysing or disabling
their thinking, this uncritical relation to Blanchot has accompanied
them as they have brought rational analysis uniquely close to the
syncope which lies at the origin of every *cogito*. With the likes of Nancy
and Derrida, what amounts to a sufficient and evolving theory of
what the *syncope* refers to effectively exists. Time and again, in their
writing, the language of rational analysis skirts the edge of its own
unthinkable origin. If this has been possible, I would argue that it is
because the *syncope* in response to Blanchot, which is integral to their
thinking, is precisely what orients it in relation to the *syncope* which
they locate outside of thought, as its origin. Their *syncope* in relation
to Blanchot is thus granted an autonomy in relation to the thinking

in which it happens. In acting as hosts to Blanchot by suspending rational judgement through *syncope*, they allow their *syncope* to acquire subjectivity in discourse. In the thought of Foucault, Derrida or Nancy, two subjects therefore operate simultaneously, though across more than one time-frame. Furthermore, this is not a relation between equals. Because everything Blanchot wrote is shadowed by a voice which says 'I am dead', what they admit into their reflections by effectively abdicating intermittently as rational subjects is not itself just *syncope*, but a particular relation between rational discourse and *syncope*. In other words, their *syncope* in relation to Blanchot introduces into the hiatus formed when reflection is suspended a reflexivity of its own. What it is about Blanchot's thinking that guides theirs by way of their *syncope* in relation to it is thus what gives it its peculiar form. The nature of this singular reflexivity becomes particularly apparent in Jacques Derrida's relation to it.

*

Derrida's relation to Blanchot displays both of the attitudes which make his contemporaneity difficult to approach. As with Foucault and Nancy, there is an uncritical espousal of Blanchot's thinking which has still to be explored in all of its detail.[27] Yet within that stance, Derrida showed himself capable of keeping his distance. The mild but firm stricture contained in the 1999 interview is anticipated by a footnote in *The Politics of Friendship* (1994).[28] And as far back as 1965, while acknowledging the 'profundity' of Blanchot's study of Artaud in *The Book to Come*, he denounced what he termed the 'essentialism' of his analyses.[29] In each case, however, his reflections perform a deflection of critique. In *The Politics of Friendship*, the tentatively framed reservations concerning the category of fraternity, while directed at Bataille, Blanchot and Nancy, take detailed issue with Nancy's text only. In 1965, the accusation of essentialism concerns texts written by Blanchot between 1948 and 1958. What Blanchot was writing *at the time* is thus ignored, even though it offered a perspective on writing and difference which Derrida would make his own.[30] In short, if Derrida's espousal of Blanchot's thought is accompanied by what appears to be a certain independence of mind, the *syncope* whereby he opens up his own discourse to invasion by Blanchot's discourse[31] would seem to disorient it somewhat. This raises the possibility that what allows Derrida simultaneously to acquiesce entirely in Blanchot's thinking while keeping it at arm's length is not a strategy or practice to which he can simply lay claim in his own name, but is rather an effect, or more precisely, the trace of something purely autonomous, not to say alien to philosophy, which Blanchot's writing brings with it; something of which, consequently, Derrida can be said not to be conscious, philosophically speaking at least.

In order to illustrate what must for the moment remain a tentative argument, I shall look at a text by Derrida in which his relation to Blanchot plays a major role, and one which, in return, Blanchot hailed as 'unforgettable':[32] 'Of an Apocalyptic Tone Newly Adopted in Philosophy' (1983).[33] The first half of Derrida's study explores Kant's observations on the recent intrusion of a voice into philosophy which perturbs the voice of reason in us with its seductive oracular tones (36). 'All that is so much literature', says Derrida summing up Kant's attitude, before going on: 'We know this scene well today' (42). Derrida's text thus pivots significantly at its mid-point, shifting focus away from the tension between philosophers who heed the voice of reason and the purveyors of an oracular tone which places philosophy in mortal danger, towards a tension lying within philosophy today between what he calls two voices of the other in me: that of reason and that of the oracle. These may be distinguishable in Kant's terms as *voice* versus *tone*, but from the *neutral* position which Derrida seeks to adopt,[34] the better to focus on the concordat through which Kant offers his adversaries 'a neutral ground of reconciliation', they emerge as equally present in all thinking today ('every slightly organised discourse is found (...) on both sides, alternately or simultaneously' (45)).

The shift which occurs as Derrida's text pivots at its mid-point is therefore huge and far-reaching. Not only is Kant's historical moment overlaid with the present in which Derrida philosophizes, the difference between philosophers and non-philosophers is shifted to within the contemporary philosophical subject, where the two voices, or voice and tone, are at all times indiscernible. Then, Derrida pushes this move to its ultimate and boldest extreme: since the contract which Kant proposes involves each side agreeing to avoid what could cause the death of philosophy, death itself becomes the horizon of philosophy in general. From Hegel to Marx to Nietzsche therefore, 'the West has been dominated by a powerful programme that was also an untransgressible contract between discourses of the end' (48). As a consequence, the voice of philosophy today is no longer a voice at all, but a universal 'langage eschatologique', in other words: an apocalyptic tone.

This leaves Derrida with a problem, which he does not define directly, but which the movement of his analysis implies: if Kant offers his 'oracular' adversaries a neutral position from which to resist what is 'inadmissible' (45) (the end of philosophy), what becomes of that position when, from having served to ensure the predominance of the voice of reason for Kant's modernity, it is overturned so that it is the apocalyptic tone which comes to predominate today? Is not neutrality itself apocalyptic henceforth? Where then must Derrida's position be established, if his own thinking is not inevitably to be defined and dismissed as just another sort of apocalyptic discourse: 'all language on apocalypse is also apocalyptic and cannot be excluded from its object' (61)? His answer could not be more resolute:

today (...), we cannot and we must not — this is a law and a destiny — forego the *Aufklärung*, in other words, what imposes itself as the enigmatic desire for vigilance, (...) for a truth that at the same time keeps within itself some apocalyptic desire (...). (51)

We must acquiesce totally in the programme which the Enlightenment has handed down to philosophy, while recognising that the desire for vigilance which is our Enlightenment heritage is enigmatic in so far as it is also and unavoidably an apocalyptic desire. Vigilance would then consist in demystifying or deconstructing apocalyptic discourse by turning apocalypse against itself. Unable not to hear and heed the 'Come' with which the apocalyptic tone endlessly seduces him, the philosopher must respond with the same question again and again: 'with a view to what and to what ends?' (53). Taking the Apocalypse of John as the basic *scene* of this historical moment in philosophy, Derrida advances a complex interrelation between a 'Come' uttered in advance of all thought and all language, in an apocalyptic tone without subject or content, and a 'Stay awake' (*Veille*) which is endlessly that of the voice of Enlightenment (the voice of philosophy) in each individual in so far as he is already dead (54).

As the second half of his argument progresses, Blanchot appears in Derrida's text across a widening span. What is significant in the light of the present argument, however, is not the role Derrida gives to Blanchot, but rather the fact that the 'Blanchot' he invokes is shadowed by another, nameless and impersonal (non-)figure who, at one level, is recognisably Blanchot (for Derrida's reader), but at another is not him — not because Derrida's text sometimes does not name him, but because in writing 'Of an Apocalyptic Tone' Derrida would sometimes appear to be oblivious of the fact that it is

Blanchot he is citing. This division occurs from the very moment the name 'Blanchot' enters Derrida's argument, and originates in a resolutely 'philosophical' gesture on his part. Following the post-Kantian eschatological-apocalyptic programme down through Hegel and Marx to Nietzsche, Derrida comes inevitably to the figure of the 'last man', whose voice has displaced the voice of reason with its tone: 'Isn't the voice always that of the last man?' (49). He then moves forward in time to embrace Heidegger in his eschatological programme, repeating his question about voice and the 'last man' before going on: 'Foregoing a reading of Blanchots' *Last Man* with you, I recall (...) this fragment from the *Philosophenbuch*' (49; translation modified). In a telling series of moves, a philosophical question is here repeated as a means of excluding from consideration a work of fiction dealing with the same question, in favour of a work of philosophy for which the last man is the same as the last philosopher. No sooner does Blanchot come onto the scene as an author of narrative fiction, therefore, than his name is the site of a movement of deflection.

If Derrida does not read *The Last Man* with his audience, there can be no doubt that he can read it and has read it. The fact remains, however, that whereas 'Of an Apocalyptic Tone' will cite Blanchot's theoretical texts with an ease and a confidence which occasionally allow them to be brought in without attribution, each time Derrida refers to Blanchot's fiction, things appear less straightforward. Enlisting Blanchot's distinction between 'narrative voice' and 'narrating voice' in the service of a detailed analysis of voice in the Apocalypse of John, he evokes the echo of the 'Come' to be heard in that text in 'all the "come"s resounding in the *récits* or *non récits* of Blanchot' (55). If his recourse to the distinction between narrative and narrating voices reflects a theoretical mastery on Blanchot's part which Derrida is happy to assimilate, the distinction expressed as '*récits* or *non-récits*', while inevitably recalling his extraordinary and illuminating analyses of Blanchot's fiction in 'Pas', 'Living On' etc.,[35] suggests, as does the (non-)reference to *The Last Man*, that when it refers to Blanchot's narrative, Derrida's text introduces into itself a quantity which it neither accommodates nor masters.

Initially and seemingly in passing, Blanchot's fiction is given equivalent status to his theoretical analyses. Having displaced *The Last Man* in favour of Nietzsche's 'last philosopher' Derrida writes: '"The end is beginning", we read in *The Madness of the Day*' (50). Rather than lending assistance to his deconstructive project, however, Blanchot's fiction is here presented as a source for the voice he is seeking to demystify. And from here on, this division into two 'Blanchots' will cease to be something which Derrida masters. Here is how he characterizes 'the finest diversity of apocalyptic ruses':

The subject of eschatological discourse can have an interest in foregoing its own interest, or else can forego everything in order to leave you stuck with its death, and bequeath you its corpse in advance (...). (52; translation modified)

Then, after repeating the question which should be asked of anyone adopting the apocalyptic tone: 'with a view to what and to what ends?' (53), Derrida repeats the quotation from *The Madness of the Day*, this time without attributing it, before, as he puts it, translating this tone into discourse:

The end is soon, it is imminent, signifies the tone. (...) We're all going to die, we're going to disappear, and this death sentence cannot fail to judge us, we're going to die, you and I, the others too (...), all those who don't share this secret with us, but they don't know it. It's as if they were already dead. We're alone in the world (...), come, let us be for (...) a moment before the end the sole survivors. (53–4)

It is following this that he refers to the category of 'narrative voice' and invokes 'Blanchot's *récits* or *non-récits*' (55).

There is a pattern discernible here, which clearly reveals two levels or moments in the relation of Derrida's argument to Blanchot: an overt one, in which from the reader's point of view boundaries are marked out and respected, and one which is not so much covert as uncharted. At the theoretical level the division is only apparent. Whether Derrida is borrowing explicitly (narrative voice/narrating voice), or anonymizing a quotation ('the apocalypse is disappointing'(66)[36]), or else displacing his borrowing onto a hypothetical reader ('Perhaps you will be tempted to call this disaster' (66)), the relation between his text and Blanchot's is productively contained within the overall deconstructive strategy which he has mapped out. At the level of Blanchot's fiction, however, division becomes radical divergence. No doubt reflecting the strain placed on philosophical discourse by the end which he sets himself: namely to limit his attention to a 'Come' which is uncontainable by philosophy (64) and which he simultaneously locates in three different textual sites — the Apocalypse of John, Blanchot's *récits* and his own commentary on them in 'Pas' and 'Living On' — Derrida's citations of Blanchot's fiction do more than just reflect the overt/unattributed alternation visible at the level of theory: that alternation is the site of what appears to be a falling away of his deconstructive project. For when his attributed citation of *The Madness of the Day* is repeated as part of his own text, this leads to a curious haunting of his argument by the language of Blanchot's fiction. His previous attempts at approaching the 'Come' which philosophy cannot contain, by setting up 'a milieu of resonances, responses, citations referred, referring to texts of Blanchot (...) or others' (64), are something he claims he cannot reconstitute on this occasion. However, it is precisely that milieu that haunts the passages I have quoted, in which Derrida gives voice to the seductive tone of apocalypse. The expression 'bequeath you its corpse in advance', the reference to a 'death sentence', to dying, being 'already dead' but also living on, resonate with echoes from and references to Blanchot's narratives.[37] These are unattributed, however. As a result, the translation into discourse by Blanchot's narratives of the contentless apocalyptic tone whose seduction ('Come') it is Derrida's project to demystify and deconstruct, is inseparable from the hypothetical voice into which Derrida translates the apocalyptic tone in his own text. Derrida's deconstructive project is thus put at risk by the very strategy it employs. If every voice that takes on the apocalyptic tone must attract the question 'with a view to what and to what ends?', by allowing Blanchot's voice to invade his own discourse until it loses its identity and becomes the voice of apocalyptic tone itself, there ceases to be a subject to whom that question may be addressed. So complete is Derrida's espousal of Blanchot that the *syncope* whereby his voice is intentionally interrupted as it seeks to give voice to apocalyptic tone, is at the same time a *syncope* in which intention itself is suspended, and during which the voice in which tone exerts its oracular seduction is one in which Derrida has already succumbed to that seduction as it can be heard in the voice of Blanchot's fiction.

In 'Of an Apocalyptic Tone' the effect on the discourse of those thinkers I have said espouse Blanchot in the 1970s and 1980s is clearly perceptible. Enlisted in the cause of allowing philosophy to display awareness of, and ultimately articulate, a moment which exceeds philosophy, Blanchot's writing introduces into the discourse of philosophy something which it is not just unable to accommodate, but which escapes all of the complex discursive manoeuvres whereby philosophy seeks to bring what exceeds it into relation with it. In espousing Blanchot, Derrida and those like him therefore accommodate a moment of *syncope* which is effectively *on the loose* in their philosophy, and which marks it independently of any programmatic intention or rational project on their part.

To return to my earlier point therefore: both those who seek to relegate Blanchot to the past, and those who on the contrary assimilate him into the present of their own discourse, respond to Blanchot by means of oblivion. Any attempt by a reader today to approach directly what makes Blanchot a contemporary for him or her consequently remains caught at the mobile edge which oblivion traces out. What 'Of an Apocalyptic Tone' reveals is that there is something more than merely circumstantial about that edge: it is present first and foremost in the writing of those contemporaries who espouse Blanchot's writing unconditionally. Far from marking particular historical moments in Blanchot's perception and reception, that edge of oblivion defines fundamentally Blanchot's relation to the present for all rationally constructed discourse which has sought to be contemporary with it up to now.

If both the simple and the complex versions of the obliviousness of his contemporaries deflect thinking away from what actually happens in Blanchot's writing, an earlier question therefore returns: what is it about Blanchot's writing that makes such aversion seem inevitable? Is he, as Heidegger said of Nietzsche, '*too* contemporary'?[38] What is actually going on over the edge traced out by oblivion? What discursive activity is philosophy not just unable to accommodate, but unable to know it cannot accommodate? It is here that Blanchot's refusal of biography acquires its full significance. By appropriating the biographical gesture while emptying it of content, he augmented all of his writing with a preliminary 'I am dead' thanks to which the present of his contemporaneity remains fractured. It is in that gesture, I would argue, that the cause of the obliviousness of those who espouse him is to be found. It is that which the discourse of reason cannot accommodate, and in relation to which it can only lose its bearings. But let us be clear about what it is precisely about the dual utterance 'I am alive', 'I am dead' that induces oblivion as the inevitable rational response to it. In *Specters of Marx*, quoting Stirner on the subject of an Ego 'inhabited and invaded by its *own spectre*', Derrida argues that this hypothesis may be extended to every *cogito*.[39] In other words, the *syncope* without which, according to Nancy, the *cogito* would not exist is endowed by Derrida with a spectral subjectivity. Moreover, it is capable of language, as he indicates when he speaks in a footnote of 'the strangely murmured implication of death (not only of an "I am mortal" but of an "I am dead") in the declaration of the "I am"' (237, n. 3). He then refers his reader in 1993 to Chapter VII of his early essay *Speech and Phenomena* (1967), where he writes: 'The statement "I am alive" is accompanied by my being dead, and its possibility requires the possibility that I be dead; and conversely'.[40] To say that it is the implicit 'I am dead' of Blanchot's refusal of biography which is inassimilable for rational thought, so that when confronted with it, thought can only swoon, would thus seem in the end to be saying no more than Derrida said about thought in general at the beginning of his career, and allowed to determine his philosophy throughout his life.

However in *Speech and Phenomena*, the way Derrida accommodates the sentence 'I am dead' within his argument reveals very clearly that the process of assimilation has strict limits. The quotation above is followed by a firm statement of the philosophical validity of what he has just claimed: 'This is not an extraordinary tale by Poe but the ordinary story of language' (97). And somewhat surprisingly, it is precisely that story by Poe in which the words 'I am dead' are uttered, 'The Facts in the Case of M. Valdemar' (1845),[41] that provides the third of the epigraphs to his book. In other words, what Derrida has to set aside ('an extraordinary tale by Poe') in order that the validity of his philosophical assertion may be assured is not simply negated, but placed at the threshold of his philosophy. It is as if the general assertion that an 'I am dead' accompanies every living act of cognition (including therefore the one Derrida is performing) inevitably generates, as a condition of its generality, a version of that same assertion which defies generalization because it was proffered once only (and therefore is not iterable) in the singularity of a work of narrative fiction. It is thus something of which philosophy must remain oblivious, but which haunts it from just beyond its threshold.

What happens on this threshold to Derrida's philosophy makes it possible to see what it is about the murmured 'I am dead' guarding the threshold to all of Blanchot's writing that induces oblivion in any discourse which seeks to be contemporary with it. It is the fact that, into the generalizing field of philosophical discourse (to which Derrida remains robustly committed) it introduces the singularity of an act of narrative. If philosophy can for its own purposes generalize that singular act by calling it 'ordinary', something excessive or supplementary (something *extra*ordinary) about its singularity remains on the loose in the work of those who espouse Blanchot's writing. In *Speech and Phenomena*, Derrida's instinct as a philosopher, having banished this singular excess from the field of his argument, is to corral it on the margins in the form of an epigraph. Throughout his career, however, during which his espousal of Blanchot's writing is total and uncritical, that margin refuses to remain in place. Rather, it runs through his philosophy, suspending it unexpectedly and intermittently substituting for the sustained and orderly voice of reason, the traces left in language by the 'I am dead' proffered by Blanchot which does not only guard the threshold to Blanchot's writing in general, but also generates a series of works of narrative fiction which accompany the development of his thinking as what gives it its sole raison d'être.[42]

The question remains, however: what exactly is it about narrative that brings about a *syncope* if it is not expelled from the generalizing field of philosophical discourse? As Derrida has shown with unequalled originality in a vast body of work, philosophy can entertain a productive relation to what entails its eclipse. In subtle and versatile analyses, he and others have succeeded over their careers in pin-pointing, characterizing and above all acting upon the *syncope* which thought presupposes and which their uncritical espousal of Blanchot makes into a real dimension of their philosophical practice. In short, a willed host-parasite relation to Blanchot is inseparable from the originality and impact of their work. What is it then that escapes even the most lucidly reflective contortions of their thinking, so that *syncope* coincides simultaneously with every *cogito* they enact? The answer, I would say, is *time*—the singular temporality with which the statement 'I am dead' haunts every 'I am' for Derrida, and whose narrative character Blanchot explores in a series of works of fiction during twenty years of his writing life. For the present in which 'I am' and 'I am dead' are simultaneously uttered is a present not just divided, but dislocated, torn apart by the two incompatible temporal perspectives which it is forced to accommodate. It is thus neither the past nor the present understood chronologically, but a 'now' in which 'I am' and 'I was' disastrously collide, and which thus traverses their continuum as what both distorts and interrupts it fundamentally. *That* is what, however asymptotically close their analyses may come to it, the *philosophy* of Nancy, Derrida and others can relate to only by way of a *syncope* over which they have no control.

Derrida comes extraordinarily close to recognising this original temporality in what he says about the gift in *Given Time*. A gift is always a gift of time, it '*gives time*'.[43] And he goes on: 'The thing as given thing, the given of the gift arrives, if it arrives, only in narrative [*le récit*]' (41). Earlier, this event has been characterized as follows:

For there to be a gift event (we say event and not act), something must come about or happen, in an instant, in an instant that no doubt does not belong to the economy of time, in a time without time, in such a way that the forgetting forgets, that it forgets *itself*, but also in such a way that this forgetting, without being something present, (...) is not nothing. What this forgetting and this forgetting of forgetting would therefore give us to think is something other than a philosophical, psychological or psychoanalytical category. Far from giving us to think the possibility of the gift, on the contrary, it is on the basis of what takes shape in the name of the *gift* that one could *hope* to think this forgetting. (17)

In espousing Blanchot obliviously, what Derrida (like others) forgets, and forgets he forgets, is that in his writing, which is from the outset a posthumous narrative, Blanchot gives his reader the time of his life.

NOTES

1   Maurice Blanchot, *L'Attente l'oubli* (Paris, Gallimard: L'Imaginaire, 1962), 83; *Awaiting Oblivion*, translated by John Gregg (Lincoln and London, University of Nebraska Press, 1997), 57. 'But it's my life you want. I would need to have nothing more to live to have nothing more to say.' — 'Not exactly your life; on the contrary, it is your life that I am keeping in reserve.' — 'So, you want more than my life' (translation modified).
2   For important studies of suddenness and the present, see Karl-Heinz Bohrer, *Suddenness. On the Moment of Aesthetic Appearance*, translated by Ruth Crowley (New York, Columbia University Press, 1994), and *Das absolute Präsens* (Frankfurt-am-Main, Suhrkamp, 1994).
3   Jean-Paul Sartre, '*Aminadab*, or the fantastic considered as a language', *Literary and Philosophical Essays*, translated by Annette Michelson (London, Radius Books, 1968), 56–72 (57).
4   *Je suis partout*, 534, 18 October 1941, 8.
5   Ramon Fernandez, review of Eduard Wintermayer, *L'Europe en marche, Panorama*, 5, 18 March 1943, quoted in Lionel Richard, *Le Nazisme et la culture* (Paris, Maspero, 1978), 291.
6   Gaëtan Picon, *L'Usage de la lecture I* (Paris, Mercure de France, 1960), 199.
7   Georges Mounin, 'Maurice Blanchot et la poésie toujours mal entendue de Char' [1958], *La Communication poétique* (Paris, Gallimard, 1969), 236.
8   See Philippe Sollers, 'De quelques contradictions', *Tel Quel*, 38 (Summer 1969), I–IX.
9   See my 'Bibliographie I' and 'Bibliographie II', in *Gramma*, 3–4 and 5 (1976), 223–45 and 124–32.
10 Jeffrey Mehlman, 'Of Blanchot at *Combat*', *Legacies of Anti-Semitism in France* (Minneapolis, University of Minnesota Press, 1983), 6–22.
11 See in particular *Ligne de Risque*, 16 (September 2001). The title of the issue is 'La mort, cette imposture' (Death, this sham).
12 'I have always tried [...] to *appear* as little as possible', letter to Blandine Jeanson, 18.2.86, in *Photographes en quête d'auteurs* (Paris, Agence VU, 1986), 49. See also p. 33 of this issue.

13 See *Le Pas au-delà* (Paris, Gallimard, 1973), 53; *The Step Not Beyond*, translated by Lycette Nelson (Albany, SUNY, 1992), 35: 'We write in order to lose our name' (translation modified).
14 *L'Entretien infini* (Paris, Gallimard, 1969) ends with a brief postface in which Blanchot claimed that the texts it contains were 'already posthumous' and hence 'almost anonymous' (637). See *The Infinite Conversation*, translated by Susan Hanson (Minneapolis and London, University of Minnesota Press, 1993), 435.
15 Ann Jefferson, *Biography and the Question of Literature in France* (Oxford, OUP, 2007), 16–17, 21.
16 See Jean-Paul Sartre, *Words*, translated by Irene Clephane (Harmondsworth, Penguin, 1967): 'I am my own death notice' (129); 'I was looking at my life through my death' (145).
17 Pierre Guyotat, whose *Eden, Eden, Eden* (Paris, Gallimard, 1970) Barthes described in a preface as 'a free text, free of any subject, any object, any symbol' (9), recently published an autobiographical work, *Coma* (Paris, Mercure de France, 2006), which begins: 'The account which follows is something I have carried about in me since, while recovering from an attack which had placed me at death's door, I forced myself to speak once again in my own name' (9).
18 Yannick Haenel and François Meyronnis, 'Editorial', *Ligne de Risque*, 16 (September 2001), 1–3 (3).
19 Roland Barthes, 'Vie et mort des revues', an interview by Maria-Teresa Padova (1982), *Œuvres complètes*, edited by Eric Marty, revised edition, 5 vols (Paris, Seuil, 2002), V, 774–81 (780).
20 'La mort politique', *Comité*, 1 (October 1968), 8. Also in *Ecrits politiques, 1958–1993* (Paris, Léo Scheer, 2003), 108–10 (108).
21 Vincent Kaufman, 'Pourquoi j'ai oublié Blanchot', *Furor*, 29 (September 1999), 17–32. I examine this text in more detail in 'Accuser le coup', *Les Lettres romanes*, 'Maurice Blanchot, la singularité d'une écriture', numéro hors série (2005), 117–29.
22 See Didier Eribon, *Michel Foucault*, translated by Betsy Wing (London, Faber, 1992), 58: 'Foucault once described the 1950s to Paul Veyne: "At that time, I dreamt of being Blanchot".'
23 See Chapter V of *The Archaeology of Knowledge* (1969), translated by A.M. Sheridan Smith (New York, Pantheon Books, 1972), whose dialogue format clearly recalls certain of the texts included in *The Infinite Conversation*.
24 See Jean-Luc Nancy and Philippe Lacoue-Labarthe, *The Literary Absolute* (1978), translated by Philip Barnard and Cheryl Lester (Albany, SUNY Press, 1988). The conclusion to this work repeatedly acknowledges the *enabling* influence of Blanchot's writing about German Romanticism. At the end of Nancy's *Le Discours de la syncope. Logodaedalus, I* (Paris, Galilée, 1976) (148), and at the beginning of his *Ego sum* (Paris, Galilée, 1979) (24), the same

passage from Blanchot's 'Le "discours philosophique"' (*L'Arc*, 46 (1971), 1–4) is cited: 'philosophical discourse "is perhaps merely an inexorable way of losing and of becoming lost"'.
25 *Le Discours de la syncope*, 13.
26 For example: 'In [Blanchot] there are very discreet things about friendship, fraternity that I have also occasionally found suspect (not to mention directly his political past). There are questions; but basically, it is in relation to Blanchot that I feel the fewest jolts, or highs and lows' (from an interview with Derrida by Dominique Janicaud in *Heidegger en France, II* (Paris, Albin Michel, 2001 [1999]), 89–126 (106).
27 For important approaches to the issue, see Herman Rapaport, *Heidegger and Derrida* (Lincoln and London, University of Nebraska Press, 1991), and Timothy Clark, *Derrida, Heidegger, Blanchot* (Cambridge, CUP, 1992).
28 *The Politics of Friendship*, translated by George Collins (London, Verso, 1997), 48–49.
29 See 'La parole soufflée', in *Writing and Difference* (1967), translated by Alan Bass (London, Routledge, 2001), 212–45 (217).
30 As early as July 1960, Blanchot could write: 'we speak by way of that difference which, as we speak, makes us defer speaking' (*The Infinite Conversation*, 32 (translation modified)).
31 For an example of this, see *Aporias*, translated by Thomas Dutoit (Stanford, Stanford University Press, 1993), 87: 'See in particular *Awaiting Oblivion* (1962), *The Step Not Beyond* (1973) (...) and *Writing the Disaster* (1980) (...). It would now be necessary to re-read and cite these texts from beginning to end.'
32 Blanchot, *La Communauté inavouable* (Paris, Minuit, 1983), 26; *The Unavowable Community*, translated by Pierre Joris (Barrytown, Station Hill Press, 1989), 57.
33 'Of an Apocalyptic Tone Newly Adopted in Philosophy', translated by John P. Leavey, Jr, in *Derrida and Negative Theology*, edited by Harold Coward and Toby Foshay (Albany, SUNY Press, 1992), 25–71. All page references will henceforth be given in the main body of the text.
34 'Not to take sides (...) — I shall do no such thing — between (...) literary mystagogy and true philosophy' (42).
35 See *Parages*, revised edition (Paris, Galilée, [1986] 2003).
36 See 'L'Apocalypse déçoit', in *L'Amitié* (Paris, Gallimard, 1971), 118–27; 'The Apocalypse is Disappointing', in *Friendship*, translated by Elizabeth Rottenberg (Stanford, Stanford University Press, 1997), 101–8.
37 In Chapter II of *Thomas l'obscur* (Paris, Gallimard, 1941), the protagonist finds himself interred alongside his own corpse. *L'Arrêt de mort* (1948) and *Au moment voulu* (1951), translated by Lydia Davis as *Death Sentence* and *When the Time Comes* (Barrytown, Station Hill Press, 1978 and 1986), are just two of Blanchot's narratives which echo through Derrida's text.
38 Martin Heidegger, *Nietzsche. Volume I: The Will to Power as Art*, translated by David Farrell Krell (San Francisco, Harper Collins, 1991), 4.

39 *Specters of Marx*, translated by Peggy Kamuf (New York and London, Routledge, 1994), 166.
40 'Speech and Phenomena', translated by David B. Allison, in *Speech and Phenomena and Other Essays* (Evanston, Northwestern University Press, 1973), 1–104 (96–7).
41 See Edgar Allan Poe, *Tales of Mystery and Imagination* (London, Everyman, 1968), 280–9: 'Yes;—no;—I have been sleeping—and now—now—*I am dead*' (288).
42 The ending to *Le Très-Haut* (Paris, Gallimard, 1948), translated by Allan Stoekl as *The Most High* (Lincoln and London, University of Nebraska Press, 1996), clearly echoes the end of Poe's tale. As he is shot dead the narrator cries: 'It is now, now that I speak' (258).
43 Jacques Derrida, *Given Time. 1, Counterfeit Money*, translated by Peggy Kamuf (Chicago, University of Chicago Press, 1992), 41.

R/M, 1953[1]

CHRISTOPHE BIDENT

Abstract:
French literary criticism in the twentieth century is marked by two names: those of Roland Barthes and Maurice Blanchot. Each of them cut an individual path through the dense and variegated cultural terrain of their era, and few authors escaped their attention. Their paths generally ran in parallel, and they rarely opposed each other, yet their dialogue was never easy, and the impression remains that between them, there was never really a meeting of minds. Taking 1953 as a crucial year, this article will attempt to situate both the convergences and the divergences which mark their respective careers, by considering them in relation to a single question: that of the neuter.

Keywords: Barthes, Blanchot, the neuter, politics, writing, fiction, friendship

Maurice Blanchot, Roland Barthes, Roland Barthes, Maurice Blanchot: the history of French literary criticism in the twentieth century revolves around these two names. They accompany that history, while forging it and polarizing it: nothing biographical, thematic, scientific or philosophical is foreign to either of them. Between the birth of the elder of the two (1907) and that of the younger (1915), Proust wrote *Against Sainte-Beuve* (1908/1910). Between the death of the younger of the two (1980) and that of the elder (2003), the great critical journals began to fall apart and the time for summing up had come. In the meantime, Barthes and Blanchot punctuated the century with hundreds upon hundreds of articles. Their many books were excitedly read and discussed, sometimes admiringly, sometimes adversely. Few authors, starting with their contemporaries, escaped their analyses. Some were singled out to be defended, even exhumed. This critical militancy, in turn impassioned and serene, will follow often parallel and rarely opposing paths. Yet the sense remains that between Blanchot and Barthes there was more of a passing nod than an encounter. Of course they read, knew and appreciated each other. They also sometimes ignored or irritated each other. Their dialogue was not easy, and their respective journeys are not alike.

Personal, biographical or political elements might account for this dissimilar similarity. Each of them suffered from tuberculosis before he was thirty and spent time in a sanatorium, that state of 'abstraction in relation to the world'; but Blanchot went for treatment in the Pyrenees while Barthes went mostly to the Alps.[2] Later, in the 1960s, they lived very near each other in the sixth *arrondissement*: in rue Servandoni, in rue Madame; but they did not go to the café on the place Saint-Sulpice together, at the heart of their 'village'. And so, a few feet away from each other but never with four hands, each would play his favourite composer, Schumann, on his piano.[3] They lived their literary lives as a celibacy that was sapped by the solitude of the one, and eased by the homosexuality of the other. More or less from a distance, Blanchot's elder brother played the domestic and protective role which Barthes's mother fulfilled close by him. Blanchot's acquaintances were often those of Barthes, and vice versa, but they had none of their closest friends in common. They sometimes published in the same journals, but they were principally involved with neither the same titles nor the same publishers. On one occasion, they became involved together in a common publishing venture, the 'International Review', but the heart of one of them was in it more than the other's was, and in the end it failed. It was an attempt at prolonging the political venture of the Manifesto which had spoken out against a war that each of them had denounced. But one was the main author of this *Declaration on the Right to Insubordination in the Algerian War*, while the other did not sign it. They never failed to send each other their books, elegantly inscribed. But Barthes spoke much more in his about Blanchot than Blanchot ever referred to Barthes in his. This was perhaps to do with those they were in dialogue with. For Blanchot it was Levinas, Bataille, Antelme, Mascolo, Des Forêts and Derrida. For Barthes it was Dort, Robbe-Grillet, Greimas, Sollers and Kristeva. And the modes in which they conducted their dialogues differed. With the hugely popular professor at the Collège de France, the melancholy solitude of writing eventually formed a contrast with the engagement in active discussion to be found in the fragments published by the reclusive individual, invisible to almost everyone.

I interrupt these alternating portraits, which are beginning to seem like destinies, the better to focus on two close but diverging conceptions of historicity and community reflected in them. Put succinctly to begin with: Blanchot was a man of the absolute, Barthes a man of plurality. For the one, either total commitment or *refusal*, involvement in events or cloistered isolation; being driven up against the unavowable, yet believing in the spacing of literature, perhaps in a new version of the Republic of Letters, in any case, hope sustained beyond all hopelessness. For the other, between unwavering adhesion to dialectical materialism and uncompromising rejection of all fascist regimes, a broad interval opening on to the suspension of meaning, the randomness of languages, a fund of images and utopian or atopian assemblages of quotations. Blanchot raises up ideological form into the impossible time of poetry. Barthes protects himself from it through the Oriental gesture of the non-desire-to-grasp [*non-vouloir-saisir*]. Their relation to political involvement entails a critical relation to language.

Once again I interrupt this confrontation, this time so as to relocate it within the play of writing. The association of these two names, Barthes and Blanchot, Blanchot and Barthes, prompted me to begin this article with the lowest common denominator of their work, literary criticism. However, the work of each of them unquestionably extends beyond the field of criticism: by way of the question of sociology, structural theory and the promise of the novel in the case of Barthes; by way of the question of politics, aesthetic theory and the practice of the fictional *récit* in the case of Blanchot. Not to mention the dramatization of knowledge by each of them, and fragmentary writing as the two-fold outcome of ultimatums, vigilance and remembrance. Seen from whatever angle or whatever slant, Blanchot and Barthes freed up extravagant spaces of literature within which many imitators became lost. That is why the question of their legacy is more urgent today than ever, in the painful period following their demise, in the uncertain era of *intellectuals under scrutiny* and within the spectral inevitability of publishing ventures: complete works, correspondence, performances, websites, photographs and exhibitions. Is it an accident that *Chaque fois unique, la fin du monde*[4] begins with Barthes and ends with Blanchot, the death of each framing that of so many others? Or that its author, Jacques Derrida, put his signature to the book so soon (a year, month for month) before his own death?

I shall therefore attempt to *situate* both the convergences and the divergences, so as to bring them into line with a *question*. This question is that of the neuter. I shall not claim to examine it here in its entirety. For that, it would be necessary to follow closely in Barthes and in Blanchot the different stages of the discovery, the writing and the theorization of the neuter. I shall do no more than name them. However, in so far as this study aims to bring Maurice Blanchot and Roland Barthes face to face, naming the different moments or epochs of the neuter in their works entails bringing out what should perhaps be called the *discordemes* of a field of vision. In what precedes, I singled out three which seem to me to be major: the difference in their relation to the political, the difference in their relation to writing fiction and finally, the difference in the way each of them considered the work of the other: what appears as an immense unfamiliarity with Barthes's work on Blanchot's part, and the conflicting interest in Blanchot shown by Barthes.

With a brief appeal to analytical determinism, I might say that everything happens during the earliest phase of their encounter. We are back in 1953. Barthes is not yet thirty-eight. He publishes *Writing Degree Zero*.[5] He has read *The Work of Fire*,[6] which was published four years earlier, and this has left its mark on two chapters of his first book, which Blanchot, who will soon be forty-six, reads in his turn and reviews in the *Nouvelle Nouvelle Revue française*, that 'totally reactionary' journal, as Barthes will write two years later (I, 596).[7] Their communication at a distance thus begins on an ambiguous note. In his book, indeed, Barthes proceeds to offer double-edged praise for a 'white writing that is freed from all subservience to a specific order of language', but which is a victim of the power of social forces which prey on the writer, leaving him 'a prisoner of his own formal myths' (I, 216/218).[8] This white writing, which he also describes as 'neutral' or a 'degree zero', is attributed by Barthes more to Camus, Cayrol and even Sartre, than to Blanchot, whom he singles out for his key analyses of Mallarmé and Kafka.[9] By exclusively quoting these critical passages and neglecting the novels and *récits*, Barthes performs a two-fold disqualification of Blanchot's writing: basically, if it is 'white', it is a prisoner, if it is not white, it is not worthy of interest. Blanchot loses no time in delivering his riposte: his *NNRF* article takes the form of praise accompanied by remonstration. The praise he offers is relative: in 1953, Blanchot speaks only of 'a recent essay which it would be interesting to reflect upon', and it is only in the version to be found in *The Book to Come* that he replaces this formula with a nobler and almost prophetic acknowledgment, referring to 'one of the rare books in which the future of literature is inscribed'.[10] The praise is relative therefore, and the remonstration real: the article recommends going 'further than degree zero', and Blanchot frames his commentary on Barthes with two long meditations on Mallarmé and Proust, which aim to leave behind the issue of semiotics and re-evaluate the notions of experience and the neuter. Blanchot opens with a warning: 'Literature is a realm of coherence and a common territory only for as long as it does not exist, that is: does not exist for itself and conceals itself. As soon as it appears in the distant presentiment of what it seems to be, it shatters into pieces and turns in the direction of a dispersal where it refuses to allow itself to be recognized by means of precise and determinate signs'.[11] Blanchot thus states from the outset that his conception and that of Barthes are incompatible. Blanchot seems to catch Barthes red-handed in the act of being dispassionate about literary experience — perhaps because Barthes in fact does not write, at least not novels, not récits, not literature. This is clearly visible in the concluding sentences (I quote from the 1953 text):

> The experience called literature is a total experience, a question which brooks no limit, nor allows itself to be stabilised or reduced to a question of language for example (unless from that perspective everything begins to tremble). It is the very passion of its own question and it requires of anyone who is attracted by it that they enter entirely into that question (...). It may be that what Roland Barthes calls the degree zero of writing approximates to the moment when literature could take hold of itself; but in that case, at such a point it would not simply be a writing that was white, absent and neutral, it would be the experience of 'neutrality' itself, which can never be heard, for when neutrality speaks, only the one who silences it can prepare the conditions under which it might be heard, and yet what there is to be heard is that neutral speech, what has already been said, cannot stop being said and cannot be heard, a torment whose presentiment the pages which Samuel Beckett has written bring close to us.[12]

The article thus closes with the name of Beckett. At a banal level, this is a way of announcing next month's chronicle, which will be about *The Unnamable*; above all though, it is a rather curt reminder of a writer whom Barthes did not deign to mention in *Writing Degree Zero*.

How can we explain this preliminary and almost prophetic incompatibility, the immediate appearance of a discordeme? In 1953, Barthes and Blanchot are not at the same stage in relation to the neuter. In January, Blanchot publishes 'Essential solitude', an article no less essential itself, which is part of the relaunch of the *NRF* and will provide the opening chapter of *The Space of Literature* two years later.[13] It contains the first significant appearance of a reflection on the neutrality of writing, which is immediately applied in texts on Mallarmé and Kafka that continue those to be found in *The Work of Fire*. And yet, if the neuter or neutrality are each starting to acquire a dominant position, this is far from being their first occurrence in Blanchot's work, nor the first time they have insistently surfaced in his thought. In close dialogue with Bataille's 'non-knowledge' (*non-savoir*), Levinas's *il y a* and even Sartre's 'nausea', Blanchot has already approached these paradoxical expressions of consciousness, which raise the question of the existential status of inner experience and the legitimacy of literary experience. It is they which gave a spectral quality to the protagonist of his first novel, Thomas: 'never had the rays of life penetrated a more neutral, less vulnerable body'.[14] They provide the substance of the style of *The Madness of the Day* (1949)[15] and the object of the descriptions in both *When the Time Comes* (1951) ('[the] zero point of a furious desire') and *The One Who was Standing Apart from Me* (1953) ('to limit and circumscribe the void', 'the uninterrupted and the incessant').[16] Like Barthes, Blanchot admired Camus's novel *The Outsider* while the War was on. Each of them wrote an article at the time: discreetly in Barthes's case, in the journal of his sanatorium, more visibly in Blanchot's, the piece being included in *Faux pas*.[17] A little later on, still at a distance from each other, Barthes and Blanchot both showed interest in the writing of Jean Cayrol — once again, a neutral, 'Lazarean' writing with, for a background, the disaster of the prison camps of World War Two. These parallel preferences did not dictate a common approach, however. Barthes was attentive to the signs of writing, to the way in which a form of literature indicates that it is literature and brings itself to the attention of History. This explains his doubts regarding the historical relevance of writing at 'degree zero': capable of conveying a resistance to the power to destroy the world, it runs the risk of either fostering its own mythology, or giving rise to its own allegory.[18] The first risk explains why Barthes keeps his distance from Beckett, the second will determine the bitterness of his polemic with Camus when *The Plague* appeared. That is why Barthes remained ambivalent about how to qualify writing: 'white', as he sometimes wrote, 'neutral' as he wrote mostly, 'at the zero point' more rarely, though this will prove most effective as the title of a book in which, it should be recalled, there is very little on the subject of literature.

1953 is also the year in which Barthes began to write for *Théâtre populaire*. The very next year, he rapidly discovered the theory (Brecht's) that would validate, retrospectively as it were, his approach to literature: a theory of the exposure, the explication and the distancing of signs. Blanchot too will take an interest in Brecht. Initially entitled 'Brecht, or dislike for the theatre', his 1957 study curiously complements Barthes's analyses of Brechtian theory. Barthes admires the 'non-signifying background' of Brechtian scenography, which avoids a naturalistic saturation with meaning, makes possible the materialist presence of beings and objects and contributes to the dialectical function of performance (I, 1066–7).[19] The role that Blanchot gives to the neutrality of the Brechtian image is comparable to the one which Barthes bestows on the neutrality of scenography:

The image is no longer what allows us to have the object as absent, but is rather what holds us by means of absence itself, in that place where image, always at a distance, always absolutely close and absolutely inaccessible, eludes us and opens on to a neutral space where we can no longer act, opening us in our turn on to a sort of neutrality where we cease to be ourselves, and oscillate strangely between I, He and no one.[20]

It is this suspension of fascination which contributes to the effect of the performance; it is this poetic interruption which 'prepares the ground for a new and preliminary understanding'.[21]

Does the 'discordeme' then result from two readings which concur only by intersecting in the contradictory figure of the chiasm? Barthes became absorbed by the theatricality of signs while remaining sensitive to the literarity of Flaubert and Mallarmé. Blanchot became absorbed by the division of language without ever divorcing it from its historical effectiveness: the poem is 'absence of response' and 'understanding of the future' (in this respect the whole of the last part of *The Space of Literature* could be reread, in particular the final pages on Hölderlin and René Char).[22] Over many years, though in extremely different modes, Barthes and Blanchot will thus be haunted by the relation between the dialectic of the possible and the neutrality of the impossible, between the affirmation and the suspension of meaning. Signs of a reconciliation will only begin to appear in the seventies, years when Blanchot was producing his fragments, and Barthes was giving his lectures.

How will Barthes and Blanchot emerge from the year 1953? It is illuminating to dwell briefly on the indecision which *also* affected the public gestures whereby one began his writing career and the other continued his. This is the turbulent context of the 'discordemes'. We are in the midst of the Fourth Republic. In France, governments regularly fall. War has not really begun in Algeria. It is still in Viet-Nam. Stalin dies on 5 March. That is the month in which Barthes published *Writing Degree Zero*, as well as two articles in the first number of Maurice Nadeau's journal *Les Lettres nouvelles*. Two months earlier, Blanchot had published a first article in the first number of Jean Paulhan's journal, the *NNRF*. Two months later, Barthes published his first article in the first number of *Théâtre populaire*, Jean Voisin's journal, which had links with Jean Vilar's 'Théâtre National Populaire'. There Barthes met Bernard Dort, who admired Artaud, but also Beckett and Blanchot.[23] Roger Blin staged *Waiting for Godot* on 3 January. *Théâtre populaire* was publishing Brecht and Ionesco. All this indicates that decisions were not yet taken, that history was not yet written, that the lines were not yet drawn. And it further indicates that the publications, the allegiances, the friendships and the stances which were those of Barthes and Blanchot were what gave their orientation, provisionally at least, to the periodic reflections as journal critics which each will subsequently draw on to construct a decisive body of thought. Barthes will publish in *Les Lettres nouvelles* and *Théâtre populaire* until the end of the fifties; what came next is well known: the turn to semiology, the close relations with *Tel Quel*, the election to the Collège de France. Blanchot's articles will regularly appear in the *NNRF* until the beginning of the 60s; then came the slow, progressive disappearance of his journal-based writing, the publication of a compendium like *The Infinite Conversation* and the gift of memory contained in *Friendship*;[24] then the construction of his work on the basis of a withdrawal and a silence which were broken only by the year 1968. Blanchot takes part in the May demonstrations; he enjoys marching in the street with the students, calling them 'tu', joining in their charges while shouting 'hop! hop! hop!', and raising a fist in solidarity with the workers who are positioned at the windows of the occupied factories. As is well known, Barthes on the contrary found such spontaneity repugnant. But one has only to reread the rare articles he published in 1968 to realise to what extent he is embarking on a calling into question of Western thinking, and how these texts also determine a calling into question of his own thinking. They are 'The Reality Effect' in *Communications*,[25] 'Lesson in Writing' in *Tel Quel*,[26] 'The Death of the Author' in *Manteia*[27] and 'Linguistics and Literature' in *Langages*.[28] Barthes had been through the era of semiology and the functions of sense, when the 'degree zero' of phonology, semantics, logic and structural anthropology had played an essential role (in this respect, the passages on neutralization in *Elements of Semiology*[29] and *The Fashion System*[30] would also need to be reread). This time, the aim is to escape semiological positivity and bring to the fore the dialectic of sense posited and sense frustrated, of plenitude and suspension, of the plural and the neuter. This, in Barthes's vocabulary, is the obvious and the obtuse, polysemia and asemia, expenditure and reserve, tumescence and holes, panache and exemption, the empire and the retreat of signs. It is in this sense that Barthes can write in one of his 1968 texts: 'writing is that neuter, that composite, that oblique through which our subject escapes, the black-and-white where all identity gets lost, beginning with that of the very body doing the writing' (III, 40).[31] In the preceding years, that was also what Blanchot had written.[32] In his numerous texts,

Blanchot had put a repeated gesture to the test: in his articles, a search for how each writer brings out and apportions the neuter in an original creative work; in his *récits*, a pursuit of the anonymous movement whereby each singular ordeal [*épreuve*] dissolves into an indefinite experience. He therefore gave noun status at that time to *the* neuter, against philosophy which could be said to have always been afraid of it, and in favour of writing, which was alone in being receptive to the particular mode of its manifestation. I am thinking in particular here of the sections of *The Infinite Conversation* devoted to narrative voice, and also to the voice of poetry and that of theatre.

Their paths had thus diverged, and so had their ways of constructing their works. If Blanchot and Barthes ever had occasion to meet between 1953 and 1968, this could only have been during the attempt at publishing an 'International Review'. In a late interview in 1979, Barthes gave an account of this venture which still displayed the ambiguous feelings that linked him to the person and the work of Blanchot:

> I'll be frank with you here: if it was a venture that interested me — and I'm surprised to discover I continue to feel that now —, for me it had a lot to do with Blanchot, do you see? You know, I'm always quite pessimistic about these collective undertakings; but this one interested me because it allowed me to observe a man like Blanchot — a man whose thinking is extremely sharp, extremely lofty, a superior way of thinking about literature, solitude, negativity if you like — getting involved in activities which displayed all the imperfections of activism. (...) [T]here were numerous preparatory meetings and they all bore the mark — it was very fine actually, and rather terrible — of a sort of... fate, a negative *fatum*, which came from... Blanchot; basically therefore, at a second level let's say, the undertaking was fated necessarily to come to nothing. That is the paradox which we perceived, if you follow me! A sort of staging of negativity. And it was very fine, but rather fatiguing, as well as trying. (V, 779–80)[33]

This account, displaying a voyeurism that was all the more active for being exhausting, contrasts with what those close to Blanchot have said, namely how much he wanted the project to succeed, and how ill its failure made him. It is surprising to hear Barthes theatricalize and mythologize Blanchot's activism. Especially considering that if this activism fatigued him, he drew substantial benefit from it, as he had just acknowledged at the time of this interview, when in *A Lover's Discourse* he referred to 'a previous conversation' with Blanchot: 'I had to wait for Blanchot to have someone talk to me about Fatigue' (V, 149).[34]

Perhaps Blanchot noticed this attitude, with its mixture of fascination and weariness. Perhaps he recalled that Barthes had not signed the 'Manifesto of the 121'. No doubt he continued to read him and to follow the progress of a theoretical method whose arrogant pretensions gave rise later on to a rare flight of invective: 'You theorists should know that you are mortal, and that theory is already death in you.'[35] This was his way of repaying in kind a man who had contributed to depicting his work as 'a magnificent and deserted sign'.[36] He remained silent about work which borrowed his language only so as to transform it. His writing proceeded by way of fragments and tangents in relation to psychoanalysis and philosophy, whilst Barthes distanced himself from both sciences and ideologies. They had both admired Foucault's *History of Madness*, as well as Derrida's first books. But Derrida broke with Sollers, and any opportunity for direct dialogue became remote.

It was therefore Barthes who would return to Blanchot, to the neuter in Blanchot. In the 1970s, he tended to uncouple the neuter from its links to the degree zero:

The Neuter is thus not the third term — the degree zero — of an opposition which is both semantic and conflictual, it is, *at another link in the infinite chain of language*, the second term of a new paradigm, the full term of which is violence (combat, victory, theatre, arrogance). (IV, 707)[37]

In the lectures on *The Neuter*, this is what Barthes will call 'the active side [*l'actif*] of the Neuter': the just measure of a relation to the world which seeks constantly to free itself of all aggression and all oppression, which displays differences without hierarchy, which touches by dint of not touching and maintains by means of restraint — 'an ardent, burning activity', 'an extreme concentration of energy'.[38] In *The Pleasure of the Text*, the neuter was already on the side of pleasure: 'never tire of speaking of the *suspensive* force of pleasure (. . .). Pleasure is a *neuter*' (IV, 260).[39]

In the lectures, the neuter has the capacity to unsettle any principle of representation and systematization. It is defined at the outset as something capable of outwitting any paradigm. Political, historical, ethical and aesthetic implications constantly interfere, and the lecture can be read as a neutralizing mechanism, for the active neutralization *of* the reactive neutralization exerted by all power, be it political, media-based, ideological or 'ideospheric' as Barthes puts it. The meaning of his return to Blanchot can thus be understood, particularly when Barthes quotes this passage from *The Infinite Conversation*: 'The demand of the neuter tends to suspend the attributive structure of language, that relation to being, whether implicit or explicit, which is, in our languages, immediately posited as soon as something is said.'[40] This necessity for an ontological critique calls for what alone can convey the demand and communicate the pleasure of the neuter: writing. Hence Barthes states further on: 'Writing is precisely that discourse which can reliably thwart the arrogance of discourse.'[41] When one recalls that *Writing Degree Zero* presented itself as 'an introduction to what could be a History of Writing',[42] the change of position is considerable. Barthes has gone from a historical enquiry to an ontological one: from a forecast to a critique, not to say a deconstruction; from having reservations about neutral writing to being certain of the neutral power of writing. He can now set to work on *The Preparation for the Novel*: a 'writing of the Neuter' perhaps, 'a white Work' of course, whose simplicity should make it accessible to a wider public, but whose hero remains Mallarmé.[43]

We are now in the closing pages of *Roland Barthes*. Here, Blanchot is simultaneously rejected and admired. The expression from 1950, 'a magnificent and deserted sign', returns in the form of a 'clandestine heroism'. Barthes admires the literary heroism of Mallarmé, Kafka and Proust, a heroism without arrogance which has nothing in common with social, military or militant heroism. And to this heroism, which is 'called on today to be *clandestine*, unsaid', Blanchot provides 'the sole and final testimony'. A week later, however, during the final lecture in the series, Barthes once again invokes the figure of the *fatum*: 'Blanchot, the admirable theorist (even if my project is opposed to his) of that sort of disappointment or tragic exhaustion of literature: the work can no longer be anything other than what I have to say about it.'[44] It is 23 February 1980; these are the last words Roland Barthes will utter in public.

And yet there is nothing more coherent than this contradiction when it is at work. The chiasm of dialogue having disappeared, there emerged a monologue in which the sole speaker could treat the other only in oxymoronic mode. The alliance offered to Blanchot by Barthes was thus a curious one. Close examination of the numerous references to Blanchot in Barthes's writings and interviews would be revealing. I shall conclude by surveying them rapidly.

These references follow a twin curve, both emphatic and negative. The impulse to adhere sometimes appears unbounded. Barthes even seems to have heard the lesson or remonstration from 1953. He opens the second part of *Criticism and Truth*, at the point where he moves from *refutatio* to *confirmatio*, by citing three exemplary writers:

Mallarmé, Proust and Blanchot (II, 781).[45] The names which framed Blanchot's commentary on *Writing Degree Zero* now precede Barthes's recognition of Blanchot's writing. In an interview with Raymond Bellour for the *Lettres françaises* in March 1967, Barthes intensifies his praise: 'Blanchot belongs to what is unequalled, inimitable and inapplicable. He belongs to writing, to the transgression of science which constitutes literature' (II, 1302).[46] When he adopts this tone, Barthes grants Blanchot a historic place in the history of writing. Expressions such as 'since Blanchot' and 'from Mallarmé to Blanchot' proliferate.

This is not always the case, however. Barthes is also capable of violently backing away, and erasing his own acts of recognition. A case in point is his revision of the article entitled 'Baudelaire's Theatre'. This text was published twice: first in 1954 in *Théâtre populaire*, then in 1955, by the Club du Meilleur Livre, as the preface to an edition of the poet's *Complete Works*. Towards the end it contained a decisive dual reference to Blanchot: 'the pure murder of Literature, which we know since Blanchot to be the torment and the justification of the modern writer'; and speaking of Baudelaire: 'that sociability which he pretended to profess and to flee, according to the dialectic of a choice which Sartre and Blanchot have conclusively analysed'.[47] But when he revised the text for inclusion in *Critical Essays* in 1964, Barthes carried out a two-fold deletion. Where it appeared the first time, Blanchot's name is replaced by that of Mallarmé; the second time, it disappears, leaving only Sartre's (II, 309).[48] And such changes are common. In 1971, Jean Thibaudeau asked Barthes in an interview for *Tel Quel*: 'which are the critical systems or theories of literature that influenced *Writing Degree Zero*', before suggesting the names of Paulhan, Blanchot, Sartre and Lukács. Barthes's response is astonishing: 'I knew neither Paulhan, nor Blanchot, nor Lukács, I didn't even know their names (except perhaps for Paulhan's)' (III, 1028).[49] Yet of the three of them, Blanchot alone is cited in the book! Just as incredible is the systematic exclusion of Blanchot's name from the surveys of the situation of criticism in France which Barthes gave to foreign journals. In 1959, he publishes in *Politica*, a Yugoslav journal, a piece entitled 'New Directions in Literary Criticism in France'. He contrasts criticism that reviews what has just come out [*une critique de lancée*] (Taine, Plekhanov) and 'criticism of structures' (Goldmann, Sartre, Bachelard, Poulet, Richard). He does not mention Blanchot (I, 977–80).[50] In 1963 he publishes 'The Two Criticisms' in *Modern Language Notes*: positivist criticism is contrasted with ideological criticism, university criticism with interpretative criticism, transcendent criticism with immanent criticism, one that posits an 'elsewhere' for the work with one that works 'in a domain which is purely internal to the work'. Again he cites Sartre, Bachelard, Goldmann, Poulet, and Richard, but also Starobinski, Weber, Girard, though yet again, not Blanchot (II, 496–501).[51] In the same year, he paints a similar picture in 'What is Criticism' for the *Times Literary Supplement* (II, 502–7).[52] Still in 1963, it takes questioning by *Tel Quel* in 'Literature and Signification' to transform this critical typology, and this time contrast the 'critics of significance' on the one hand with Blanchot alone on the other (II, 516–9).[53] But Barthes objects to this contrast, maintaining that the question of the suspension of sense can already be found in the critics of significance. In this way, he contrasts criticism that posits a meaning with criticism — Blanchot's — that 'nihilates' it. We are back with the debate in *Writing Degree Zero*: what lies outside of sense [*le hors-sens*] always ends up being recouped by '*non-sense* which is indisputably a form of sense' (II, 518).[54] What lies outside of sense can only be maintained as a hypothesis that is necessary theoretically, and socially provisional. That is the limit he establishes for Blanchot's work: 'by refusing the work any semantic "solidification", Blanchot merely succeeds in tracing out the empty imprint of meaning'. But in an interview he gave to *France-Observateur* the following year — the year of the double erasure — he evokes the 'very great works (...) of Mallarmé and Blanchot', which were written 'from within this empty imprint' (II, 616).[55] And in 'Literature and Signification' he refers very rapidly, though in a way that is inhabitual, to Blanchot's *récits*: 'Blanchot's work (whether critical or "novelistic") thus represents, in its own way, which is singular (though I believe it may have its counterparts in painting and music), a sort of epic of meaning, which might be called Adamic, since it is that of the first man from *before meaning*' (II, 518–9).[56] Was it Blanchot then, the writer referred to in 1953 in the closing lines of *Writing Degree Zero*, the language of whose writing 'offered perhaps the perfect figure of a new Adamic world where language would no longer be alienated'?[57]

The diverse statements about Blanchot by Barthes could thus be read as a *mythology* to which he never found the key. That is no doubt why Barthes encouraged Daniel Wilhem at the beginning of the seventies in his bold project: to write a thesis on 'narrative voice' in Blanchot.[58] This was the voice that had 'fatigued' him. The voice that he had believed to be exclusively political, and whose literary potential he glimpsed on the threshold of the novel of the Neuter. The voice which had located, *for him*, his own 'discordemes'.

Perhaps Blanchot played for Barthes the role played by Zambinella for Sarrasine. RB, MB: this would be their R/M, their very own bar of signification. Reflecting that, I shall conclude with this statement which transposes a sentence of Roland Barthes's (III, 207): 'Barthes receives the Blanchotian M according to its true nature, which is the wound of lack'.[59]

Translated by Michael Holland

NOTES

1. The first version of this article was written for a conference in Brazil organised by André Quieroz, Fabiana de Moraes and Nina Velasco e Cruz, with the title 'Barthes/Blanchot: um encontro possivel?'. The proceedings were recently published in Portuguese by Editoras 7 Letras (Rio de Janeiro). The French version is unpublished.
2. Roland Barthes, *Comment vivre ensemble, Cours et séminaires au Collège de France (1976–1977)* (Paris, Seuil/IMEC, 2002), 71.
3. Barthes seems unaware that he shares this rare passion with Blanchot: 'the only Schumann-lovers I know are Gilles Deleuze, Marcel Beaufils and myself' (Preface to *Musique pour piano de Schumann* de Marcel Beaufils (Paris, Phoebus, 1979), in *Oeuvres complètes*, vol. V (Paris, Seuil, 2002), 725. I shall refer to Barthes's texts in this second edition of the *Oeuvres complètes*. References will be in the main text, with the volume number in Roman numerals and the page number in Arabic numerals.
4. Jacques Derrida, *Chaque fois unique, la fin du monde* (Paris, Galilée, 2001).
5. Roland Barthes, *Le Degré zéro de l'écriture* (Paris, Seuil, 1953); *Writing Degree Zero*, translated by Annette Lavers and Colin Smith (London, Jonathan Cape, 1967).
6. Maurice Blanchot, *La Part du feu* (Paris, Gallimard, 1949); *The Work of Fire*, translated by Charlotte Mandell (Stanford, Stanford University Press, 1995).
7. 'Suis-je marxiste?', *Les Lettres nouvelles* (juillet-août 1955). It should be said that he had just been attacked on two occasions in its pages: in May 1955, Jacques Lemarchand attacked *Théâtre populaire*, and Jean Guérin (alias Jean Paulhan no doubt) attacked *Mythologies* in June.
8. *Le Degré zéro de l'écriture*, 55, 57; *Writing Degree Zero*, 82, 84 (translation modified).
9. Strangely, Barthes's inclinations change between 1950 and 1953: in the first version of the text Blanchot's writing is placed on a par with that of Camus, while his studies of Mallarmé are not referred to (see 'L'écriture et le silence' [Writing and silence], *Combat*, Thursday 23 November, 1950, 4).
10. Maurice Blanchot, 'Plus loin que le degré zéro', *La Nouvelle Nouvelle Revue française*, 9 (septembre 1953), 489; 'The Search for Point Zero', *The Book to*

Come, translated by Charlotte Mandell (Stanford, Stanford University Press, 2003), 205.
11 'Plus loin que le degré zéro', 487; *The Book to Come*, 203–4 (translation modified). The sentence is identical in both versions.
12 'Plus loin que le degré zéro', 493–4, *The Book to Come*, 209 respectively. The section is slightly modified in the final version.
13 'La solitude essentielle', in *L'Espace littéraire* (Paris, Gallimard, 1955, collection 'Idées'), 7–28; 'The Essential Solitude', in *The Space of Literature*, translated by Ann Smock (Lincoln and London, University of Nebraska Press, 1982), 21–34.
14 Maurice Blanchot, *Thomas l'obscur* (Paris, Gallimard, 1941), 113.
15 Maurice Blanchot, *La Folie du jour* (Montpellier, Fata Morgana, 1973); *The Madness of the Day*, translated by Lydia Davis (Barrytown, NY, Station Hill Press, 1981).
16 Maurice Blanchot, *Au moment voulu* (Paris, Gallimard, 1951), 83; *When the Time Comes*, translated by Lydia Davis (Barrytown, NY, Station Hill Press, 1985) 35 (translation modified); *Celui qui ne m'accompagnait pas* (Paris, Gallimard, 1953), 12, 125; *The One Who was Standing Apart from Me*, translated by Lydia Davis (Barrytown, NY, Station Hill Press, 1993), 4, 66 (translation modified).
17 'Le roman de l'étranger', in Maurice Blanchot, *Faux pas* (Paris, Gallimard, 1971 [1943]), 242–7; 'The Novel of the Stranger', in *Faux pas*, translated by Charlotte Mandell (Stanford, Stanford University Press, 2001), 217–21.
18 It would be of advantage to reread Roland Barthes's first publication on the literary page of *Combat* on 1 August 1947. Its title is already 'Writing Degree Zero'. The perspectives in this initial approach are astonishing. They reveal in their way that the question of the neuter is for Barthes, from the outset and as he sets out, a question that is simultaneously aesthetic, historical, political and philosophical.
19 Preface to Bertolt Brecht, *Mère Courage et ses enfants* (Paris, L'Arche, 1960).
20 'L'effet d'étrangeté', in Maurice Blanchot, *L'Entretien infini* (Paris, Gallimard, 1969), 528–39 (536–7); 'The Effect of Strangeness', in *The Infinite Conversation*, translated by Susan Hanson (Minneapolis and London, University of Minnesota Press, 1993), 360–7 (366) (translation modified).
21 *L'Entretien infini*, 538; *The Infinite Conversation*, 367 (translation modified).
22 See 'La littérature et l'expérience originelle', in *L'Espace littéraire*, 281–379; 'Literature and the Original Experience', in *The Space of Literature*, 213–47.
23 During the first half of 1952, Bernard Dort published a review of *When the Time Comes* (*Les Cahiers du Sud*, 311, 134–5). For a more general account of Dort's admiration for Blanchot see Chantal Meyer-Plantureux, *Bernard Dort, un intellectuel singulier* (Paris, Seuil, 2000).
24 Maurice Blanchot, *L'Amitié* (Paris, Gallimard, 1971); *Friendship*, translated by Elizabeth Rottenberg (Stanford, Stanford University Press, 1997).

25 'L'effet de réel', *Communications*, 11 (March 1968), 84–9. Also in *Le Bruissement de la langue. Essais critiques, IV* (Paris, Seuil, 1984), 179–88; 'The Reality Effect', in *The Rustle of Language*, translated by Richard Howard (Oxford, Basil Blackwell, 1986), 141–8.

26 'Leçon d'écriture', *Tel Quel*, 34 (Summer 1968), 28–33; 'Lesson in Writing', *Image-Music-Text*, translated by Stephen Heath (London, Fontana, 1977), 170–8.

27 'La mort de l'auteur', *Manteia*, 5 (1968). Also in *Le Bruissement de la la langue*, 63–70; 'The Death of the Author', in *The Rustle of Language*, 49–55.

28 'Linguistique et littérature', *Langages*, 12 (December 1968), 3–8.

29 Roland Barthes, *Eléments de sémiologie* (Paris, Seuil, 1964); *Elements of Semiology*, translated by Annette Lavers and Colin Smith (London, Jonathan Cape, 1967).

30 Roland Barthes, *Système de la mode* (Paris, Seuil, 1967); *The Fashion System*, translated by Matthew Ward and Richard Howard (New York, Hill and Wang, 1983).

31 'La mort de l'auteur', *Le Bruissement de la langue*, 63; *The Rustle of Language*, 49 (translation modified).

32 And it is in that sense that Barthes quoted him in *Critique et vérité* (Paris, Seuil, 1966); *Criticism and Truth*, translated by Kathrine Pilcher Keuneman (London, Athlone, 1987). See also the preface to *Essais critiques* (Paris, Seuil, 1963), 9–18; *Critical Essays*, translated by Richard Howard (Evanston, Northwestern University Press, 1972), xi–xxi, which extends the indirect dialogue begun ten years earlier (e.g. the sections on the last reply, the opposition between 'I' and 'one', the Orphic metaphor (II, 273–82).)

33 'Vie et mort des revues', an interview with Maria-Teresa Padova, *Scarabée International* (Spring, 1982).

34 Roland Barthes, *Fragments d'un discours amoureux* (Paris, Seuil, 1977), 133; *A Lover's Discourse. Fragments*, translated by Richard Howard (London, Jonathan Cape, 1979), 116.

35 Maurice Blanchot, *L'Ecriture du désastre* (Paris, Gallimard, 1980), 73; *The Writing of the Disaster*, translated by Ann Smock (Lincoln and London, University of Nebraska Press, 1986), 43.

36 In December 1950, Barthes contrasted the knowledge of the 'sciences of man' with the vain ritual of literature: 'literary writing is becoming more and more a magnificent and deserted sign' (*Combat*, 14 October 1950, 7). The expression describes quite effectively the locus of his fascination with Blanchot.

37 *Roland Barthes par Roland Barthes* (Paris, Seuil, 1975), 135–6; *Roland Barthes by Roland Barthes*, translated by Richard Howard (London, Macmillan, 1977), 132–3 (translation modified).

38 Roland Barthes, *Le Neutre. Cours au Collège de France (1977–1978)* (Paris, Seuil/IMEC, 2002), 116–22, 32, 104; *The Neutral. Lecture Course at the*

Collège de France, translated by Rosalind E. Krauss and Denis Hollier (New York, Columbia University Press, 2005), 81–6, 7, 71 (translation modified).
39 Roland Barthes, *Le Plaisir du texte* (Paris, Seuil, 1973), 102; *The Pleasure of the Text*, translated by Richard Miller (London, Jonathan Cape, 1976), 65.
40 *Le Neutre*, 76; *The Neutral*, 45. *L'Entretien infini*, 567; *The Infinite Conversation*, 386 (translation modified).
41 *Le Neutre*, 206; *The Neutral*, 162 (translation modified).
42 *Le Degré zéro de l'écriture*, 10; *Writing Degree Zero*, 12.
43 Roland Barthes, *La Préparation du roman. Cours et séminaires au Collège de France (1978–1979 et 1979–1980)* (Paris, Seuil/IMEC, 2003), 41, 378–83.
44 *La Préparation du roman*, 359, 380
45 *Critique et vérité*, 45; *Criticism and Truth*, 63.
46 'Sur le *Système de la mode* et l'analyse structurale des récits', an interview with Raymond Bellour, *Les Lettres françaises*, 2 March 1967. 'On *The Fashion System* and the Structural Analysis of Narratives', in *Le Grain de la voix* (Paris, Seuil, 1981), 62–80 (52); *The Grain of the Voice. Interviews 1962–1980*, translated by Linda Coverdale (London, Jonathan Cape, 1985), 43–55.
47 'Le théâtre de Baudelaire', *Théâtre populaire*, 8 (July–August 1954), 51.
48 *Essais critiques*, 41–7 (47); *Critical Essays*, 25–32 (31). Also in *Barthes: Selected Writings*, edited by Susan Sontag (London, Fontana, 1982), 74–81 (80–1).
49 'Réponses', interview with Jean Thibaudeau, *Tel Quel*, 47 (Autumn, 1971), 89–107.
50 'Voies nouvelles de la critique littéraire en France', *Politica* (May 1959).
51 *Modern Language Notes*, 78 (1963), 447–52. In *Essais critiques*, 246–51; *Critical Essays*, 249–54.
52 *Times Literary Supplement* (1963). In *Essais critiques*, 252–7; *Critical Essays*, 255–60.
53 *Essais critiques*, 258–76; *Critical Essays*, 261–79 (translation modified).
54 *Essais critiques*, 269; *Critical Essays*, 272 (translation modified).
55 'Je ne crois pas aux influences', an interview with Renaud Matignon, *France-Observateur*, 16 April 1964. In *Le Grain de la voix*, 30–3 (32); 'I don't believe in influences', *The Grain of the Voice*, 25–9 (27) (translation modified).
56 *Essais critiques*, 269; *Critical Essays*, 272 (translation modified).
57 *Le Degré zéro de l'écriture*, 65; *Writing Degree Zero*, 94.
58 Daniel Wilhem, *Maurice Blanchot: la voix narrative* (Paris, U.G.E., collection '10/18', 1974).
59 *S/Z* (Paris, Seuil, collection 'Points', 1970), 113; *S/Z*, translated by Richard Miller (London, Jonathan Cape, 1975), 107 (translation modified).

From the Star to the Disaster

KEVIN HART

Abstract:
Franz Rosenzweig's *The Star of Redemption* comes before the Shoah and Maurice Blanchot's *The Writing of the Disaster* comes after it. The one addresses itself with hope to the figure of a star; the other meditates on the state of being without a guiding star. The figure of Emmanuel Levinas stands between these two works, since *Totality and Infinity* is marked by Rosenzweig's critique of totality and *The Writing of the Disaster* is in part a response to Levinas's philosophy. Both Rosenzweig and Blanchot propose a new way of thinking, one that calls unity into question. This essay seeks to clarify what 'thought' means for Rosenzweig and for Blanchot. In what ways do Rosenzweig and Blanchot converge? In what ways do they diverge?

Keywords: Blanchot, Rosenzweig, Levinas, Shoah, double truth, disaster

Almost sixty years separate the publication of Franz Rosenzweig's *Der Stern der Erlösung* (*The Star of Redemption*) (1921) and Maurice Blanchot's *L'Ecriture du désastre* (*The Writing of the Disaster*) (1980). It is difficult to say if these two books should be seen as utterly distinct, the atheist laying aside as completely hopeless the intense spiritual hope of the observant Jew, or if they are fundamentally in accord, the Frenchman confirming and extending, though in a new direction, the crucial intuitions of the German. It is hard to specify the relation that would encompass the two, in part because each is a work that remains solitary, largely outside the hubbub of philosophical and theological discussion, and Blanchot does not refer to Rosenzweig in *The Writing of the Disaster* and only in passing elsewhere. Yet it is enticing to think that Blanchot's idea of the 'relation without relation', worked out in dialogue with Emmanuel Levinas, may help us to think these two books together without thereby making them into a false unity.[1] Could it be that they abide, like two separated voices, in a relation that is marked by a violent interruption — the Shoah — that nonetheless keeps them together? Also, though, it is possible that there is another, more mediated relation in play. It is intriguing to think that Levinas himself is the one who keeps these two works in relation for us, the one opening the space in which *Totalité et infini* (*Totality and Infinity*) (1961) could be written, and the latter responding in part to that work and its profound companion, *Autrement qu'être* (*Otherwise Than Being*) (1974).² In thinking of *The Star of Redemption* and *The Writing of the Disaster*, with the Shoah and Levinas between them, we might better understand the change in thinking that was glimpsed last century in these two works, a change that Rosenzweig dubbed 'the new thinking' and that Blanchot called simply 'thought'.³

If the two books are joined, it is mostly along a common, hyperbolic line of criticism. For both Rosenzweig and Blanchot question one of the most deep-seated assumptions of philosophy, that there is a unity of thought.⁴ Right at the beginning of *The Star*, we are reminded that, '[i]t is the unity of thinking that enforces its right by asserting the totality of the world against the multiplicity of knowledge. The unity of the logos founds the unity of the world as a totality' (S, 18). Accordingly, 'he who questions the totality of being, as is the case here, refutes the unity of thinking. He who does this throws the gauntlet to the whole venerable brotherhood of philosophy from Ionia to Jena' (S, 18). Later, he declares with equal confidence, '[w]e have broken the All to pieces, and now each piece is an All unto itself' (S, 34), and resigns himself to the 'imperfect work of our knowledge' (S, 34). Exactly what this fragmentation means for us is spelled out much later: 'The mythical God, the plastic world, tragic man—we are holding the pieces in our hands. We have really shattered the All' (S, 93). Idealist philosophy from Parmenides to Hegel has come to an end, it seems, and Rosenzweig does not hesitate to call it pagan philosophy, since it affirms immanence over transcendence.⁵ His philosophy (and he insists that it is a philosophy, not a theology) is one of transcendence.⁶ It involves an ascent, sure, though no *theosis*, and is principally a philosophy of God's free descent into the world, one broad enough to include the Shekina and the Incarnation. From the beginning of its second part, once the logic of the 'system' has been expounded, it is a positive philosophy, in Schelling's sense of the expression, a philosophy in touch with the here and now.⁷

Idealism serves as a figure of philosophy as such for Rosenzweig, and once it has been overcome there opens the possibility of thinking anew, and one project of this new thinking is reconceiving the nature of unity. The world is not constituted by thought, as traditional idealism has claimed; it is not monological, formed from within by the logos, but is more than logical, or—as Rosenzweig has it—metalogical; it includes the logos yet precedes it and cannot be encompassed by it. In terms of method, also, philosophy can no longer be monological but must become dialogical; the philosopher must turn from producing the great System in the solitude of his study or before the podium in a lecture theater and be transformed into a *Sprachdenker*, a speech-thinker, someone in whom philosophy emerges out of conversation with others. The new thinking begins with the recognition that lived existence, communal as well as individual, is prior to essence. Yet this new beginning is itself prompted by something given in experience, namely the fear of death. Only by rejecting the assurances that philosophy gives us that death is really a shelter from life can we begin to think freshly, both about the world and our actions in it. Just as the world is metalogical, so too men and women are metaethical, beings who practice ethics rather than draw their humanity solely from it.[8]

The cosmos, as conceived by the Greeks, is '*securus adversus deos*' (S, 22), insulated from the gods, and this is not because the Greeks turned away from their divinities but because Olympus was always a world unto itself, without any need to refer to the villages and fields below. For all the Greeks' talk of the gods, and for all our talk of classical mythology, the Greeks in fact developed 'a world without gods' (S, 42), even when the gods ruled the whole world. The Greeks lived without Apollo and Zeus having to establish concrete relationships with mortals. Similarly, Christian theology has also been set against God to the extent that it has construed God as existing *a se*, eternal, immutable, omniscient, omnipotent, and not needing to form any relations with human beings.[9] No matter when and where it takes place, thinking is safe from the disturbance of the divine whenever it believes that it can explain the whole from within its limits. For the Greeks, the gods are the highest beings of the cosmos. For Islam, God is unconditioned and perfect, utterly apart from the world. And for those Christians whose theology depends on Plato and Aristotle (presumably without the adjustments made by Aquinas), God is the highest ground of being.[10] In all these cases, divinity is not beyond the cosmos as its Creator.

Rosenzweig introduces this thought somewhat abstractly. First, he states his general position with respect to the idealist strain in philosophy: 'So thinking, moreover, which is itself the unity of its own internal multiplicity, establishes the unity of being, and certainly, it is not in the degree where it is a unity, but a multiplicity' (S, 19). Rather than entertain a world that is nothing other than mere multiplicity, however, he looks elsewhere for unity: 'But now, the unity of thinking insofar as it directly concerns thinking alone and not being, falls outside of the cosmos of being = thinking.

This cosmos itself, insofar as it is the overlapping of two multiplicities, now has its unity entirely beyond itself' (S, 19). So Rosenzweig breaks with Schelling, for whom (at least in the Stuttgart seminars of 1810) 'cosmos' is co-ordinate with 'system'.[11] The unity beyond the cosmos that Rosenzweig discerns as the basis for his system — the 'new thinking' — can be presented only by way of paradox. As we are told in the *Urzelle*, '[t]his something attached to reason beyond (said *logically*: "beyond") reason is a unity, which is *not* the unity of two: not to be formulated as equation, rather unity *aside* from duality, the equals sign in both equations, but, with respect to the difference of its application there'.[12] We should not identify the divine *Urgrund* or dark abyss from which God creates Himself with the God who freely enters into a relationship with us.

As can be seen from this allusion to Schelling's later philosophy of religion, Rosenzweig does not escape German idealism (as Heidegger hoped to do) so much as modify it; and he does so by pitting it against itself and drawing from time to time on others of its critics, especially Kierkegaard and Nietzsche. One piece of idealism he takes is Kant's doctrine of the noumenal world. It is there, beyond the cosmos, where God abides, although we can approach Him through prayer and not merely through moral action. Schelling of course would not subscribe to the idea of the noumenal world, Kant being for him the clergyman of *Clara* who denies any relation between this world and the next. Yet Rosenzweig picks and chooses among idealist systems, taking only what is needed for the new thinking. Another, more important piece for him is Schelling's notion of the *Urgrund*. Rosenzweig allows these thoughts to point him outside the absolute idealism of Hegel, that increasingly determinate process of thinking about thinking.[13] Unity will come, he says, only from outside the cosmos. And when we pass '[t]owards the "outside"', Rosenzweig says, 'the world is thus deprived of that truth' that has sustained the idealist strain of philosophy in all its variations over the centuries (S, 21).

That Rosenzweig borrows from Kant and Schelling does not commit him to either philosophy in its broad lines or in all the details that gather round a motif. For one thing, he rejects the philosophy of time as Kant develops it in the 'Transcendental Aesthetic' of the *Critique of Pure Reason* (1787). No longer is time conceived as a pure form that is given *a priori*.[14] Instead, time is deformalized, and for Rosenzweig the *a priori* horizon is to be replaced by one that is informed by Schelling's notion of the three ages in his *Die Weltalter* (1811–15) and by the experience of the Jews. In his great fragment on the three ages, Schelling tells us very little about the second of his three ages, the present, and — assuming that we reject *Clara* (1810?) as the start of the third book — nothing at all about the future. Yet he tells us a great deal about the first, a past that was never present, an 'eternal past' that belongs to God before creation.[15] Excited by this idea, Rosenzweig interprets it in the direction of Lurianic Kabbalah. The *Urgrund*, pure self-identity, an essence that does not yet exist, posits itself as both an object and a subject, and thereby comes into being. That much is Schelling. The view that God comes into existence by way of withdrawing from His essence so that He can freely relate to us in history is Rosenzweig's Kabbalistic reading of Schelling, an interpretation that grounds the philosophy of transcendence that he develops.[16]

Time, for Schelling and for his Jewish admirer, is not successive, reaching a concrete determination of *Geist*, so much as overlapping: we live in the three ages of the world in different ways although at one and the same time. *Die Weltalter* begins by declaring, '[t]he past is known, the present is discerned, the future is intimated'.[17] For Rosenzweig, the past is Creation, the present is Revelation, and the future is Redemption. As we have seen, metalogic changed the nature of *ontologica specialis* as inherited from Christian Wolff's *Vernünftige Gedanken von Gott, der Welt und der Seele der Menschen, auch allen Dingen überhaupt* (1719), so that God, Man, and World no longer comprise a whole ordered from within by thought but a system of relations instead. Now, with the deformalization of time, we have another triangle, one formed by the apexes of Creation, Revelation and Redemption, and it intersects with the first. And so the Star of David appears, newly charged with philosophical dignity, and since all six categories are common to the two religions, it encompasses Christianity as well as Judaism. Rosenzweig calls it 'the Star of Redemption'.

It seems, then, as though Rosenzweig challenges the unity of thought in philosophy only to recast it at the level of theology. This is the conclusion that will be reached if one quickly reads *The Star*, for all its criticisms of Hegel, as a deeply Hegelian work, as though the first two parts of the book, 'The Elements' and 'The Path', are sublated in the third part, 'The Configuration'.[18] Even so, 'theology' would be not quite the right word here, if only because the Hegelian *Aufhebung* retains the content of theology while changing its form into philosophy. Also, while Rosenzweig plainly draws from Hegel, he does so, as we have seen, while also adapting from others and using what he takes to contest the dialectic and its drive toward totality. The unity that is conferred from the viewpoint of theology comes from beyond the cosmos, and certainly beyond the range of the dialectic: Rosenzweig's God is not intelligible as *Geist*. Besides, whatever unity Rosenzweig affirms in the third book of *The Star* is one that takes account of human being as already doubled and of redemption itself as divided. We are doubled, he thinks, insofar as only a human being is a self ('B = B', as his logic has it) capable of experiencing revelation, and therefore able to say 'I'; and yet, '[a]ll relation finds its foothold only between third persons; the system is the world in the form of the third person'.[19]

More complicated is the division in redemption itself, which is required for Judaism and Christianity both to be true. One difficulty that stems from the rejection of thought is that it is not clear on what basis either Judaism or Christianity can maintain its integrity as a religion. How can the God beyond the cosmos, beyond totality, confer unity on either Judaism or Christianity? Let us limit ourselves simply to the Christian religion, and to one of the main challenges it has faced in maintaining doctrinal coherence. Rosenzweig approaches the question historically, in a quasi-Hegelian dialectical narrative, by considering how Christianity overcomes the challenge of having a divided essence, of its truth being distributed between faith and reason. The problem does not emerge with Augustine, he thinks, because Christianity was able to convert pagan philosophers with its discourse of love. Against pagan philosophy, however, love was impotent. With the Emperor Justinian's closure of Plato's Academy in Athens in 529, and a more general suppression of paganism, *philosophia* became 'an opponent as intangible as a phantom and yet very colourfully visible and hung as it were like a painting on the wall, against which the power of action — and here, the power of love — was inadequate to win the victory' (*S*, 298).

It is an elegant conceit, and Rosenzweig allows it to develop fully: 'Before the picture on the wall, medieval Scholasticism had put up a curtain that it could open and close; for it was only a curtain before that most dreadful thought — precisely in the Christian sense most doubtful, because it was a hindrance to the mission — of a twofold truth, a truth of reason opposite the truth of faith' (*S*, 298). The allusion is to the spectre of *duplex veritate*, double truth, the modern name of a philosophical stance that was popularized by Ernest Renan in his *Averroès et l'averroïsme* (*Averroes and Averroism*) (1867). Whether it was distinctly held or not, the philosophical view certainly precipitated a crisis in the Church. The earliest and most dramatic instance of it is the condemnation by Etienne Tempier, Bishop of Paris, in 1277 of some Masters of Arts in the University of Paris. The Bishop objected to those radical Aristotelians who said that certain things are 'true according to philosophy, yet not according to the Catholic faith, as if these were two contrary truths' (*vera secundum philosophiam, sed non secundum fidem catholicam, quasi sint duae contrariae veritates*).[20] Two Masters, Siger of Brabant and Boethius of Dacia, were named, although no attempt was made to distinguish what they actually taught from what their enemies said they taught.[21]

Moving quickly and lightly over his material, Rosenzweig suggests that the Church 'seemed again to disintegrate for these three centuries, in fact four centuries, counting the aftermath' (S, 299). 'Disintegrate' is far too strong a word, and Rosenzweig completely ignores the synthesis of *fides et ratio* provided by Aquinas that was to sustain the Catholic Church through the centuries. It might be noted also that Rosenzweig bypasses without comment Aquinas's teaching that the divine *esse* could abide with all possible perfections without the cosmos; one does not need to appeal to Schelling's dark abyss when one has Aquinas's doctrine of God. That said, Rosenzweig is entirely correct to point out that the spectre of *duplex veritate* reappeared in the sixteenth century. In the eighth session of the Fifth Lateran Council on March 11, 1513, Leo X addressed all philosophers, admonishing them that they were not to teach that the rational soul is mortal 'at least according to philosophy (*secundum saltem philosophiam verum*)', for theology teaches that it is immortal. 'And since truth cannot contradict truth (*Cumque verum vero minime contradicat*)', Leo says, 'we define that every statement contrary to the enlightened truth of the faith is totally false and we strictly forbid teaching otherwise to be permitted'.[22] Leo did not name Pietro Pompanazzi in his decree but an interpretation of the philosopher's teaching that the immortality of the soul was certain for faith but not for reason was undoubtedly in his mind.[23] Pompanazzi's book, *Tractatus de immortalitate animæ*, was not published until 1516, and when it appeared Leo obliged the philosopher to retract his teaching.

For Rosenzweig, the upshot of the Fifth Lateran Council was the overcoming of 'the evil thought of twofold truth' (S, 299), by faith, and this led directly to the upsurge of Protestantism and the irruption of another problem there. Again, Rosenzweig draws from Schelling (though surely with a bow to Joachim of Fiore as well), this time to give himself the three ages of Christendom: the Petrine (or Catholic) age, beginning with the Edict of Milan in 313; the Pauline (or Protestant) age, beginning with Luther's posting of the ninety-five theses to the door at the Wittenberg Castle Church in 1517; and the Johannine age, which has been developing since 1800, the symbolic year that for Rosenzweig marks the fulfillment of German Idealism and the beginning of *Weltanschauungsphilosophie*.[24] With the final banishing of the *duplex veritate*, we see the passage from the Petrine to the Pauline Church. 'Faith had quite simply forgotten the body in the spirit. The world had slipped away from it', we are told. 'Of course, it had gotten rid of the doctrine of twofold truth. But in return, it dealt in a twofold reality, that is to say of the purely inner reality of faith and the purely outer reality of an increasingly worldly world; the greater the tension between the two, the better this Protestantism felt' (S, 299–300). This is the world first of Luther and then, over a century later, of Kant's attempt to limit reason in order to supply a place for moral faith.[25]

When fully elaborated, German idealism was to reject this exclusive attention Christianity gives to faith, whether it be Luther's *fiducia* or Kant's moral faith. (Rosenzweig is presumably thinking of Hegel's acidic remark in 1802 that, with Kant, Jacobi and Fichte, '[p]hilosophy has made itself the handmaid of a faith once more'.[26]) And, with this rejection, Christianity was to take another turn, this time towards what Rosenzweig calls the 'Christianity of the future' (S, 300) or the 'Johannine completion' (S, 302). It is worth noting that Rosenzweig does not take into consideration Hegel's criticism of the very idea of a noumenon, whether the deity or something else beyond the cosmos: it is unintelligible to us, and therefore beyond both reason and faith.[27] Suffice it to say that Christian faith, bearing witness to Christ, is 'faith in the way' (S, 363), and is able to unite 'those who bear witness into a union in the world' (S, 363) by way of the invisible Church. 'And so faith establishes union of individuals as individuals for a mutual task, a union is rightly called *Ekklesia*' (S, 364). It is a distinctly Protestant understanding of 'church'. Protestant also is the way in which God confers unity on the church, namely by 'the illumination of prayer' (S, 414) and the 'yearly cycle' of liturgical prayer (S, 414). No reference is made to the life of sacraments.

And so the Hegelian story of the overcoming of *duplex veritate* comes to an end, and in doing so it leaves us with Christianity — and Protestantism, first of all — as the religion of 'the eternal way in the world' (S, 363), a way that is given *sub specie aeternitatis*, caught between an absolute past and an absolute future. 'Both, beginning and end, are for him at every moment equally near, because both are in that which is eternal; and only for this reason does he know himself at each moment to be [the] central point' (S, 360). Judaism survives as the other true monotheism, and is by contrast with Christianity the religion 'of the eternal life of the people' (S, 363). Islam, the third Abrahamic religion, drops out of consideration without a satisfactory reason for its disappearance. Both Judaism and Christianity are held to be true, and since no attempt is made to reconcile their conflicting truth claims, the unity of thought has been undone. Each religion gains its unity not from participating in a frozen eternity but by being in a free relation with the living God. So the primal elements of God, World and Man are not fused from within by thought but are brought into a relationship with one another by way of Creation, Revelation and Redemption. The pattern that Rosenzweig calls 'the Star of Redemption' is a 'new unity' and a 'new totality' (S, 273), a gathering that is given in lived and therefore shifting relationships, not guaranteed by an appeal to a timeless whole.[28]

Drafted on postcards during World War I, *The Star of Redemption* was composed during one of Europe's greatest catastrophes, and begins, as we have seen, with a meditation on the fear of death. Yet Rosenzweig's voice speaks to us from before 1933, in a world innocent of the disaster that is the Shoah, a disaster for the Jews yet also for Christians — and all the more so if it is not experienced as a wound that goes to the heart of Christian theology and Christian practice. Levinas was surely right to say that the German guards in the camps knew their catechism.[29] No such innocence exists in Blanchot's *The Writing of the Disaster*, and it cuts to a level beneath confession, eschewing any hope in keeping Judaism and Christianity in the one configuration. It is a book of experience, of what 'experience' of the disaster might be: first of all, experience *par excellence*, exposure to peril, yet also, since it is not a lived event, non-experience, an attunement to the Outside that is suffered in a state of radical passivity in which one loses the power to say 'I'.[30] When Levinas reflects on the book, he underlines his friend's concern with 'an event which is neither being nor nothingness' which Blanchot calls 'disaster' and which 'signifies neither death nor an accident, but as a piece of being which would be detached from its fixity of being, from its reference to a star, from all cosmological existence, a *dis-aster*.'[31] For Levinas, the disaster is a version of the *il y a*, the grim persistence of being even in the absence of being, and certainly Blanchot meditates on the *il y a* in important moments of the book.[32] Levinas makes no mention, however, of his friend's engagement with the ethical concerns developed in *Totality and Infinity* and *Otherwise than Being*. Nor does he note that *The Writing of the Disaster* broods on the Shoah, interlacing it with Blanchot's signature themes, which Levinas identifies obliquely, of dying, writing, and the approach of the Outside.

If we read *The Writing of the Disaster* with *The Star of Redemption* as a lens, we will quickly identify several motifs that come sharply into focus. First of all, we will note the attack on the unity of thought, the fear of '"false" unity' (*D*, 2; 8), the affirmation of an irreducible doubling of the subject (an 'I' and a 'he' or 'it' [*il*]), and, as we shall see, a new version of the *duplex veritate*. Like Rosenzweig, Blanchot is not simply arguing against Hegel; he incorporates him into his vision, though all the time denying his System any hope of sublating his fragmentary non-system. Second, we will observe that Blanchot rejects the comforting notion of the cosmos. 'Would the cosmic be a little heaven in which to survive, or with which to die universally, in stoic serenity? A "whole" which shelters us, even as we dissolve therein, and which would be natural repose — as if there were a nature outside of concepts and names?' (*D*, 75; 121). He affirms the Outside, the non-place where being perpetually empties itself as image and in which possibility finds no traction and which eternally returns in writing and in the recognition of the human relation. Attuned to the Outside, 'I' am divided, lose all my possibilities, and experience time differently, as though it were a stagnant pool rather than a stream. Such is the disaster. Yet Blanchot differs sharply from Rosenzweig in rejecting the possibility that one can find God beyond the cosmos or that the Outside is divine. That transcendence occurs, he concedes, though he says that its success occurs 'only in a negative form' (*D*, 91; 143), namely what Jean Wahl calls 'transdescendance', which for Blanchot is the Outside or the Neutral.[33] An implacable atheist, Blanchot denies 'the idea of salvation, of redemption' (*D*, 13; 27), suspecting that such ideas breed fear, and suspecting also that atheism, unless conceptually clarified by way of the Outside, is merely 'a privileged way of talking about God' (*D*, 92; 145).

Third, it is apparent just on opening *The Writing of the Disaster* that it is a fragmentary work, having learned if not from '1800' then certainly from '1798', the first year of the *Athenaeum* (1798–1800) and the affirmation of the fragment. The possibility for thought opened in 1798, Blanchot thinks, is not the production of masterly aphorisms of the sort that Friedrich Schlegel dreamed of in Fragment 206 ('A fragment, like a miniature work of art, has to be entirely isolated from the surrounding world and be complete in itself like a porcupine') or that Rosenzweig imagined ('and now each piece is an All unto itself').[34] It is something far more daring. Blanchot specifies what is at issue in Schlegel's fragment on fragments in three statements, each of which is phrased negatively, for Schlegel seeks to lead the fragment back towards the aphorism. This failure of nerve comes down to

(1) considering the fragment as a text that is concentrated, having its center in itself rather than in the field that *other* fragments constitute along with it; (2) neglecting the interval (wait or pause) that separates the fragments and makes of this separation the rhythmic principle of the work at the structural level; (3) forgetting that this manner of writing tends not to make a view of the whole more difficult or the relations of unity more lax, but rather makes possible new relations that except themselves from unity, just as they exceed the whole.[35]

In terms of form, at least, what will constitute 'thought' for Blanchot is precisely the putting into play of these three statements in an affirmative manner.

When that play, 'this mad game of writing' (*ce jeu insensé d'écrire*) as Mallarmé called it, begins, we will gradually pass from the fragment to the fragmentary, from Schlegel to Nietzsche, from internal relations, characteristic of idealism, to 'the third relation' in which neither dialectic nor fusion has a role to play.[36] We will slowly change how we read and write and, therefore, how we think. If we read the 'Note' that introduces *The Infinite Conversation* (1969), we hear a voice that speaks in the tone of someone announcing a new age of the world. Once it has emerged from idealism, and oriented itself towards 'the aleatory force of absence', writing will 'devote itself solely to itself as something that remains without identity, and little by little brings forth possibilities that are entirely other: an anonymous, distracted, deferred, and dispersed way of being in relation, by which everything is brought into question'.[37] Like Rosenzweig, totality will be rethought by way of relation; unlike him, however, there will be no 'new totality', only the 'relation without relation'. And finally, like Rosenzweig, Blanchot will affirm the eternal past, not, however, as Creation but as the immemorial past as Levinas understands the expression: the groundless ground of ethics.

In *The Writing of the Disaster* this affirmation of the fragmentary becomes the counterpart of the grand systems of German philosophy of which *The Star of Redemption* was perhaps the last as well as being one of the first works to make out what may be beyond systems. *The Writing of the Disaster* will not form a star of redemption but will talk about living in a world without a star to guide us and without redemption. Blanchot will name 'the four winds of spirit's absence', an atheistic equivalent of the four horsemen of the Apocalypse in Revelation 6: 1–8, traditionally known as Pestilence, War, Famine, and Death, and renamed by him:

> These names, areas of dislocation, the four winds of spirit's absence, breath from nowhere — the names of thought, when it lets itself come undone and, by writing, fragment. Outside. Neutral. Disaster. Return. Surely these names form no system. In their abruptness, like proper names designating no one, they slide outside all possible meaning without this slide's meaning anything — it leaves only a sliding half-gleam that clarifies nothing, not even the outside, whose frontier is nowhere indicated. (*D*, 57–8; 95)

No fifth horseman, the Messiah, will come, according to Blanchot, for the Messiah is already here and will 'come' only when we listen to him. 'Anyone might be the Messiah — must be he, is not he' (*D*, 142; 215). We are not to speak of the Messiah 'in Hegelian language' (*D*, 142; 215), presumably the language that construes Judaism as the religion of sublimity, because his coming announces not the end of history but a time that is 'more future (...) than any prophesy could ever foretell' (*D*, 142; 215).[38]

Could Blanchot be alluding to Rosenzweig, among others? It is doubtful, if only because Rosenzweig speaks rather differently about the Messiah than Hegel does. 'Opposite Israel', he says, 'the eternally beloved of God, the eternally faithful one and eternally complete one, there stands the one who eternally comes, eternally waits, eternally wanders, eternally thrives, the Messiah' (*S*, 326). And later he evokes the idea of the 'remnant' of Israel who will welcome the Blessed One. 'If the Messiah comes "today", the remnant is ready to receive him' (*S*, 427). There is no doubt that Rosenzweig awaits the Messiah. Not so Blanchot. For him, the coming of the Messiah is a way of evoking an absolute future, the time of the eternal return of the Outside, which only ever approaches and never installs itself in a present moment. Accordingly, Blanchot can elsewhere say that 'prophetic speech is that speech in which the bare relation with the Outside could be expressed, with a desolate force, when there are not yet any possible relations, primal powerlessness, wretchedness of hunger and cold, which is the principle of the Covenant, that is to say, of an exchange of speech from which the surprising justice of reciprocity emerges'.[39]

Prophetic or Messianic speech therefore expresses the disaster, not redemption, and we better understand what 'disaster' means, what the approach of the neutral Outside 'means', when we reflect on the

Shoah. The defining characteristic of Auschwitz, Blanchot suggests, is 'senselessness', not horror (D, 83; 132), that is, living without being able to project a horizon from one's *ego cogito*, living in the complete absence of possibility understood as 'I can'. In the camps people were subject to a time that was an endless, grey present, without past or future: a stagnant pool. Stripped of the power to say 'I', they found themselves in another way of being, one that surprisingly breaks with totality. It is marked by what Blanchot calls the 'relation without relation', a rapport between two people that holds them together and apart, without one person having dialectical mastery over the other or fusing immediately with him or her in the elation of romantic love. Unable to speak, and least of all to speak in the language of their guards — to 'play their game', as we say — they were nonetheless able to hold in reserve a 'true *speech*' [*vraie* parole] of justice that could not be given voice in the camps.[40] It was this speech that could finally be spoken by the survivors, and that he calls Messianic because it bears testimony to the relation through which we identify the other person as irreducibly human, without the mediation of religion, myth, ideology, value, sentiment, or power. 'The thought of the disaster', he writes, forms a silence in which 'the other who, keeping still, announces himself' (D, 12–13; 27). Thought, then, requires us to recognize that anyone *might* be the Messiah, the one who heralds the realm of justice, and *should* be the Messiah. Although Robert Antelme does not use this language, and respects the difference between the death camps and the labour camps, Blanchot points to his friend's *L'Espèce humaine* (1957) as exemplary of the thought of the disaster.[41]

The disaster makes us pass from expecting 'the Messiah' to each of us accepting the role of being 'a messiah'. This thought also finds support in Blanchot's reading of Levinas. What Blanchot chiefly takes from his friend is summed up in one, strong sentence in *The Writing of the Disaster*: 'The responsibility with which I am charged is not mine, and because of it I am no longer myself' (D, 13; 28). I am not responsible for the other person in the sense that I ever agreed to look after him or her, or that I concurred with a bill of human rights, composed in some past present, that constrains me to help him or her, or that I anticipate a just State in some future present that can come into being if and only if I and others do a decent amount of social work. Instead, the responsibility for the other person that I assume comes to me from a past that was never present and never will be. One might say it is Schelling's 'eternal past', and in a sense it is, although for Levinas God deflects direct approaches into an ethical relation with the orphan, the widow and the stranger. God 'comes to mind' only in moral action, and does not appear as Creator or directly as Lord.[42]

'Creation' is not a word that Blanchot rejects, although he uses it in an unusual way, as when, writing of reading, he evokes somewhat dramatically 'the experience of creation (...) the torments of the infinite'.[43] In his reflections on Levinas, however, we may say that he speaks of 'creation' without ever quite using the word, as though the concept hovers over the page, quietly whispering 'creation' in order to denote not the origin of the cosmos so much as the birth of responsibility in me. It is certainly not the creation of my soul or my 'true self'. On the contrary, the other person does not call on me, a singular, indispensable individual, and in doing so confirm my uniqueness. Instead, I am merely 'the first come or the least of men; by no means the unique being I would like to be' (*D*, 18; 35). If I am to be a messiah it is not because of any special commission I have been given by God or any particular quality that I may have that makes me more fit for the task than the next person. Any truly responsible person would be a messiah, and the unspoken challenge that Blanchot puts before us is that perhaps we are still waiting for a messiah to come.

In the Preface to *Totality and Infinity* Levinas says, 'We were impressed by the opposition to the idea of totality in Franz Rosenzweig's *Stern der Erlösung*, a work too often present in this book to be cited'.[44] To the extent that Blanchot engages Levinas — that is, often and intensely — *The Star of Redemption* remains darkly in the background of his reflections, shaping them without drawing attention to itself or when and how it does its work. Perhaps Rosenzweig's voice can be indistinctly heard from time to time, as part of a chorus, in Blanchot's polemic against unity and the One. Yet there is at least one moment when Blanchot is closer to Rosenzweig than Levinas is, and that is on the issue of the unity of truth. In *Totality and Infinity* Levinas skirts the old problem of *duplex veritate* when he argues that justice precedes truth. 'The transitivity of teaching, and not the interiority of reminiscence, manifests being; the locus of truth is society. The *moral* relation with the Master who judges me subtends the freedom of my adherence to the true'.[45] There is no gulf between the truths of reason and the truths of faith at issue here. Rather, truth is considered only as a figure of freedom — the freedom of the intellect to comprehend phenomena and render them intelligible — and Levinas's claim is only that, because the other person resists being regarded as a phenomenon, my freedom is posterior to my responsibility and is limited by it. Blanchot does not contest this position. However, he proposes something that comes to seem very close to *duplex veritate*, not a division between faith and reason but between two relations that are irreducible to one another, each of which claims to be true.

In his poem 'With happiness stretchd across the hills' (1802), William Blake says 'a double vision is always with me'.[46] Blanchot quotes the line (slightly mistranslated) in French in a short, early piece on Blake: '*Il y a en moi une double vision*'.[47] One might well say of Blanchot that he has a 'doubled vision' in him. In *The Infinite Conversation* he maintains that we are bound by a double relation, that is, '*naming* the possible, *responding* to the impossible' (48; 69). Nothing changes in *The Writing of the Disaster*: 'there must always be at least two languages, or two requirements: one dialectical, the other not; one where negativity is the task, the other where the neutral remains apart, cut off both from being and from not-being. In the same way each of us ought both to be a free and speaking subject, and to disappear as passive, patient' (*D*, 20; 38). The first language is Hegelian and dialectical; the second is neutral and non-dialectical; and neither can gain traction with respect to the other. Nor can we distribute these languages neatly into the realms of the public and the private.[48] Each speaks its own truth, which cannot be reduced to the other and cannot be reconciled in a higher truth. The two are related only in terms of the infinite relation or 'relation without relation', and no 'new unity' can ever hold them together otherwise. Blanchot's universe, 'a term henceforth deceptive' as he admits, is 'non-finite, disunited, discontinuous' and there is nothing beyond it, no divinity and not even the Outside, capable of conferring a 'new unity'.[49] Thought must slowly re-imagine itself in this non-world.

One main difference between 'the new thinking' and 'thought' is that the former rejects the philosopher's God in order to welcome the biblical God while the latter rejects both. 'If, I say, the old [thinking] addressed the problem whether God is transcendent or immanent, then the new [thinking] attempts to show how and when He turns from the distant into the near God, and again from the near into the distant'.[50] Thus Rosenzweig; and as one of his most acute readers points out, the upshot of the new thinking is to pass from resolving, as Hegel did, the 'contradiction between an infinite and eternal God and a finite and temporal world' to thinking 'the disjunction' being 'within God himself. The paradox of eternality and temporality in God is thus the same as that which relates God and the world or the world and humanity'.⁵¹ If we are still to talk of God as one, as the Shema tells us to do ('Hear, O Israel: The LORD our God is one LORD', Deut. 6: 4), then this is a divine unity that lives with, rather than surpasses, difference.⁵² Again, I quote Ellen T. Charry, '[r]eality is not a totality or a unity as "philosophy from Ionia to Jena" had it, but a dualistic unity which is neither fully separated nor fully unified' (*FR*, 106). Blanchot may well appreciate that the 'new thinking' draws close to the relation without relation, and hence 'thought', but will doubtless reply that his atheism is based on a rejection of unity, and that for him unity is higher than the Judeo-Christian conception of God.⁵³ To which one can imagine Rosenzweig responding that, in positing Unity above God, and fighting against it, Blanchot appears to be struggling more directly against Gnosticism than against either Judaism or Christianity. The 'new thinking' and 'thought' are close when arguing against an idealism they consign to the past and, when arguing for a future, less distant from one another than is sometimes supposed except, of course, in the matter of religious hope.

NOTES

1 See Maurice Blanchot, 'The Relation of the Third Kind (man without horizon)', in *The Infinite Conversation*, translated by Susan Hanson (Minneapolis, University of Minnesota Press, 1993), 66–74 (94–105). Blanchot evokes the temptation of '"false" unity' in *The Writing of the Disaster*, translated by Ann Smock (Lincoln and London, University of Nebraska Press, 1986), 2 (8). See Franz Rosenzweig, *The Star of Redemption*, translated by Barbara E. Galli (Madison, University of Wisconsin Press, 2005) (henceforth referred to in the main text as *S*). On Blanchot's familiarity with Rosenzweig, see 'Being Jewish', *The Infinite Conversation*, 124, 128 (181, 188).
2 See Emmanuel Levinas, *Totality and Infinity: An Essay on Exteriority*, translated by Alphonso Lingis (The Hague, Martinus Nijhoff, 1979), 28. *L'Ecriture du désastre* grew out of some earlier fragments by Blanchot, 'Discours sur la patience *(en marge des livres d'Emmanuel Levinas)*', *Le Nouveau Commerce*, 30–1 (1975), 19–44.
3 See Franz Rosenzweig, 'The New Thinking' (1925), *Philosophical and Theological Writings*, translated and edited by Paul W. Franks and Michael L. Morgan (Indianapolis, Hackett Publishing Co., 2000), 109–39, and Blanchot, *The Writing of the Disaster*, 1 (7).
4 Also see Franz Rosenzweig, 'The New Thinking', 134–5. For a fuller account of the unity of thought, see my essay 'The Third Relation', presented at the Cerisy conference on Blanchot in July 2007.

5 See Franz Rosenzweig, '"*Urzelle*" to the *Star of Redemption*' (1917), *Philosophical and Theological Writings*, 50, 69.
6 See Franz Rosenzweig, 'The New Thinking', 110.
7 See, for example, F. J. W. Schelling, *On the History of Modern Philosophy*, translated by Andrew Bowie (Cambridge, Cambridge University Press, 1994), 133.
8 For Franz Rosenzweig's discussion of the metalogical and the metaethical, see *The Star of Redemption*, 19–21, 16–17.
9 Rosenzweig moves very quickly over complex material. His remarks on Arabic scholasticism are perhaps more to the point than his allusions to Christian scholasticism. See *The Star of Redemption*, 124–7. Certainly Rosenzweig allows that God may love Creation, even though He does not depend ontologically on it. See *The Star of Redemption*, 176–8. For Aquinas's views on the relations between God and Creation, see *Summa theologiæ*, I, q. 13 art. 7, c; I, q. 28, art. 1, ad 3; I, q. 45 art. 3, *On the Power of God*, translated by Lawrence Shapcote (1932; rpt. Eugene, OR, Wipf and Stock, 2004), I, q. iii, iii, and *Truth*, 3 vols, translated by Robert W. Mulligan (1954; rpt. Indianapolis, Hackett Publishing Co., 1994), I, q. 4 art. 5, reply.
10 On this theme, see Robert Sokolowski, *The God of Faith and Reason: Foundations of Christian Theology* (Washington, DC, The Catholic University of America Press, 1995), ch. 2–4.
11 Schelling, 'Stuttgart Seminars', *Idealism and the Endgame of Theory: Three Essays*, translated and edited by Thomas Pfau (Albany, State University of New York Press, 1994), 197.
12 Franz Rosenzweig, '"*Urzelle*" to the *Star of Redemption*', 56.
13 Rosenzweig's insistence that the divine nature is not 'a "dark ground" or anything else that can be named with Eckhart's, Böhme's, or Schelling's words' indicates his transformation of a concept, not an avoidance of naming his source for it. See *The Star of Redemption*, 34. Also see the comment on Schelling in '"*Urzelle*" to the *Star of Redemption*', 56.
14 See Immanuel Kant, *Critique of Pure Reason*, translated by Norman Kemp Smith (London, Macmillan, 1933), Transcendental Aesthetic, §4.
15 See Schelling, *The Ages of the World*, translated and introduced by Jason M. Wirth (Albany, State University of New York Press, 2000), 39. The discussion of the present is confined to the 1815 lecture *Über die Gottheiten von Samothrake*.
16 Stéphane Mosès offers an admirable discussion of Rosenzweig's debt to Schelling in his *System and Revelation: The Philosophy of Franz Rosenzweig*, foreword by Emmanuel Levinas, translated by Catherine Tihanyi (Detroit, Wayne State University Press, 1992), 39–45. It should be noted that in *Of Human Freedom* (1809) Schelling takes a dim view of the divine withdrawal. See his *Of Human Freedom*, translated by James Gutmann (Chicago, Open Court Publishing Co., 1936), 11, 28–9.
17 Schelling, *The Ages of the World*, xxxv. Also see pp. 76, 80.

18 See, for example, Else-Rahel Freund, *Franz Rosenzweig's Philosophy of Existence: An Analysis of 'The Star of Redemption'*, translated by Stephen L. Weinstein and Robert Israel, edited by Paul R. Mendes-Flohr (The Hague, Martinus Nijhoff, 1979), 5.
19 Rosenzweig, '"*Urzelle*" to the *Star of Redemption*', 60. For the interpretation of 'B = B', see *The Star of Redemption*, 78.
20 *Chartularium Universitatis Parisiensis*, I, 543, no. 473.
21 See Roland Hissette, *Enquête sur les 219 articles condamnés à Paris le 7 mars 1277*, Philosophes médiévaux, 22 (Paris, Publications Universitaires, 1977). Fernand Van Steenberghen points out that Boethius of Dacia states '(*philosophorum*) sententia in nullo contradicit sententiae christianae fidei nisi apud non intelligentes' and '*Ideo nulla est contradictio inter fidem et Philosophum*', *Thomas Aquinas and Radical Aristotelianism* (Washington, DC, The Catholic University of America Press, 1980), 97.
22 Leo X, *Damnatur omnis assertio contraria veritati christianæ fidei illuminatæ*, in *Decrees of the Ecumenical Councils*, edited by Normal P. Tanner, 2 vols (London, Sheed and Ward, 1990), I, 605.
23 The view that Pomponazzi held a doctrine of double truth was propagated by Ernest Renan in the third edition of his *Averroès et l'averroïsme: essai historique* (Paris, Calmann-Lévy, 1867). Martin L. Pine launches a defense of Pomponazzi, arguing that he did not hold a theory of double truth, in his *Pietro Pomponazzi: Radical Philosopher of the Renaissance* (Padova, Editrice Antenore, 1986).
24 See *The Star of Redemption*, 114. The best account of the three ages, and in particular what '1800' means for Rosenzweig, is offered by Franks and Morgan in their edition of Rosenzweig's *Philosophical and Theological Writings*, 27–43. I am indebted to their discussion.
25 It is doubtful, however, that the *duplex veritate* was banished in this period. One of its strongest statements is given by Luther in his 'The Disputation Concerning the Passage: "The Word Became Flesh" (John 1: 14)' (1539), translated by Martin E. Lehmann, *Luther's Works*, vol. 38, *Word and Sacrament, IV*, edited by Martin E. Lehmann, general editor Helmut T. Lehmann (Philadelphia, Fortress Press, 1971). See especially the second thesis: 'In theology it is true that the Word was made flesh; in philosophy the statement is simply impossible and absurd' (239).
26 G. W. F. Hegel, *Faith and Knowledge*, translated and edited by Walter Cerf and H. S. Harris (Albany, State University of New York Press, 1977), 56.
27 See *Hegel's Logic: Being Part One of the 'Encyclopaedia of the Philosophical Sciences' (1830)*, translated by William Wallace, with a foreword by J. N. Findlay (Oxford, Clarendon Press, 1975), §§44, 45.
28 Peter Eli Gordon proposes the suggestive expression 'temporal holism' for the 'new totality' that Rosenzweig has in mind. See his *Rosenzweig and Heidegger: Between Judaism and German Philosophy* (Los Angeles, University of California Press, 2003), 203.

29 See Emmanuel Levinas, 'Interview with François Poiré', *Is It Righteous to Be? Interviews with Emmanuel Levinas*, edited by Jill Robbins (Stanford, Stanford University Press, 2001), 40–1.

30 For examples of the approach of the Outside, see Maurice Blanchot, *When the Time Comes*, translated by Lydia Davis (Barrytown, NY, Station Hill Press, 1985), 4 (13–14), and *The One Who Was Standing Apart from Me*, translated by Lydia Davis (Barrytown, NY, Station Hill Press, 1993), 24 (47–8).

31 Emmanuel Levinas, *Ethics and Infinity: Conversations with Philippe Nemo*, translated by Richard A. Cohen (Pittsburgh, Dusquesne University Press, 1985), 50.

32 See Maurice Blanchot, *The Writing of the Disaster*, 65, 116 (108, 178) (henceforth referred to as *D*). I leave aside the important and delicate question as to the relations between the *il y a* and the Outside. Suffice it to say that for Levinas the *il y a* can be overcome and this passage is needed for ethics to begin while for Blanchot the human relation subsists in and through the Outside.

33 See Jean Wahl, *Existence humaine et transcendance* (Neuchâtel, Editions de la Baconnière, 1944), 37.

34 Friedrich Schlegel, *Philosophical Fragments*, translated by Peter Firchow, with a foreword by Rodolphe Gasché (Minneapolis, University of Minnesota Press, 1991), 45. Blanchot quotes this fragment in 'The Athenaeum', *The Infinite Conversation*, 359 (527).

35 Maurice Blanchot, 'The Athenaeum', 359 (527).

36 Blanchot quotes Mallarmé's expression as an epigraph to *The Infinite Conversation* as well as in the first numbered paragraph in 'The Absence of the Book', *The Infinite Conversation*, 422 (620). For Mallarmé's phrase, see his *Œuvres complètes*, edited by Henri Mondor and G. Jean-Aubry (Paris, Gallimard, 1945), 481.

37 Maurice Blanchot, 'Note', *The Infinite Conversation*, xii (vii).

38 Hegel says nothing about the Jewish conception of the Messiah in his Berlin lectures on the philosophy of religion. See, however, his remarks on the Messiah as a concept formed by way of political expectations in his early essay 'The Positivity of the Christian Religion', *Early Theological Writings*, translated by T. M. Knox, introduced and fragments translated by Richard Kroner (Philadelphia, University of Pennsylvania Press, 1971), 158–9.

39 Maurice Blanchot, 'Prophetic Speech', *The Book to Come*, translated by Charlotte Mandell (Stanford, Stanford University Press, 2003), 80 (111). Blanchot adds a little later, 'speech prophesies when it refers to a time of interruption, that *other* time that is always present in all time and in which people, stripped of their power and separated from the possible (the widow and the orphan), exist with each other in the bare relationship in which they had been in the desert and which is the desert itself—bare relationship, but not unmediated, for it is always given in a prior speech' (81).

40 Maurice Blanchot, 'Humankind', *The Infinite Conversation*, 134 (197).
41 See Robert Antelme, *The Human Race*, translated by Jeffrey Haight and Annie Mahler (Malboro, VT, The Malboro Press, 1992), 5.
42 See the essays in Levinas's collection *Of God Who Comes to Mind*, translated by Bettina Bergo (Stanford, Stanford University Press, 1998).
43 Maurice Blanchot, 'Reading', *The Space of Literature*, translated by Ann Smock (Lincoln and London, University of Nebraska Press, 1982), 196 (259).
44 Emmanuel Levinas, *Totality and Infinity*, 28.
45 Emmanuel Levinas, *Totality and Infinity*, 101.
46 *The Complete Poetry and Prose of William Blake*, edited by David V. Erdman, new and revised edition, with a commentary by Harold Bloom (Los Angeles, University of California Press, 1982), 721.
47 Maurice Blanchot, 'The Marriage of Heaven and Hell', *Faux Pas*, translated by Charlotte Mandell (Stanford, Stanford University Press, 2001), 29 (38).
48 See Maurice Blanchot, 'On One Approach to Communism', *Friendship*, 296 n. 3 (112 n.)
49 Maurice Blanchot, 'Ars Nova', *The Infinite Conversation*, 350 (514).
50 Franz Rosenzweig, 'The New Thinking', 122.
51 Ellen T. Charry, *Franz Rosenzweig and the Freedom of God* (Bristol, IN, Wyndam Hall Press, 1987), 106.
52 Charry points out with good reason that 'although [Rosenzweig] did not exempt God from his metalogical principle, neither did he draw all the conclusions about God that were implied by his presuppositions', and suggests that drawing his conclusions would distance him from orthodoxy. See her *Franz Rosenzweig and the Freedom of God*, 107.
53 See Maurice Blanchot, 'The Absence of the Book', *The Infinite Conversation*, 433 (635).

Blanchot in *The International Review*

CHRISTOPHER FYNSK

Abstract:
This essay contains a consideration of Maurice Blanchot's contribution to the collective project that came to be known as *The International Review*. It focuses on Blanchot's insistence that the project be collective and international, and pursues Blanchot's effort to provide a thought of the fragmentary that will answer these imperatives. With special attention to the question of literature, the essay concludes with a consideration of Blanchot's own proposed contribution, his famous piece 'Berlin'.

Keywords: Blanchot, nuclear terror, critique, fragmentary writing, literary responsibility, translation, Marxist dialectic, *il y a*, Berlin

The circumstances surrounding the attempted creation and eventual abandonment of *The International Review*, as it came to be called, are now well established and documented.[1] For a period of several years in the early 1960s, a number of prominent intellectuals from Europe and North America pursued actively the project of simultaneous publication in at least three languages (French, German and Italian) of a literary journal of a radically innovative form. Active commitments at an organizational level came from individuals such as Hans Magnus Enzensberger, Uwe Johnson, Roland Barthes, Dionys Mascolo, Maurice Blanchot, Louis-René des Forêts, Elio Vittorini and Francesco Leonetti, and throughout the relevant documents we find mention of associations involving figures such as Michel Leiris, Leszek Kolakowski, Pier Paolo Pasolini, Italo Calvino, Alberto Moravia, Ingeborg Bachmann, Martin Walser, Günter Grass, Carlos Fuentes and Iris Murdoch. The projected scale of participation was immense, and the documents speak consistently to the awareness that what was sought was an entirely new form of literary intervention.

The essential facts regarding the participation of Maurice Blanchot in this venture are also established, and I will pause over them only to note that this ambitious international project gripped Blanchot's attention at a moment that followed very soon after his public re-entry into the French political world in response to de Gaulle's seizure of power in May 1958. Having participated in the drafting of the *Déclaration sur le droit à l'insoumission dans la guerre d'Algérie* [Declaration Concerning the Right of Insubordination in the Algerian War] (to which he lent the title and the crucial notion of a *right* to insubordination in the course of an intense effort at joint writing), and having faced the juridical pressure that ensued, Blanchot concluded that French intellectuals were traversing a critical juncture that required new forms of commitment and collective action. Thus, in addition to a powerful brief statement published in October 1958 in the second issue of *Le 14 juillet*, 'Le refus',[2] we have a letter to Sartre applauding his intention of transforming the format of *Les Temps modernes* in response to the new political and intellectual configuration.

Blanchot's letter to Sartre is a crucial document for understanding his thinking in this important moment of renewed political intervention. It does more, in fact, than applaud Sartre's recognition of the importance of literature for this political moment, and his acknowledgement of 'the new relations involving political responsibility and literary responsibility, as manifested by the *Déclaration*' (L, 219). It calls upon Sartre to respond to what Blanchot describes as the emergence of a new consciousness of the role of intellectuals. The *Déclaration*, Blanchot writes, recalling Sartre's own reaction, had brought to the fore a historical and socio-political exigency that revealed in the action of its signatories a new 'power of decision' to which they were summoned to respond (L, 218). In the same movement, their acts had revealed, through the 'impersonal force' of the *Déclaration*, a new form of collective being; the *Déclaration* figured for them 'an anonymous community of names' (L, 218). Sartre was now invited to embrace the change that was occurring, and to help mark it for the intellectual world as a public event by joining a new project that would be committed to a practice of 'total critique':

I believe (...) that a review of *total critique*, critique in which literature would be grasped in its proper meaning (also with the help of texts), where scientific discoveries, often very poorly set forth, would be subject to the trial of a general critique, where all the structures of our world, all the forms of existence in this world would come into a single movement of examination, research, and contestation — a review, therefore, where the word 'critique' would also recover its sense, which is to be global, would have today, precisely today, an importance and a force of action that would be very great. (L, 220)

When Blanchot concludes his letter to Sartre by evoking the shared presentiment of an approaching crisis 'that will only render more manifest the critical situation that is our own' (L, 220), we have all the elements of the thinking that will justify the step toward the project of *The International Review*.

When the step is made, however, Blanchot gives his name to something more than we might have anticipated. He dramatically redefines the character of the event to which he has invited Sartre to respond, and he rethinks the nature of a collective response. He tells us, more precisely, *how* a new thought of literary responsibility in an international context will be elaborated. The coherence of this thinking — at least a crucial line of it — is arresting, and if I should succeed in drawing it forth in these few pages, it may catch the reader's attention forcefully enough to prompt the question as to whether this text holds a kind of summons for contemporary thought.

*

It is evident that the step to which I have alluded comes via Blanchot's association with Dionys Mascolo, one of the editors of *Le 14 juillet*. Blanchot's response to Mascolo's initiative in this last venture could not have been more absolute: 'I want to express my accord. I refuse all of the past and I accept nothing of the present'.[3] These sentences make a bridge with Blanchot's thought of refusal, but the solidarity they express also marks an assent that carried Blanchot into a dialogue concerning the new international initiative.

Whether it is in fact Mascolo who prompted in Blanchot this attention to the international character of the crisis he had evoked in his letter to Sartre, or whether the exchange was more complex (the internal working papers devoted to the project of the review attributed to Mascolo and Blanchot respectively are very similar, and we must not forget the other associates in this collective project), it is clear that Blanchot's political understanding was at least momentarily *seized* by this motif. The strength of Blanchot's recognition of the urgency of an international perspective is given immediately in the opening paragraph of his reflections on the meaning and projected form of the review, as he defines what he calls the 'gravity' of the project at hand. Citing the motif of a 'change in times' that he also developed in dialogical form in a brief text of 1960,[4] Blanchot 'ontologizes', we might say, the *sense* of urgency he evokes in his letter to Sartre: 'We are all aware that we are approaching an extreme movement in these times, what I would call a change in times' (*L*, 179).[5] He then declares that this sense of crisis does not relate solely to the French context, or to that of any other particular site, but rather derives from the fact that all problems are now of an international order, and that every international problem is now 'insoluble'. Thus, to the argument of his dialogical essay 'On a Change of Epoch', which addressed the meaning of the global sway of a new order of *Technik*, Blanchot brings an overlying development that adds an essential and dangerous ambiguity to every situation. The essay on the 'Change of Epoch' had in fact touched on the presence of the nuclear menace and situated it within the enumeration of the fundamental symptoms of a change in times; but the new statements allude to a different understanding of this menace in the context of the Cold War, and seem to give a more determining character to factors such as the unstable stricture of 'nuclear deterrence'. Little analysis is offered of the governing 'state of tension', but it is difficult to read the statement that it excludes any traditional idea of peace and cannot be resolved by a 'good classical war' (*L*, 180) without bringing to bear a thought of the question of nuclear terror.

The latter theme will not be further developed in Blanchot's working papers for the *Review* (though we find another reference to it in the closing notes via a question regarding its bearing on a 'change in meaning in the notion of violence' (*L*, 190–1)). The emphasis shifts, rather, to the implications of the fundamental assertion that the *Review* must 'gather itself upon the gravity of its task' by responding to the enigma of a change in times. Blanchot starts, here, with a striking statement: 'The project is essentially collective, as it is so on an international scale' (*L*, 180). The phrasing is muted enough to forestall a question about the adequacy of the explanation that follows it (to which I will return). But when it is paired with an equally challenging sentence that occurs after a subsequent reference to the imperative of discussion and dialogue for a collective venture of this kind, it becomes clear that Blanchot is genuinely confronting the implications of his assertion that the extremity of the moment requires a particular form of collective response. The sentence to which I have referred opens the second paragraph of the second part of Blanchot's reflections on the exigencies defining the project, and the form of response that must be sought:

For the current project for a review, this necessity [of discussion and dialogue] imposes itself still more; as an international review, it must be so in an essential manner; not only multinational, nor universal in the sense of an abstract universality, nor drawing from the problems a vague and empty identity, but a placing in common of literary, philosophical, political and social problems as they pose themselves in the determination of each language and in each national context. (*L*, 181)

In brief, and to repeat, we are told that the project is *essentially* collective because it is collective on an international scale, and that the project can only be essentially international if it achieves a genuinely international form of collectivity. An impatient reader could assume, from this nearly tautological formulation, that Blanchot is simply adapting his thinking to the circumstances of the project and that a rather banal necessity dictates this focus on collective interaction. But I would argue that Blanchot has in fact fundamentally recast his commitment to collectivity as it is stated in the letter to Sartre. He has done this under the pressure of his claim, dramatically stated in the concluding paragraph of the first section, that what is at stake in this project is 'a search for truth, or else a certain just demand, perhaps one of justice, for which the literary affirmation, by its interest in the centre, by its unique relation to language, is essential' (*L*, 180–1). Any effort to articulate the truth of this extreme moment will bring forth a new meaning of collectivity, inasmuch as a just response cannot be thought either merely locally or through some universalizing formulation.[6]

The question of the review's collective functioning is indissociable from the question of its form, and must therefore be pursued further if we are to grasp the meaning of Blanchot's statement that this review might be said to be essentially in search of its form (*L*, 188). I hinted above that Blanchot's initial explanation of the meaning of a collective organization did not seem to meet the strength of his appeal to it. The explanation reads as follows: 'This means, not that we seek a thought that would be common to all, all the participants, but that, through a placing in common of our efforts, our questions, and our resources, above all through an internal movement carrying us beyond our own thought, we might bring forth new possibilities' (*L*, 180). Such an argument is already implicit in the letter to Sartre: a collective undertaking will carry individuals beyond their solitary trajectories and into a space of exchange where a movement that is not proper to any individual claims their thinking. But what does a 'placing in common' (the phase appears twice) imply in the international context Blanchot evokes? How will a collegial structure or a multiplication of discussions and exchanges further this movement? If the task is to exceed a genial sharing of perspectives (serving a form of cultural pluralism), and to avoid an abstract consensus or universalism, if the collective is to become truly genetic, to use Kolakowski's term,[7] then a more concrete form of exchange must be achieved.

Blanchot's initial statements about the collective structure of the review thus seem insufficient. But the course of his reflection points to a movement at the core of this venture that would realize the concreteness he demands when he evokes terms such as 'truth' or 'justice'. We already catch a glimpse of what is involved when Blanchot refers early in his papers to the manner in which literary, philosophical, political and social issues must be 'placed in common' from the grounds of the way they are posed in 'the determination of each language' (*L*, 181). But to take the meaning of these words forward, we need to pause over Blanchot's comments on the scope of this endeavour and the place of literature.

We have seen that the endeavour is conceived as *international* — a description that may be said to have a potentially global extension, even if the collectivity devoted to it in this case remains merely European in its constitution and primarily attentive to European issues. Every problem or question, Blanchot tells us, has an international determination; this is one defining trait of the 'change in times' that must be thought. But the ambition of the review, in Blanchot's understanding, reaches beyond this international determination of every socio-political issue; it seeks to think every question or problem from the perspective of the *whole* and with an attention to what *exceeds* the whole:

There are very few things that must interest us in this review, or in other words we must not give the impression that we are interested in and curious about everything. Or rather, we must be interested only in the whole, there where the whole is at stake, and always rediscover this interest in and passion for the whole; then, we must ask ourselves if the essential interest does not also go to what is outside the whole. (*L*, 180)

These words will be developed in subsequent pages in terms of a divergence between a horizon of questioning that is embraced by dialectic (conceived in a sense that is essentially determined by the Marxian legacy, but also surpasses it) and an 'exigency' of literature and art that carries us beyond this horizon. Readers of Blanchot will be familiar with this divergence between the order of the possible covered by dialectical reasoning and the order of literary experience, a 'fundamental' order of research engaging a 'power without power' that is 'perhaps not subsumed by possibility' (*L*, 182). They will also be familiar with Blanchot's insistence that both orders must be affirmed in what they entail of an irreducible responsibility:

There seems to result from this an irreducible difference and even discordance between a political responsibility that is a responsibility at once global and concrete — accepting Marxism as nature and dialectic as a method of truth — and literary responsibility, a responsibility that is a response to an exigency that can only take form in and by literature.

This discordance does not have to be reduced from the outset. It is a given; it exists as a problem, a problem that is not frivolous, but which must be born with difficulty, a problem all the more difficult for the fact that each of the discordant terms engages us absolutely and in that their dissonance, in a sense, engages us as well. (L, 183)

These last words form point 5 of part II of Blanchot's working reflections. Point 6 affirms quite simply that there exist 'elements of a solution' that the review will have to explore.

The solution Blanchot will explore in the subsequent pages of his reflection will not take a form that might in any way be described as a surreptitious return of dialectic. It also gives the notion of a 'placing in common' of problems, questions and approaches a radical twist, since it defines both the space of this encounter or juxtaposition and the nature of the dialogical interchange in which it might unfold, or which might result from it, in ways that deny any simple conceptual or affective accord. The notion by which Blanchot explores this solution, the notion of the *fragment*, will set the question of the review's collective and international character on an original path.

The appearance of the motif of fragmentary writing first appears via a proposition that the review's central undertaking (something that would constitute its spine or guiding 'element': its *fil conducteur*) would consist of parallel chronicles, one a reflection of the 'intellectual course of things', established by each editorial group and focusing essentially on literary events (taking this phrase in a broad sense), the second more dialogical and critical, unfolding the political situation and 'general movement of the world' (L, 184). The proposal suits brilliantly Blanchot's dedication to the question of a change in times, though we cannot presume that it is properly Blanchot's. Nor can we assume that the description of the serial structure of the chronicle, or the appeal to the 'short form' in music, are really to be attributed specifically to Blanchot. But the appeal to the fragmentary dimension of these very contemporary forms carries us into a distinctly Blanchotian space.[8]

I do not mean to suggest that Blanchot's motif of the fragment effectively overwhelms the proposals for the envisioned chronicle addressed to the 'Cours des choses'. An intriguing suggestion for the constitution of a kind of counter-history through a juxtaposition of soberly edited items of information ('the elements of a truthful and more secret history' (L, 186)) should be noted in this regard. But the meaning and purpose of the chronicle, as stated by Blanchot, would seem only to be served, in the strongest sense, by the notion of the fragment that Blanchot advances in these pages, for only the fragment achieves the address to 'the whole' and 'what is beyond the whole' in a way that meets the literary responsibility Blanchot seeks to articulate in and through the review:

> The purpose of the review [*le sens de la revue*] is to try to prepare a new possibility, one that would permit the writer to *say* the 'world' and everything that takes place in the world, but as a writer and in the perspective proper to the writer, with the responsibility that comes solely from the writer's truth: therefore a form of responsibility that is totally different (though no less essential) from the one that brutally characterized relations between literature and public life following 1945, known under the simplistic name of 'Sartrean engagement'. (*L*, 185)

Blanchot's manner of evoking the possibility that the review is to prepare indicates strongly that the term 'world' has taken something of a Heideggerian inflection and points to a totality of experience that can only be given in its factical 'totality' by a literary engagement with language. Of course, 'totality' is a precarious and ultimately unsatisfactory word here, for it must accommodate not only what Blanchot designates in the opening paragraph of his reflections as an 'insoluble' state of affairs (as determined by international tensions), but even a form of experience that involves what Blanchot will call, in his definition of the fragment, an essential discontinuity.[9] I will turn shortly to a powerful example of the kind of discontinuity Blanchot seeks to think. But I want first to emphasize Blanchot's attention to the way this 'saying' of the world in a change in times must entail a particular engagement with language as such (to use Benjamin's term), or the 'being' of language, and thus its 'original power' or 'power without power' to proffer something like 'world'.[10]

Blanchot's reference to the question of language is relatively discreet, but it is insistent, and it surfaces fairly dramatically when Blanchot turns to the problem of translation and declares that the translator will be, in a certain sense, 'the true writer of the review...' (*L*, 187). This declaration is predicated upon an understanding of translation as an 'original' form of literary activity that Blanchot illustrates with a powerful evocation of Hölderlin's translations of *Oedipus* and *Antigone*. The latter discussion, strongly reminiscent of Benjamin in respect of the question of the difference between languages, clearly signals at what level the question of language is being engaged in this essay. The translator's intervention in language must touch upon the singular character of any individual language. All literary 'saying' must reach this level.

It is not insignificant that the most extended discussion of the fragment — a discussion that reaches the same rhetorical pitch as the preceding one on translation — appears immediately after the points made about the 'difference between languages' (a difference which includes an *historial* dimension: 'the languages are never contemporary with one another' (*L*, 187)) and the subsequent remarks on the extremity of 'the example of Hölderlin' (*L*, 187). The understanding of the problem of translation points to an always fragmentary saying of being. This is clearly a critical issue for an international undertaking that seeks a 'placing in common' of socio-political or ethico-political issues and seeks responses ('to say the world') with a global reach. 'How can one maintain in a translation [the] difference of historical level?', Blanchot asks (*L*, 187). Then there is the problem of dialects — a problem 'never adequately resolved' (*L*, 187), and differently pressing for each of the languages involved in the undertaking. A traditional understanding of the task of translation, even a relatively sophisticated one, would not indicate here an insurmountable problem. But Blanchot's reference to the fragment serves to draw out the issue as one with radical implications for this collective project. Clearly, Blanchot wants to link the question of the difference of languages to the topic he broaches under the phrase 'essential discontinuity' in his enumeration of the different ways in which one might grasp the fragment.

But a very significant step is made when he moves to define this notion of discontinuity, for he appears to open the notion of 'saying the world' to those dimensions of experience that would unsettle even what he has evoked thus far in respect to translation. Thus, he speaks of a literature of the fragment that is

situated outside the whole, either because it supposes that whole as already realized (...), or because it senses, to the side of forms of language in which the whole is constructed and speaks — a speech of knowledge, work, and salvation — an entirely different speech freeing thought from being merely a thought in view of unity, demanding, in other words, an essential discontinuity. (*L*, 188)

This statement does not indicate that he has left behind the question of the difference of languages (the saying of this difference would already lead into the space he evokes); but it does seem to point at the same time toward a more radical understanding of difference, and ultimately toward his understanding of the *il y a*, or his later thought of the neutral.

To use a Blanchotian abbreviation, we could say that this 'step' has all the distended complexity of Blanchot's *pas au-delà*. A consequent development of this complexity and its meaning for the present occasion would carry us into an immense digression as regards Blanchot's argument in the texts we are reading. But it would also take us to the heart of the question Blanchot seeks to address when he remarks on the divergence between literary and political responsibility. Can a 'saying of the world' include the writing of the neutral or the *il y a* and achieve a form of ethico-political responsibility? Blanchot clearly thinks it can. A *full* and *just* response to the discontinuities of factical existence in the world is possible by way of the fragment, presuming that the 'entirety' of meaning that must be conveyed in each fragment is grasped in its becoming. In brief, Blanchot wants to affirm the essential finitude of every act of 'saying the world', and is thereby led to understand the elaboration of the review's chronicle as a calculated arrangement, and further, a *relay* of singular events of writing. Collective work at an international level must be thought from the grounds of this structure of fragmentary communication.

It is time to focus a bit more precisely on this question of the fragment, and for this purpose I would like to turn from the 'working pages' I have been commenting to a brief text by Blanchot — a fragment — prepared for *The International Review*: his stunning meditation on 'Berlin'.[11] This is a text that says very precisely what it means to live an insoluble problem, and is no less precise about what it means to try to say this. We find here, in fact, an explicit discussion of the fragment.

The text reads initially as an enumeration of the levels — political, socio-economic, 'metaphysical', existential, linguistic — at which we might understand the problem of 'division'. Punctuated with an insistent 'this is not all', the writing is intense and jagged, leaving its shifts of perspective without mediation:

Berlin is not only Berlin, but also the symbol of the division of the world (...). That is not all. Berlin is not a symbol, it is a real city in which human dramas unknown to other big cities are played out; here, division should be named tearing apart. (B, 346)

Blanchot offers no resolution of perspectives as he moves between the declaration that Berlin is 'for all' (all thinking human beings, as he says at a later point (B, 348)) the problem of division, and evocations of the singularity of the experience of dwelling in this place (for each of its citizens) that offers no possibility of dwelling. Blanchot's emphasis, however, does not fall simply on discontinuity; it falls, rather, on the *indivisible* character of this problem of division. No individual aspect of Berlin can be rendered truthfully in isolation, he suggests. Thus, while no full mediation of perspectives is possible, 'Berlin' demands in thought and in writing a 'complete' formulation. The problem of division presented by Berlin must be rendered, each time there is an effort to render it, in its totality. This can only be done fragmentarily:

> In other words, each time we are confronted with a problem of this nature (there are, after all, others), we must remember that to speak of it in a just manner is to speak of it in such a way that we allow the abrupt wanting of our words and our thoughts to speak, we must allow to speak the impossibility of speaking of it in a supposedly exhaustive manner.[12]

The *situation* that is Berlin, an irreducibly existential situation or site of 'world' that surrenders to no transcendental perspective, demands, each time, and powerfully, an effort to say the *indivisible* of this worldly situation. Thus it demands a form of speech or writing that testifies to this exigency — brings this exigency to speech — as it remarks its own inability to meet it: a writing that must convey both the intransigence of this demand (the imperative of saying the totality of the experience that is Berlin) and the *impossible* of this demand. The 'divisions' of Berlin cannot finally be subsumed in any dialectical account; they are irreducible inasmuch as they are traversed by fundamental discontinuities of language and a human experience that Blanchot describes as an irremediable tearing. The only possibility of saying this world inheres in a saying that communicates its own finitude and thus *relays* the impossible exigency to which it answers, offering meaning in and as an irreducible becoming. Fragmentary writing would relay 'the affirmation that meaning, the entirety of meaning, is not to be found immediately either in ourselves or in what we write, but that meaning is still to come, and that, by questioning meaning, we consider it a pure becoming and a pure future of questioning' (*B*, 350).

A full account of Blanchot's understanding of fragmentary writing at this moment would have to bring together both of the traits I have emphasized: arrangement and relay. It would have to work through both Blanchot's commitment to the collective editorial practice he envisions for the constitution of the 'Cours des choses' (which involves the juxtaposition of disparate statements), and his understanding of the manner in which such statements, both in their solitude and in their conjunction, would convey the essential finitude of their saying.[13] This thought of fragmentary writing should then be extended into a discussion of Blanchot's struggle with the question of dialectic. The motif of 'division' in the text on Berlin signals this problem clearly enough, as does a striking reflection on the problem of *abstraction* presented by a wall that sought to establish, along an oscillating line of enigmatic passage and exchange, a visible and tangible division.[14] An immense question of a philosophical-historical order opens here that vastly exceeds the space of the present essay. How do we assess Blanchot's adherence to the language of dialectic in this moment of return to a form of writerly political activism, and how do we think it together with the muted references to Heidegger's thought of language and *Technik*, and with what Heidegger offers to Blanchot regarding the necessity of fragmentary writing and the place of art for the question of truth (offered by Heidegger in response to Hegel)? I will pause here over merely one point: Blanchot's insistence in this moment that the 'truest' or most 'just' political intervention is a *literary* intervention that will guide (like a *fil conducteur*) a necessary reflection. It is striking, in the pages I have commented here, how insistently Blanchot suggests that literature must constitute the first step in the search for a 'solution' to the problem of the discordance that inheres between political responsibility and literary responsibility. And it is no less striking how insistently the motif of the *question* is itself submitted to pressure as Blanchot undertakes the search for a suitable form for the review (cf. *L*, 188–9). The radical character of Blanchot's efforts on behalf of this review lies here, I believe: in this intransigent commitment to the search for a way of 'saying' the world that escapes the abstraction of political or 'sociological' representation.

I will not attempt to explore the grounds for the failure of this collective venture, for they too require a broad and detailed historical analysis. It would be necessary to explore the way in which the German and Italian committees found themselves unable to embrace the French proposals for a 'placing in common' by reason of their understanding of the very singularity of their respective situations and intellectual tasks. The divisions between intellectual groups in their national situations proved considerably more recalcitrant than Blanchot had anticipated, and for reasons that cannot be reduced to issues of personality or material constraints. The German committee, in particular, understood the literary tasks before them in ways that eventually ruled out any joint address to socio-political issues (the situation was considerably aggravated by the construction of the Berlin wall). The Italians, for their part, were less distant, but still wary of French abstraction and mysticism. *Plus ça change*, one is tempted to say. The fundamental issue of situational difference (a genuine challenge to the fragmentary 'solution' proposed by Blanchot) seems to have given way, as a question or problematic, to quarrels shaped by national prejudice.

Have global movements (realignments of economic and political power, but also shifts in communicative structure and possibilities) changed these conditions, or pointed to a new necessity of something like collective response on an international level? A cautious answer in the affirmative seems possible, though it is not at all clear that an urgent need for such a response has quite emerged in intellectual circles (nor can we expect this need to emerge as long as the meaning of a *political* intervention on the part of intellectuals remains so diffuse). What is urgently required, however, is a reflection on the possibilities of drawing forth such a sense of urgency. How do we prepare the grounds for understanding the 'power of decision' Blanchot glimpsed in the acts of the 121 signatories of the *Déclaration*? Does this task not entail an exploration of the conditions for *saying*, concretely, the abstraction, but also the opaque facticity of our contemporary world(s)? The hold of the grand theoretical narratives that prevailed in the last quarter of the last century has considerably weakened, and intellectuals, in significant quarters of the West at least, have found themselves stripped of that symbolic authority that informed the 'power' to which Blanchot referred in his letter to Sartre. But the international movement Blanchot sought to institutionalize with his efforts for *The International Review* did not presuppose broad affiliation (at least in numbers), and it did not seek to achieve a theoretical hegemony of any kind. It presupposed simply the power (without power) of literature and fragmentary writing in general to relay an exigency: the demand, emerging from a sense of ethico-political urgency (sensed with various degrees of lucidity and indissociable from experiences of pain, anxiety and various forms of existential destitution stemming from the abstraction of the modern world) that intellectuals find ways to think and say their time.

The project failed, and this failure should pose real questions for Blanchot's founding assumptions, including both his faith in the possibility of a dialectical elaboration — however *limited* — of the divisions defining the international context, and his understanding of the relationality that would be brought to language by an international response that would be elaborated through a work of translation. But I believe it would be a mistake to write off this failure as somehow inevitable for such a 'literary' venture (an attitude that could well be prompted by a remark such as Blanchot's own regarding the utopic character of this project and the necessity of embracing failure utopically (*L*, 180)). Such an assumption falls critically short of the notion of literature Blanchot sought to evoke. The project for *The International Review*, as Blanchot conceived it, may not quite *claim* the present in the manner Benjamin described when he envisioned a critical relation between past and future. But the ambition of *saying* the 'world' articulates a need that emerges ever more strongly as the abstraction of most contemporary theory comes into view — and this at a time when an inchoate sense of global change in our socio-political world is almost as visceral as the awareness of the new temperatures assailing our bodies.

NOTES

1 The key resource for this information is *Lignes*, 11 (September 1990), a volume devoted to Maurice Blanchot and containing a dossier on the *The International Review*. Introductory essays by Michel Surya and Anna Panicali sketch the breadth of the project and prepare a presentation of texts and letters by individuals active in the editorial committees. All citations of Blanchot's 'working papers' for the review (internal documents circulated among the prospective editors), as well as my citations of his letter to Sartre of December 1960, will be drawn from this volume, cited hereafter with the abbreviation *L*. Translations will be my own, but they benefit from a draft translation prepared with the help of Monique Galloway and Michael Syrotinski. For the significance of this venture, one should consult Leslie Hill's *Blanchot: Extreme Contemporary* (London, Routledge, 1997), 211–17, and Michael Holland's *The Blanchot Reader* (Oxford, Blackwell, 1995), 167–99, as well as Christophe Bident's *Maurice Blanchot: partenaire invisible* (Seyssel, Champ Vallon, 1998), 376–417.
2 This stunning essay is collected in *L'Amitié* (Paris, Gallimard, 1971), 130–1; *Friendship*, translated by Elizabeth Rottenberg (Stanford, Stanford University Press, 1997), 111–12.
3 Cited in *Maurice Blanchot: partenaire invisible*, 378.
4 This essay is collected in *The Blanchot Reader*, 174–81.
5 I will return to the place of Heidegger's thinking in these reflections as I proceed, but I would note that this motif of a 'change of times' bears a strong Heideggerian inflection, particularly as Blanchot evokes the nature of the obscure awareness of this turning. It is interesting to note, however, how circumspect Blanchot is in citing Heidegger at this juncture.
6 Blanchot's use of the word 'just' in these pages is itself worthy of attention. It evokes, for the most part, the notion of a political judgement or demand

that is both accurate and 'rightful': concretely anchored in a truthful grasp of reality and 'truthful' in an ethico-political sense. Later, we will see a reference to a form of writing that is 'just' by reason of the way it acknowledges its own limitations vis-à-vis any notion of complete adequacy or correctness; this latter notion of a 'just' expression does not surrender anything with regard to the claim to truth or concreteness evoked here.

7 Cited by Anna Panicali, *Lignes*, 168.
8 The description of the fragmentary writing that will compose the 'Cours des choses' points forward very strongly to Blanchot's own experimentation in a text such as *The Writing of the Disaster* (1980), translated by Ann Smock (Lincoln and London, University of Nebraska Press, 1986).
9 It would probably be best to speak simply of a 'whole' of experience (though this is problematic in view of Blanchot's references to 'the whole' and 'what is outside the whole'), or of an experience in which 'everything' is at stake. We see a usage like the latter in the opening paragraph of Blanchot's essay on the 'three forms of speech' in Marx, when he declares that any writer or speaker who does not feel subject to the plurality of exigencies to which these forms of speech answer will feel they are lacking with regard to everything [*manquant à tout*]. These three forms of *parole* belong to thought, politics, and science, and none are free of a movement that leads them into the exigency of writing. See 'Les trois paroles de Marx' in *L'Amitié*, 115–18; *Friendship*, 98–100.

In brief, and to foreshorten what should probably be a far broader discussion, I am inclined to find in Blanchot's reference to 'world' in the phrase 'to say the world' an ontological reach that recalls Heidegger's use of the term in the 1920s. Of course, Blanchot gives the word a strong socio-political inflection in this context; but this very 'worldly' reference (if I may be permitted this ambiguity) should be understood in relation to everything Blanchot has to say in a text such as 'Literature and the Right to Death' about the writer's engagement with 'the world as a whole' and with those dimensions of this world (including what Heidegger termed its 'facticity') that escape the abstractions of language (in *The Station Hill Blanchot Reader*, edited by George Quasha (Barrytown, Station Hill, 1999), 359–99; see, in particular, 373).

A notion of the 'everything' at stake in the kind of symbolic intervention Blanchot envisions is caught in a beautiful passage from Gérard Granel's *De l'université* (Mauzevin, Trans-Europe-Repress, 1982), in which he evokes the problem of doing politics in the age of *Technik*: 'There is nothing to be "done" against an age of Being. But there is a lot to prepare (...). And we concede that this "lot" is destined to remain nothing if it does not become everything, but this will also be (and even first of all) in taking our distance from the idea of totality. "Political power" — both the first condition of all serious action until now and the inaccessible end of an interminable militancy—like the "global discourse" to which every organization feels obliged and of which it finds itself incapable, are henceforth no longer objects for us' (65).

10 I pursue this issue as it appears in Heidegger, Benjamin and Blanchot in *Language and Relation: ...that there is language* (Stanford, Stanford University Press, 1996). More recently, I have examined Emmanuel Levinas's use of the notion of 'giving' or 'saying' the world to the other in an essay that takes up the problem of the relation between ethical saying and the problem of justice ('Sabbatical Acquiescence', *Poiesis*, 8 (2006), 18–39 (see, in particular, 31)).

11 I will cite the version of this text published in *MLN*, 109 (April 1994), 345–55. Citations will appear in the body of the text with the abbreviation *B* and will occasionally be modified. At the time, the original French text from which the first Italian translation was composed had not been retrieved (see the Editor's Note on this history, 345). Thus, the four translations presented in this issue of *MLN*, including the French, were reconstituted from the Italian—an ironic fate for this text composed for a non-existent review whose 'true writer' Blanchot identified as the translator. I might note that my reference to an 'entirety' of meaning in the previous paragraph stems from this text (348). Subsequently, Blanchot's original typescript was rediscovered by Louis-René Des Forêts and published in *Lignes* in October 2000. This is the version given in Maurice Blanchot, *Ecrits politiques* (Paris, Léo Scheer, 2003), 71–6.

12 This assertion is illustrated with remarks on the works of Uwe Johnson, literary works which communicate the very impossibility of saying the divisions they must embody: 'The difficulty itself, and, to put it more succinctly, the impossibility faced by the author of writing such books in which the division is put into play (and thus the necessity for him of getting a grip on this *impossibility* by writing it, of grasping it in writing)—this is what brings the literary operation into accord with the singularity of "Berlin", precisely by this hiatus it had to leave open with an obscure and never relaxed rigor between reality and a literary seizing of its meaning' (*B*, 354).

13 Following the argument of Blanchot's meditation on Berlin, I have emphasized the manner in which the fragment exposes, and thus relays, the exigency it conveys. But I think it might be noted that Blanchot's discussion of the collective venture proposed under the rubric 'Le Cours des choses' increasingly stresses (as we see in his letters of 1962 and 1963) the *plural* character of the writing envisioned. It may well be that Blanchot was simply attempting to secure a bare minimum of understanding across the three committees. He was fighting to preserve the idea of a collaborative structure of contributions against tendencies to see the project as an amalgamation of three edited groups of text (one from each committee on the basis of a firm contractual understanding of the number of pages, etc.). Thus, in these letters drafted as

Blanchot fought for the vision of the project, we find a particular focus on the question of collaborative *arrangement*.

In a later discussion of René Char's fragmentary writing in *The Infinite Conversation* (translated by Susan Hanson (Minneapolis, University of Minnesota Press, 1993)) we find an interesting articulation of the notion of arrangement and a thought of becoming. Blanchot speaks in this context of 'separate phrases' that 'convey in their plurality the sense of an arrangement they entrust to a future of speech'. He then continues in the same paragraph with a quite intriguing reference to a notion of justice: 'Juxtaposition and interruption here assume an extraordinary force of justice' (308).

The two traits of fragmentary writing I have emphasized certainly cohere (as we see in *The Writing of the Disaster*). But one might ask whether they ultimately lead toward different experiences of discontinuity and the 'indivisible' encountered in answering the exigency to 'say' it. It would seem reasonable to assume that fragmentary writing is itself a plural concept.

14 The only footnote in Blanchot's text reads as follows: 'The wall pretended to substitute the sociological truth of a situation, its factual state, for the more profound truth of this situation, which could be called — but only by simplifying considerably — dialectical' (*B*, 352). The body of the text goes on to state that the importance and 'scandal' of the wall in its 'concrete oppression' inheres in its abstraction and in the way it reminds us that abstraction does not derive from a faulty way of thinking or an impoverished use of language, but is rather 'our world, the one in which we live and think, day after day' (*B*, 352).

A Green Blanchot: Impossible?

TIMOTHY CLARK

Abstract:
Blanchot's work may at first seem remote from any sort of environmentalist thinking. While elements of his work share with Levinas and Heidegger a problematic privileging of the human, Blanchot nevertheless offers the basis of what might be seen as a timely 'deeper ecological' thinking, one that can engage the destructive anthropocentrism of Western thought and tradition in the very minutiae of its literary and philosophical texts. Unlike in much 'green' philosophy, no concept of nature or earth serves as foundation for Blanchot's thought. He is engaged by the 'impossible' as that which is not a matter of human power or decision, affirmed in both its ethical force and its contestation of dominant and appropriative conceptions of knowledge, rationality and invention. A comparison is offered between Max Oelschlager's representative ecocritical essay 'Earth-Talk: Conservation and Ecology', with its romantic attempt to find and celebrate modes of unalienated or 'natural' language, and Blanchot's practice of what can be seen as a more radical and questioning 'ecology' based on almost opposite conceptions.

Keywords: Blanchot, nature, impossible, deep ecology, physis, animal, anthropocentrism, ethics, environmentalism

Blanchot's work belongs with that of Martin Heidegger and Friedrich Nietzsche in locating the sources of many of the crises facing Western humanity, and now humanity in general, in deep ontological presuppositions, pervasive habits of thinking that are inherently aggressive or rapacious. Yet unlike Nietzsche and Heidegger, both of whom thematize the 'earth' in ways that have inspired environmentalist thinkers, Blanchot's work seems at first remote from anything recognisably like green issues.

Partly, no doubt, out of a reaction against pseudo-agrarian elements in Heidegger's work, Blanchot's writing, with its overwhelmingly urban climate, affirms a kind of anti-essentialist nomadism, refusing all forms of nostalgia and insidious notions of 'rootedness'. This cannot but set Blanchot challengingly against much that might seem attractive yet finally unacceptable in much environmentalist thought with terms like 'nature' and 'the earth'. That granted, it is very striking how, compared to almost any page of Heidegger or Nietzsche, Blanchot's writing is almost totally void of references to or images from the natural world. One might even imagine, reading Blanchot's *oeuvre*, that humanity and its artifacts were in sole possession of the Earth. His considerable body of work on Rilke barely takes up the issue of that poet's attention to the mode of being of animals, even when that is the explicit topic of a poem being cited ('Duino Elegy, 8').[1] To work through one end of *The Writing of the Disaster* (1980) to the other looking for any reference to non-human life is to find nothing, bar one anti-natural figure ('*A rose blossoming into a bud*'). After a striking passage at the end of *Thomas the Obscure* does any bird ever fly across a page of Blanchot?[2]

This essay tries to address the seeming absence in Blanchot of what is increasingly seen as an epochal issue — the crisis in human self-conceptions being wrought by the intensifying degradation of the planet itself. How far can Blanchot's thinking, his famous refusal of the present, encompass this issue?

Global Responsibility

One evident connection between environmentalist thinkers and Blanchot's work lies in the attention both give to the unprecedented nature of the contemporary world as one in which humanity, become truly global, enters an era of risk and self-questioning. Blanchot's meditations often show a planetary awareness, one that we would now associate with 'globalization', but which Blanchot described in relation to claims about the 'end of history' or, as below, to the thought of Teilhard de Chardin. He writes:

we have entered the final and critical stage in which economic, technical, ethical, scientific, artistic, and spiritual expansion carries humanity 'to the heart of an always accelerated vortex of totalization upon itself' [de Chardin].[3]

Such a sense of the world as a whole is now so commonplace that its distinctiveness is easily forgotten (so that we think nothing of passing in the course of a single conversation from African politics to Japanese technology to Irish music):

The words *world civilization, universal domination, planetization, collective cerebralization* are expressed or inferred in everything that we say and think. Each person sees himself as master of the entire earth and of all that has existed on earth. (F, 73)

This global consciousness, while conducive to fantasies of human mastery, is also an existential dilemma. Blanchot is very much a thinker of the paradoxy and crises of thought induced by the need to think human existence as a whole (ultimately in its finitude and powerlessness), as opposed to analytic tasks of 'understanding' directed towards specific issues with a view to enhancing a sense of human power over things. The global ecological crisis could be called precisely 'Blanchotian' in its demand that we think increasingly, not in terms of regional projects of management or conservation within received frameworks of thought, but anew about the totality of human life. As in Blanchot's essay on the atomic bomb (*F*, 101–8), the issue becomes to rethink 'humanity' as a question, a 'who?'

Blanchot's work overall offers a striking account of the kinds of conceptual and psychic forces that currently structure the minutiae of human thought and relations. His work as a critic attends in minute detail to how even seemingly common-sensical practices of reading, interpretation, and assumptions about knowledge as inherently synthetic, conceptual and systematizing etc., all link to global systems of political/social violence. Blanchot writes:

Even comprehension (...) is a grasp that gathers the diverse into unity, identifies the different, and brings the other back to the same through a reduction that dialectical movement, after a long trajectory, makes coincide with an overcoming. All these words — grasp, identification, reduction — conceal within themselves the rendering of accounts that exists in knowledge as its measure: reason must be given. What is to be known — the unknown — must surrender to the known.[4]

Insofar as these issues play themselves out in relation to the minutest attention to issues of reading and language in numerous texts, Blanchot's work as a critic could be said to practise a kind of *micro-ecology* ('think globally, act locally').

The issue of wrongs done to other living creatures and of the finitude of the earth itself remains mostly latent here. Nevertheless, the seeming opacity and resistance of Blanchot's work to 'environmentalist' issues may, paradoxically, form a challenge full of intellectual promise. Ultimately, Blanchot's work may adumbrate a thinking that meets one of the most urgent demands of post-enlightenment thought, that is, resources towards a re-enchantment of the natural world that would not at the same time be a kind of mystification, evasion or deception.

Blanchot's Neo-anthropocentrism (1)

The seemingly minor status of the natural world as an issue in Blanchot may lie partly in what might be nicknamed his neo-anthropocentrism, a term that is meant more descriptively than pejoratively. This is his version of the argument, derived from Heidegger and re-inflected by Emmanuel Levinas, on the uniqueness of the human compared to the rest of nature.

Blanchot's attention is to the uniqueness of the immediate human environment — the realm of the sign and image, the mediation of the space of language — considered not in terms of the positivity of 'culture' but as a kind of rupture in being, without nostalgia for some supposed lost relation to 'nature'. He moves outside those concepts of 'nature' and 'culture' whose *pas de deux* has long dominated environmentalist and much other discourse in the West (those about 'art' and the 'animal' for instance). A striking essay in this respect is 'The Birth of Art' (F, 1–11) on prehistoric cave painting and the emergence of modern human beings. Blanchot's fascination with pre-history (involving the uncanny fact that other species of human being have existed and disappeared) correlates with what Stuart Kendall writes of Georges Bataille in this context: 'Prehistory is universal history par excellence because it is not merely the history of the West; it is global in its sweep and implications.'[5]

Blanchot describes a double movement of distinction between the modern human and the animal. First is the emergence of technology along with some sort of social structure and the prohibitions and taboos that accompany it:

pre-man *fortuitously* does violence to the natural givens, stands erect, rises up against himself, (...) becomes an animal raised by himself, works, and becomes thus something not natural, as far from what is natural as are the prohibitions that limit what he is in order to benefit what he can be. (F, 6)

This last point recalls numerous thinkers in defining the animal/human distinction in terms of the emergence of 'culture' through determinants to behaviour based on taboos. Human social organization involves the deferral and repression of the immediate individual impulse in view of the greater benefits of cooperative work and power over wild nature. This initial 'separation between man and animal' (F, 6), however, does not suffice to make early humans into truly fellow creatures of ours. The modern human being is no *animal rationale*. A second step is called for. What is uniquely (modern) human according to Blanchot, following Bataille, is not only the power to create ritual, laws, and prohibitions and tools, but symbolically to transgress or destroy them. It is that freedom to negate, the power of beginning again, to abolish the real into the empty space of images and signs. For Blanchot, the emergence of modern humanity is indissociable here from that of language and 'art' (in the broadest sense of the creation of images and non-utilitarian designs). Here:

> the gap between man and his origin is put into question once again and in some sense recovered, explored, and experienced: a prodigious contact with all of anterior reality (and first with animal reality) and thus a return to the first immensity, but a return that is always more than a return, for he who returns, although his movement gives him the illusion of abolishing millions of years of bondage, of submission, and weakness, also becomes tumultuously conscious of this impossible return, becomes conscious of the limits and the unique force that allows him to break these limits, does not simply lose himself in the dream of total existence but instead affirms himself as that which is added to this existence and (...) can appropriate it symbolically or communicate with it by making it be. (F, 6)

The essay on the caves of Lascaux affirms that art and modern humanity are coeval, born in a common double break from the natural world. Blanchot concludes: 'Art would thus provide us with our only authentic date of birth' (F, 7).

Blanchot also repeats the claim—still in dispute[6]—that Neanderthals had no art and that this corresponded to their radical difference from modern people. Only the latter stand in their existence amidst a realm of non-being, that of the image, of detachment from positivity, or can choose 'to stand on the inside or the outside of being as non-presence' (F, 9). So the disjunction between modern humanity and the rest of the natural world includes *even another human species*. It is as 'if the division of human possibilities (...) were in some sense determined by an exigency having little to do with the movement of evolution' (F, 9) for, Blanchot observes, evolution was clearly as likely as not to produce a humanity without art, 'freedom' or 'discontinuity', but still endowed with tools, fire, clothing and instruments of communication, etc. Only modern people, not the extinct Neanderthals, could be called *Dasein* in Heidegger's sense of beings transcending positivity, one whose being is continually an issue for it.

Art's seeming timelessness, Blanchot argues elsewhere, 'alludes only to the power that we have of putting an end to the world, of standing before or after the world' (F, 33). It is as if there were latent in even the earliest cave art those epochal 1960s images of the earth from space, the fragile mottled sphere hanging in an unimaginable emptiness, images now forever associated with an emerging ecological consciousness. 'This is why', Blanchot continues, 'art is tied to all that puts man in danger, to everything that puts him violently outside the world, outside the security and intelligence of the world to which only the future belongs' (*F*, 33).

It cannot for any human being be a matter of leaving this third space, only of inhabiting and reconfiguring it in less violent ways. Any notion of a 'return' to some lost natural 'harmony' is intelligible to a reader of Blanchot only as an incoherence of thought. Hence Blanchot's remorseless arguments against all kinds of romantic nostalgia, the use of art ('an unreal thing in the world outside the world' (*IC*, 382)) for purposes of reconciliation with some supposedly 'lost' nature, some group or ethnic identity or allegiance or deeper life.

This is a Blanchot who cannot but be pitted against vast stretches of environmentalist thought, based as it usually is on a romantic programme of 'reconnection' with 'nature' or 'the earth'. Ultimately, however, Blanchot may offer a way of articulating global environmental crisis in terms that do not ultimately rest on forced claims of some lost 'kinship' and 'reciprocity' with nature.

Blanchot's Neo-anthropocentrism (2)

First, however, it is necessary to turn to some more problematic aspects of Blanchot's neo-anthropocentrism.

His meditative dialogues and essays often turn around the issue of modes for self-understanding that would enable human life to be thought without reference to illusory moral or metaphysical anchors, in 'God', 'nature', or seemingly self-evident 'values'. Kevin Hart has written of the importance of an ethics of the human relation in Blanchot's work overall, read as an attempt to 'preserve the sacred without religion' (206): 'To lose faith that life has an overarching meaning is not to dismiss mystery; it is to recognize that the human relation is mysterious, that the legitimate processes of demystification cannot find traction there.'[7] Should this exclusive focus on 'the human' be accepted? Among such a wealth of living things and places is there really no other resistance to demystification? Is 'nothing (. . .) more strange than the human relation' (*DG*, 17)? To turn back to Blanchot's pages is to find that the ethical relation, such as he engages it after Levinas, seems entirely and exclusively a matter only of one human being to another.

The central claim of Blanchot's neo-anthropocentrism lies in the unique breach that art and language make within the positivity of being. This realm of 'discontinuity' underlies Blanchot's reworking of an ethics of *autrui* that both looks to and revises Levinas. It is crucial that *autrui* speaks. '*Autrui* speaks to me' (*IC*, 55). Blanchot defines *autrui* through the radical inflection which language may bring to the relation of one human being to another: '*the recognition of the common strangeness that does not allow us to speak of our friends but only to speak to them*' (*F*, 291). At issue is the affirmation of 'a separation that is presupposed — not surmounted, but confirmed — in all *true* speech' (*IC*, 55; emphasis added), the lack of commonality between those who express themselves. Blanchot's appeal here is a norm of 'true' speech that seeks to let speak the very 'separation', rather than drive to accommodate both speakers within a shared identity, cultural horizon, common values, etc. The 'double dissymmetry' of the human relation — its refusal of linear geometry — lies in the fact that if the other (*autrui*) is never a self for me, even as he or she also transcends phenomenology, then the reverse is also true, but not in a dialectical fashion, for there is no symmetry that could become the foundation for a 'we', a common identity or platform.

Clearly, however, in positing that the emergence of the human and this affirmation of a space of discontinuity constitute the same event, Blanchot's argument about *autrui* must move within the presupposed circle of a shared *Dasein*. Only within some minimal kind of reciprocity between speakers is Blanchot's norm thinkable, affirming an infraction into the realm of shared terms, references and concepts that make up language. The 'double dissymmetry' remains *essentially and necessarily symmetrical* even as it maintains an infinity whereby one human being can never be an object or an intentional correlate of the other. The realm of the ethical seems exclusively human.

However, other aspects of Blanchot's argument implicitly destabilize his anthropocentrism. In this third space outside terms of equivalence and identity the human speakers may come to recognize

in impossibility our most human belonging to immediate human life, the life that it falls to us to sustain each time that, stripped through misfortune of the clothed forms of power, we reach the nakedness of every relation: that is to say, the relation to naked presence, the presence of the other. (*IC*, 47)

Blanchot's focus is on what remains of the human relation when stripped of all positivities of given identity or cultural belonging. This leads him, supposing himself forced to 'choose [his] ideology', to give allegiance to a revised notion of 'humanism'—the humanism of 'the cry—that is to say, the murmur; cry of need or of protest, cry without words and without silence, an ignoble cry' (*IC*, 262).

A reduction to the most basic, stripped 'humanness'—the helpless appeal of a complete vulnerability—this is what Blanchot sees in the victims of the concentration camps: 'human existence pure and simple, lived as lack at the level of need' (*IC*, 133). So, in a sense, it is in the acultural, deprived condition of being reduced to a quasi 'animal' existence, one might say, that the true claim of humanness becomes manifest, an ethical claim which no power can abolish. This 'man reduced to the irreducible' (*IC*, 133) cries out in the ethical appeal that the other makes to me, not only 'as though this Self were in my place, but [also to] become responsible for it by recognizing in it an injustice committed against everyone' (*IC*, 134). This is where some kind of re-entry of the other into the realm of 'dialectical struggle' (*IC*, 134), social identities and moral norms, systems of justice, etc., must occur. The sense of an 'injustice committed against everyone' may acquire, in court, the legal status of a 'crime against humanity'.

However it is at just this same Kantian point—of a universalization that sees in the one wrong a wrong committed against all—that the question of the human/animal distinction again becomes urgent and destabilizing. In relation to the suffering of a creature of another species, Blanchot's 'humanism' becomes problematic. How can I think 'as though this Self were in my place', and how can that sense of suffering become then the basis of an appeal to all who could likewise suffer? Who could 'all' or 'everyone' be within such a situation? It could surely never include, for instance, the stoat that needs to have killed that leveret in order to eat? Here no kind of broader 'society' exists into which the naked appeal of suffering can be taken up.

Blanchot's argument on the *autrui* and the human relation attempts to hold together two separate issues. One is the ethical claim of vulnerability, the cry of another's suffering. The other is the disruption of *autrui* within language taken as a horizon of equivalence, the refusal to be embraced within the horizon of given categories and identities and the challenge of a neutral space that escapes their purchase. These two arguments dovetail into each other forcefully in Blanchot's text, but they only do so if one assumes that the relation at issue is exclusively that of one human being to another. However, the issue of non-human suffering, vast and incalculable as it is, can make Blanchot's use of the term *autrui* look clumsy. Only within a presupposed horizon of a common belonging to modern humanity (or *Dasein*) does it make sense to use it, as Blanchot does, to name at once both a refusal of given terms and identities, in the name of the otherness of the other, *and* the powerlessness of the ethical appeal of vulnerability and suffering.

The following paragraph exemplifies another problematic part of Blanchot's neo-anthropocentrism. An interlocutor in a dialogue in *The Infinite Conversation* argues, on the topic of the *autrui*, the other (person):

[Man] alone is the unknown, he alone the other, and in this he would be *presence*: such is man (...). Each time we project strangeness onto a non-human being or refer the movement of the unknown back to the universe, we disburden ourselves of the weight of man. We sometimes imagine in a very impoverished fashion our frightened encounter in the sky of the planets and the stars with a different and superior being, and we ask ourselves: what would happen? A question to which we can perfectly well respond, for this being has always been there: it is man, man whose presence gives us all measure of strangeness. (*IC*, 60)

The argument here may seem unacceptably extreme, nor is it really qualified later in the dialogue. Are the sea, the stars, the forests really to be allowed no 'strangeness' but that which they reflect back from the human face? Even given innumerable qualifications well known to readers of Blanchot, that would still be a kind of 'deification' of the human.[8]

However, Blanchot's neo-anthropocentrism may also contain some surprising resources. Elsewhere, it is not a matter of humanity forming alone 'the unknown' or 'strange', but rather of the human relation as revealing such dimensions of existence more generally, giving access to a comparable sense of singularity in the realm of other creatures and things.

Blanchot's micro-ecological thinking concerns both a form of politics that is not a quest for power and kinds of knowledge and language that would not be a mode of synthetic force. Blanchot challenges the presupposition that being consists fundamentally in a unity, one which conveniently corresponds with notions of knowledge as conceptual synthesis. He surmises: 'why should not man, supposing that the discontinuous is proper to him and is his work, reveal that the *ground of things* — to which he must surely in some way belong — has as much to do with the demand of discontinuity as it does with that of unity?' (*IC*, 9). In other words, being cannot finally be correlated with that drive in human knowledge to synthesize, unify, and to explain under the aegis of a system of governing concepts. Singularity, disunity, opacity and the incalculable are 'fundamental' to the ultimate nature of things. The human relation remains the unavoidable mode of access to this issue, but is not the sole bearer of such singularity (*IC*, 10).

Impossibility, Physis, Nature

One of Blanchot's rare references to the natural world in *The Infinite Conversation* pivots on its very 'meaninglessness': '[A]ll modern humanism', writes Blanchot, 'the work of science, and planetary development have as their object a dissatisfaction with what is, and thus the desire to transform being — to negate it in order to derive power from it and to make of this power to negate the infinite movement of human mastery.' Thus anything (such as Bataille's notion of 'interior experience') which annuls the scope of conceptualization and human power 'lays waste at one stroke to our attempts to dominate the earth and to free ourselves from nature by giving it a meaning — that is, by denaturing it' (*IC*, 149).

Human aggression against the indifference of nature is also a denial of death. Reading so much of Western thought as the attempt to make death 'possible', that is, part of the realm of human power and meaning, aligns Blanchot with innumerable thinkers in the deep ecology movement for whom such denial underlies the planetary directives of techno-science to command nature and all its resources.[9] As Blanchot suggests, the necessity to which 'everything in the world submits' is death; or rather it is

the refusal of death — the temptation of the eternal, all that leads men to prepare a space of permanence where truth, even if it should perish, may be restored to life. The concept (therefore all language) is the instrument in this enterprise of establishing a secure reign. (*IC*, 33)

By describing something as 'impossible', then, Blanchot means not that it cannot exist, but that its existence is not the effect of any human power, decision or intention. 'Impossibility', writes Blanchot, is 'a relation escaping power' (*IC*, 38). In this sense, of course, all the basic dimensions of existence — birth, health, death, needs and passions, and the immediate recalcitrance of things — are impossible. Human beings cannot ultimately command them. The impossible is 'our ultimate dimension' (*IC*, 48) and 'impossibility is being itself' (*IC*, 47). Being alive is itself 'impossible' in Blanchot's sense!

Strange though it may sound at first, much of Blanchot's concept of 'the impossible' correlates with the Aristotelian sense of *physis* in Heidegger's reading 'On the Essence and Concept of *Physis* in Aristotle's *Physics B*, I' (1939).[10] (Heidegger's essay also begins by citing exactly the same poem by Hölderlin that will be prominent in Blanchot's essay on poetry and the impossible (*IC*, 38–48)). *Physis* is the term inadequately translated as 'nature'. It is that fundamental self-originating, ordering and resting of things within which all human life finds itself. It cannot be fully conceptualised, for it cannot even be thought without having been presupposed: 'Whatever produces itself, i.e. places itself into its appearance, needs no fabrication. If it did, this would mean an animal could not reproduce itself without mastering the science of its own zoology' (*Pathmarks*, 222).

Compare Blanchot on 'impossibility': 'impossibility [is] that in which one is always already engaged through an experience more initial than any initiative, forestalling all beginning and excluding any movement of action to disengage from it' (*IC*, 46).

A thinking of *physis* then is implicit in Blanchot's account of 'impossibility' both as being and as that in being which must precede ontology, since it cannot be negated. The switch in terminology from '*physis*' or 'nature' to 'the impossible' might seem partly a mark of Blanchot's neo-anthropocentrism (as well as of the influence of Bataille's *The Impossible*).[11] Being as impossibility is characterised entirely in terms of its relation to the human — one of non-power! To denominate everything in the universe outside human power 'the impossible' may seem merely the inverse of a hopelessly megalomaniac human-centred metaphysics. However, Blanchot, in affirming 'the impossible', is foregrounding just that element of so much Western thought.

The notion of *physis* is crucial in Blanchot's reading of the poetry of René Char. There is even a sense in which Blanchot is almost too eager to skip over 'nature' in the sense of individual creatures and things in favour of *physis* generally:

Nature has a powerful hold over [Char's] work, but nature does not only mean all terrestrial objects, or the sun, or the oceans, or the wisdom of enduring men; it is not even all things together, not the plenitude of the universe, nor the infinity of the cosmos, but that which already precedes 'the whole', is immediate and very distant, is more real than all real things and lies forgotten in every thing, the bond that cannot be bound and by which everything, the whole, is bound. Nature, in the work of René Char, is this exposure to the origin.[12]

A major question can be posed at this point. Is there then an analogy between the original underlying meaninglessness of nature — unnegatable, chastening of all human self-aggrandisement — and an element of art, Char's poetry for instance, with its own ordeal of another kind of powerlessness and contestation? As we have seen, in the emergence of art, prehistoric man found 'a prodigious contact with all of anterior reality (and first with animal reality) and thus a return to the first immensity'.

This seeming analogy would make Blanchot look close to that post-Kantian tradition of aesthetics which understands the peculiarity of the achieved work of art by reference to something similar in natural phenomena. For Blanchot, however, the impossibility of art inheres in its constitutive breach from the natural world, as in the moment of cave art. The break is a jump, one not explicable in terms of laws governing natural phenomena, even those of evolution. The 'impossibility' of art cannot be merely identified with the ultimate 'impossibility' of natural phenomena.

A better summary formulation of the relation might be this: whereas Heidegger may attribute to art a potential grounding role in human affairs, for Blanchot the impossibility in art and language may highlight that contestation of all anthropocentrism inherent in *physis* and natural phenomena. To make this issue more concrete let us turn to another of the rare occasions on which Blanchot uses an image from the natural world. Early in *The Infinite Conversation*, Blanchot contrasts two simple modes of expression:

'*The sky is blue*', '*Is the sky blue? Yes.*' One need be no great scholar to recognize what separates them. The 'Yes' does not at all restore the simplicity of the flat affirmation; in the question the blue of the sky has given way to the void. The blue, however, has not dissipated. On the contrary, it has been raised dramatically up to its *possibility*: beyond its being and unfolding in the intensity of this new space, certainly more blue than it has ever been, in a more intimate relation with the sky, in the instant — the instant of the question where everything is in instancy. Yet hardly is the Yes pronounced, and even as it confirms in its new brilliance the blue of the sky brought into intimacy with the void, we become aware of what has been lost. Transformed for an instant into pure possibility, the state of things does not return to what it was. (*IC*, 12–13)

The question affirms 'the gift and the richness of possibility' (*IC*, 13), 'gift' being effectively synonymous here with the impossibility of nature. This is perhaps a simple instance of the 'human relation' bearing upon a natural phenomenon, against the 'void' of outer space as effectively human space, in such a way as to foreground the sky in its instancy and singularity. In the seemingly trivial grammar of a question, Blanchot traces 'the illuminating force that brings being to the fore' (*IC*, 13).

Blanchot argues that Char's practice of a fragmentary, non-synthetic writing may adumbrate an irenic language, one that would preserve the unknown as unknown. On Char's 'fragmentary' and paratactic mode of writing we read:

Speech as archipelago: cut up into the diversity of its islands and thus causing a surging of the great open sea; this ancient immensity, the unknown always still to come, designated for us by the emergence of the earth's infinitely divided depths. (*IC*, 309)

The subject of this extended metaphor is speech or language. This is being compared to nature as *physis* or origin in the guise of 'the great open sea' and the 'emergence of the earth's infinitely divided depths'. This is not the familiar romantic position, however, that art or language and nature are analogous. The force of language inheres here in its action of breaking away and breaking apart: '*Speech as archipelago*: cut up into the diversity of its islands'. This diversity of fragmentation and dispersal is said to cause 'a surging of the great open sea' and of 'the unknown always still to come'. Language, then, is not a second-order *physis*. It enacts and affirms humanity's constitutive breach with nature and yet, in the process, also unblocks what is singular and non-synthetic more generally in relation to the emergence of unpredictable possibilities. In this way, one might say that the element of the unknown, first apparent in the human relation, becomes generalized through a kind of return without return to that 'first immensity'. Thus 'man, supposing that the discontinuous is proper to him and is his work, reveal[s] that *the ground of things* (...) has much to do with the demand of discontinuity as it does with that of unity' (*IC*, 9).[13]

It is in the third realm of language that a different and irenic relation to things lies latent, as well as a different relation to other sentient beings. ('Reality without the dislocating energy of poetry, what would that be?' (Char).[14]) Such language may effect a force of contestation and un-meaning which may re-enchant natural phenomena through an intensification of the sense of their otherness and giftedness.

Environmentalist thinkers often draw attention (like Blanchot) to the destructive effects of current paradigms of knowledge as ideally 'objective', mathematically quantifiable and decontextualized, a model that transforms reality into a homogenous set of formally expressed relations. Against this, Blanchot's work offers a detailed reflection on modes of thought and language that enable an irenic and irreplaceable singularization, discontinuity and openness, one irreconcilable with received modes of coherence, synthesis, logical consequence and 'development':

> A developed thought is a reasonable thought; it is also, I would add, a political thought, for the generality it strives for is that of the universal State when there will be no more private truth and when everything that exists will submit to a common denominator. (*IC*, 339)

'Poetry: dispersion that, as such, finds its form' (*IC*, 360). Such issues are at work even in that blend of the elusive and intense lucidity that forms the allure of Blanchot's 'style'. Its quality is that of the limpidity of swift streaming water, at once both monotonous and always fresh.

Blanchot's deeper ecology?

Blanchot's micro-ecology moves to identify and counter the kinds of conceptual violence inherent even in the most seemingly common-sensical or innocent modes of thought or speech. Were one to try to align this side of Blanchot's work with any contemporary school of environmentalist thought it would surely be with those 'eco-feminists' and 'social ecologists' who trace humanity's rapacious attitude to the natural world to the violence that predominates in relations between human beings themselves. Verena Conley, for instance, writes:

> The destructive urge of our culture can be linked with a patriarchy that organizes society according to a sexual model that is in fact a martial model. This martial model has its correlative in the economic model of competition and consumption that, while benefiting a few, has led to much of the planet's degradation.[15]

Nevertheless, almost all work in environmentalist philosophy and ethics would also be vulnerable to a Blanchot-style deeper ecology. A good instance of the kind of romantic position that Blanchot's work undermines is Max Oelschlager's essay, 'Earth-Talk: Conservation and the Ecology of Language'.[16] Oelschlager's text shares with Blanchot traces of Heidegger's influence as well as a common attention to language as a decisive human environment. For both, a change in conceptions of language is essential to any fundamental shift in how human beings conceive themselves. Oelschlager argues that even the very terms 'environment' and 'environmentalist' enact the presumption that humanity stands centre stage in a drama of one, surrounded by its 'environment' as a kind of scenery. It is at this point, however, that Oelschlager moves into familiar romantic territory, idealizing 'primary cultures' without literacy and writing as enacting a truer, supposedly non-dualistic understanding of the human relation to the natural world: 'it is through language generally, and through literacy more particularly, that we have been alienated from the first world' (51). Oelschlager addresses the nature/culture dichotomy split by an argument familiar to literary specialists since the time of the high romantic poets, for 'it is also through language that we can return' (51). He praises the literary practice of Gary Snyder and 'earth talk' as modes of language that understand human beings non-dualistically, as part and not master of a habitat. Oelschlager asks that we be attentive to the way 'primary oral cultures have allowed the flora and fauna "to speak"' (52).

The contrast with Blanchot could not be stronger. The issue for him is not to overcome some mind/nature dualism through a more 'natural' kind of language, but to intensify the very 'discontinuity' and interruption in being which the 'human relation', as it is borne in language, poses and is posed by. This produces some very different if still generally positive readings of some pre- or non-scientific modes of language (for example, the words of Heraclitus (*IC*, 85–92)). The human relation, borne in language, holds open a discontinuity in being more generally — an un-meaning and wildness that cannot be contained by given concepts of unity, synthesis or by that 'knowledge' which has almost always been defined by such principles.

Blanchot affirms the disturbing yet irenic force of this worklessness, as in the following fragment from *The Step Not Beyond*. This brings a strange twist to the familiar romantic topoi of the garden and lost childhood:

All words are adult. Only the space in which they reverberate — a space infinitely empty, like a garden where, even after the children have disappeared, their joyful cries continue to be heard — leads them back towards the perpetual death in which they seem to keep being born.[17]

Strikingly, it is the already lost status of Eden that emerges here as the principle of 'beginning'. A language exposed to its own finitude and the violence of the break from the immediate is also one held anew in the space of its own genesis. What is the force of this strange simile for the space in which a word or words reverberate: 'like a garden where, even after the children have disappeared, their joyful cries continue to be heard'? This movement of unworking in the language, considered as the constitutive human environment, becomes, through the acknowledgement of finitude and evanescence, an irenic affirmation of 'impossibility' as a force of beginning. The reference to children recalls the concept of 'natality' in Hannah Arendt's sense, that 'with each birth something uniquely new comes into the world'.[18] This strange space, whose cold fecundity inheres in its very finitude, stands in Blanchot's work in place of Hölderlin's 'Nature', Heidegger's *'physis'* and Rilke's *'das Offene'*.

Blanchot's *'naming* the possible, *responding* to the impossible' (*IC*, 48) might even make an excellent summary reformulation of some of the aims of the deep ecology movement. The deep ecologist Peter Reed, for instance, argues that a sense of the otherness of nature may be a better basis for deep ecology than those dubious narratives of an intensifying human identification with the earth found in Arne Naess and Warwick Fox. In Michael Zimmerman's words: 'Encountering the "austere mystery" of dominant nature can reveal our intrinsic insignificance (...). Only by cultivating this difference, rather than seeking to overcome it through wider identification, can people retain appropriate respect for the wholly Other.'[19] At the same time, Blanchot's work refuses, in its very constitution, that temptation which a deep ecologist never seems able to resist, that of making a new foundation or absolutist ground out of 'nature' or the 'earth'.

A World without Impossibility

To conclude I wish to turn to a thought experiment, taken from Edward O. Wilson's *Biophilia: The Human Bond with Other Species* (1984). Wilson writes:

Visualize a beautiful and peaceful world, where the horizon is rimmed by snowy peaks reaching into a perfect sky. In the central valley, waterfalls tumble down the faces of steep cliffs into a crystalline lake. On the crest of the terminal bluff sits a house containing food and every technological convenience. Artisans have worked across the terrain below to create a replica of one of Earth's landscape treasures, perhaps a formal garden from late eighteenth-century England, or the Garden of the Golden Pavilion at Kyoto, marked by an exquisite balance of water, copse, and trail. The setting is the most visually pleasing that human imagination can devise. Except for one thing—it contains no life whatever. This world has always been dead. The vegetation of the garden is artificial, shaped from plastic and colored by master craftsman down to the last blade and stem. Not a single microbe floats in the lake or lies dormant in the ground. The only sounds are the broken rhythms of the falling water and an occasional whisper of wind through the plastic trees.[20]

Such a landscape, corresponding perhaps to some future lunar colony, is nightmarish. 'This is a world (...) where people would find their sanity at risk' (115).

How does this thought experiment relate to Blanchot's work? As we have seen, Blanchot conceptualizes nature in terms of *physis* and the 'impossibility' of being. The natural realm is not to be hastily assimilated to a possible object of human power. Is it not the lack of 'impossibility' in just Blanchot's sense that renders Wilson's false paradise so horrific? '[T]he impossible is not there in order to make thought capitulate, but in order to allow it to announce itself according to a measure other than that of power' (*IC*, 43).

Wilson's thought experiment helps particularize what is at issue in Blanchot's notion of the impossible. Wilson's pseudo-beautiful landscape is the physical realization of complex programmes for so-called 'artificial life', that is, self-organizational algorithms that simulate life-like qualities without actually being alive. Such 'artificial life' might seem 'impossible' in the limited sense that no human brain, unaided, could model and so understand it. Yet it would still not be impossible in Blanchot's sense. Even if artificial life were indistinguishable from the real thing the sense of nightmare remains and is undeniable.

It is in this respect that Bill McGibben's polemic *The Death of Nature* seems so Blanchotian as an affirmation of and lament for the impossibility of nature. He argues that '*we have ended the thing that has, at least in modern times, defined nature for us — its separation from human society*'.[21] Nature as a whole, argues McGibben, is losing its wildness (its 'impossibility') and becoming, however clumsily, part of the sphere of human fabrication.

In altering the planet's atmosphere, humanity has rendered even the most distant mountain winds part of the sphere of human fabrication. 'Yes, the wind still blows — but no longer from some other sphere, some inhuman place' (*EN*, 49). The rain is likewise altered, perhaps just slightly chemically, but the sense of rain shifts drastically. McKibben narrates an experience of disenchantment felt one autumn when listening to the sound of rushing water in the Adirondack Mountains:

as I sat there (...) and thought about the dry summer we'd just come through, there was nothing awe-inspiring or instructive, or even lulling, in the fall of water.

It suddenly seemed less like a waterfall than like a spillway to accommodate the overflow of a reservoir. (*EN*, 96)

For people in less remote areas such disenchantments are enacted daily on the edge of every growing conurbation: a wood of mixed oak and birch, physically untouched by the major road that has been built nearby, is trashed nevertheless. Blanchot's concept of the impossible is apt as a name for what is suppressed — that which provokes us to think 'according to a measure other than that of power' (*IC*, 43). Yet, as the whole planet is transformed into an object of human use and management, 'the world outdoors will mean much the same thing as the world indoors, the hill the same thing as the house' (*EN*, 48). If genetic engineering posits a living organism as a self-replicating soft machine, it removes the creature from that realm of *physis* to which Heidegger had opposed the modern conception of organisms as merely 'artefacts that make themselves' (*Pathmarks*, 195). Would coming across a genetically engineered rabbit in the countryside, McGibben asks, be much different from finding a discarded coke can?

Blanchot offers no counter-politics of human liberation, self-affirmation or the retrieval of some lost relation to 'nature' as ground. His affirmation of the impossible offers a chastening step sideways, the cultivation of a force of natality, 'beginning' as a discontinuous, unmeaning and acultural element in the human realm generally, one that also affirms the uniqueness and singularity of natural phenomena, of *physis*. This is the 'wild' in the sense of a space outside use, something which is not part of the realm of human power. As we saw, Blanchot's neo-anthropocentrism bears elements of a problematic human exclusiveness. At the same time his work overall performs a re-enchantment without mystification of both some human artifacts and of natural phenomena, touching both with elements of his coldly non-redemptive notion of the sacred.

NOTES

1 Maurice Blanchot, *The Space of Literature*, translated by Ann Smock (Lincoln and London, University of Nebraska Press, 1982), 134 ff.

2 Maurice Blanchot, *The Writing of the Disaster*, translated by Ann Smock (Lincoln and London, University of Nebraska Press, 1986), 36. *Thomas the Obscure* [1950 version], translated by Robert Lamberton (New York, Station Hill Press, 1988), 112–14.

3 Maurice Blanchot, *Friendship*, translated by Elizabeth Rottenberg (Stanford, Stanford University Press, 1997), 73. All further references to the book will be given in the text, preceded with the abbreviation *F*.
4 Maurice Blanchot, *The Infinite Conversation*, translated by Susan Hanson. (Minneapolis, Minnesota University Press, 1993), 43. All further references to the book will be given in the text, preceded with the abbreviation *IC*.
5 Stuart Kendall, 'Introduction' in Georges Bataille, *The Cradle of Humanity: Prehistoric Art and Culture*, edited by Stuart Kendall, translated by Michelle Kendall and Stuart Kendall (New York, Zone Books, 2005), 15.
6 See Ian Tattersall and Jeffrey Schwarz, *Extinct Humans* (Oxford, Westview Press, 2001), 213–19.
7 Kevin Hart, *The Dark Gaze: Maurice Blanchot and the Sacred* (Chicago, University of Chicago Press, 2004), 5. All further references will be given in the text, preceded by the abbreviation *DG*.
8 In another passage on the ethical claim of the other person, we read: 'true exteriority is not that of objects, nor that of *an indifferent nature* or the immense universe (which it is always possible to attain through a relation of power by keeping it within the realm of my representation, the horizon of my knowledge, my view, my negation, and even my ignorance)' (*IC*, 69; emphasis added). This passage, unlike others we will turn to shortly, seems to reduce nature to an indifferent object, merely part of the realm of what can be mastered by human power or knowledge. Life itself, the capacity for sentience and suffering also seems oddly missing from this account: it moves from 'objects' to 'an indifferent nature', then to 'the immense universe'.
9 See Michael Zimmerman, *Contesting Earth's Future: Radical Ecology and Postmodernity* (Berkeley, University of California Press, 1994), 216 ff.
10 Martin Heidegger, *Pathmarks*, edited by William McNeill (Cambridge, Cambridge University Press, 1998), 183–230.
11 Georges Bataille, *The Impossible*, translated by Robert Hurley (San Fransisco, City Light Books, 1991).
12 Maurice Blanchot, 'The Beast of Lascaux,' translated by Leslie Hill, *Oxford Literary Review*, 22 (2000), 9–18 (15).
13 Reiner Schürmann writes of Char that 'In the poem all things just begin. "Le poète, grand Commenceur" (the poet, great Beginner) (...), says Char. Again, this beginning is neither mythical nor religious. The presence that it inaugurates neither founds anything nor even lasts.' See Reiner Schürmann, 'Situating René Char: Hölderlin, Heidegger, Char and the "There is"', *Boundary 2*,4 (1976), 513–34 (521).
14 'Pour un Prométhée saxifrage. En touchant la main éolienne de Hölderlin', *La Parole en archipel* (Paris, Gallimard, 1962), 125.
15 Verena Andermatt Conley, *Ecopolitics: The Environment in Poststructuralist Thought* (London, Routledge, 1997), 132.

16 In *Wild Ideas*, edited by David Rothenberg (Minneapolis, University of Minnesota Press, 1995), 42–56.
17 Maurice Blanchot, *The Step Not Beyond*, translated by Lycette Nelson (Albany, SUNY Press, 1992), 19.
18 Hannah Arendt, *The Human Condition*, 2nd edition (Chicago, University of Chicago Press, 1958), 178. For Blanchot's 'natality'/'beginning' see Timothy Clark, *The Poetics of Singularity: The Counter-Culturalist Turn in Heidegger, Derrida, Blanchot and the Later Gadamer* (Edinburgh, Edinburgh University Press, 2005), 115–23.
19 *Contesting Earth's Future*, 303.
20 *Biophilia: The Human Bond with Other Species* (Cambridge Mass., Harvard University Press, 1984), 114.
21 Bill McGibben, *The End of Nature: Humanity, Climate Change and the Natural World,* revised edition (London, Bloomsbury, 2003), 68. All further references to the book will be given in the text, preceded with the abbreviation *EN*.

'Not In Our Name': Blanchot, Politics, the Neuter

LESLIE HILL

Abstract:
Readers of Blanchot have long been aware of the importance of politics in the writer's intellectual itinerary. But though the history of Blanchot's political involvements is now quite well documented (albeit frequently misrepresented to polemical ends), much remains to be understood about Blanchot's conception of the political. Prompted in part by his support for the 'Not In Our Name' appeal, which was to be one of Blanchot's last political gestures, this essay fragment, which is part of a longer inquiry, reconstructs the writer's thinking on the question of the subject of politics and the closely related issue of the relationship between law and violence. It examines Blanchot's response to Hölderlin's translation of a famous fragment from Pindar entitled 'Das Höchste' ('The Most High') and places Blanchot's writing within the wider context of the political thought of Benjamin, Schmitt, Agamben, and Derrida.

Keywords: Blanchot, Hölderlin, Benjamin, sovereignty, law, violence, the neuter, refusal

I

Politics, Blanchot wrote in 1984, had always been his passion, and public events a constant source of provocation. But political thought or the thinking of politics, he added, was something that perhaps remained still to be discovered. Politics, in other words, corresponded to no stable, universal category. It evoked a concern inseparable from the struggles of the present, but it also implied a demand that, exceeding the present, reached into the future — a future that, according to Nietzsche, as Blanchot's friend Georges Bataille liked to remember, was essentially unpredictable and uncertain. Either way, responsibility was not something it was possible to avoid. So it was, for instance, in November 2002, only months before his death and perhaps for the very last time, that Blanchot lent his name and signature to the international campaign launched in New York earlier that year under the heading: 'Not in Our Name', which voiced in those terms its opposition to the 'war on terror' declared by the Bush administration and its European allies, culminating shortly after in the British-American invasion of Iraq.[1]

In the first instance, the purpose of the watchword was to appeal to an alternative, more original, more authentic, sovereign political subject, and this no doubt explains its implicit evocation of the American constitution, which famously begins, as many have observed, with the inescapably aporetic words: 'We the People of the United States. . .'.[2] But this was not all. Something else spoke in the campaign, more in tune with the challenges posed by the new world order it sought to confront. For alongside the call for a more fully present political subject, there lingered a residual doubt as to the possibility of any properly identifiable, communal first-person plural at all. In this respect, what the declaration 'Not in Our Name' suggested was not simply that 'we' were deprived of political representation. Implicit within it, intentionally or not, was the more radical suspicion or hope, in this beginning twenty-first century, that 'we' — whoever the word may be thought to designate — might henceforth no longer be arraigned as an 'us' and identified as such on the basis of species, race, nationality, class, gender, or any other mark of communal affiliation. And if 'we' were nevertheless intent on making 'our' voices heard, it was perhaps only as a tardy memory or citation from former times: as a '"we"' without 'we', inassimilable to any communal 'us'. What signed itself 'not in our name', in the words of the New York pledge, could not, then, by that very token, speak in 'our' name. It could only intervene by bearing witness to an essential exclusion, which was nothing less than a radical absence of name. The question it raised, in other words, was the abiding political question of the whole twentieth century and of the early twenty-first century too — not: what do we want, when do we want it, how shall we get it?, but: who are we, and what, if anything, are 'we' called?

The key question, in other words, was not that of the subject of politics, as addressed or interpellated by the authority of the State, positioned as a self-present national entity, and invoked as a largely fictitious source of political legitimacy — but, innumerably, that of another or the other. 'Qui vient après le sujet?', 'Who comes after the subject?', Blanchot and others were asked by Jean-Luc Nancy in 1988. Blanchot's response, by his own admission, was necessarily insufficient. It was nonetheless far-reaching. For in it he evoked the impersonality of the *neutre* or neuter, that category without category that exceeded the positing of any present subject and marked the coming of the non-self-identical future only in so far as, by way of the *neutre*, 'appeal was thereby made to the coming [*avènement*: the coming of a messiah or new epoch] of what does not arrive [*ce qui n'arrive pas*: does not occur], of what might be said to come without ever arriving [*viendrait sans arrivée*], beyond being [*hors être*] and having so to speak slipped its anchor [*comme par dérive*]'.[3] And in an extraordinary mise-en-abyme, Blanchot concluded, he said, by borrowing from the philosopher Claude Morali the title of one of that author's books, *Qui est moi aujourd'hui? (Who is Me Today?)*, and the quotation from which that title was derived — which some fifteen years earlier had first appeared, in Blanchot's hand, in the pages of *Le Pas au-delà* (though the point, precisely, was that there was never any first time nor place of origin where writing or words were concerned), and in which an anonymous narrator had wondered, in a digressive hypothesis released from the authority of any main clause, as follows: 'As though the muffled and yet joyful sound of children playing in the garden echoed forth as they called to one another: "Who is me today?", "Who's going to be me? [*Qui tient lieu de moi*: who is standing in for me, i.e. who is playing at being the first person singular?]". And the reply, joyful, endless: *him, him, him* [*lui, lui, lui*].'[4]

II

This was not the first time that Blanchot had turned his attention to the question of sovereignty and of the subject of politics. Throughout the 1930s, in his career as a political journalist and dissident revolutionary nationalist, he had arguably done little else. Much of course in recent years has been written about Blanchot's politics during the period between 1931 and 1944, but while the main episodes in Blanchot's prewar career are now well documented, relatively little attention has been paid so far to the conceptual implications of Blanchot's political thinking in general, with commentators contenting themselves all too often with hasty misrepresentation, inept generalization, and misplaced polemic, as the work of Jeffrey Mehlman, Steven Ungar, Philippe Mesnard, or, more recently, Richard Wolin, sadly confirms.[5]

Soon after the Liberation, as readers will know, Blanchot quickly began to concentrate his energies on his own fiction and literary criticism. This has often had the effect of distorting understanding of Blanchot's relationship to the political. The image of the writer that has dominated as a result is that of an artist retreating from politics during the immediate postwar period in order to devote himself solely to literature and preferring to veil the memory of his prewar extremism in what some critics, with more fidelity to stereotype than to historical fact, have denounced as a guilty silence. This version of events is, however, misleading at best. It assumes that politics and literature can be securely and reliably delimited, and that, in any case, the relationship between the political and the literary is one of uncomplicated opposition, as though what was merely literary could not by essence also be political, and vice versa. Plainly, nothing could be further from the truth. Indeed, as I have suggested elsewhere, there is every reason for considering *Le Très-Haut*, for instance, Blanchot's third and final novel, written shortly after the Liberation, and delivered to the publisher in May 1947, far from being a symptom of aesthetic disengagement, as an urgent political novel about politics.[6]

What *Le Très-Haut* makes clear is that the absent centre upon which Blanchot's postwar writing turns is not the writer's own past history nor any belief in aesthetic transcendence. It is the crucial problematic that for Blanchot and many of his contemporaries was inseparable from politics as such: the question of the law, its status and demands. For it was in the name of the law that throughout the 1930s Blanchot the political commentator attacked the ineffectual contractual politics of the League of Nations, on which French foreign policy — this 'politique de juristes' he called it in February 1935 — was largely based, together with the unstable parliamentary democracy given over to endless compromises and factional intrigues that was in its image, and both of which, in the face of Fascism, were to be found cruelly wanting. For in the meantime, France's national interest and the interests of a stable peace went undefended, and when it was thought crucial by some, like the journalist Maurice Blanchot, to intervene by force of arms in March 1936 to prevent Hitler's remilitarization of the Rhineland, all Albert Sarraut's Radical French government and Stanley Baldwin's Conservative British government thought it appropriate to do was to demur politely and concede. The fact was, Blanchot maintained, if it was not to be treated everywhere with contempt, the law had to be defended: if necessary by force.

Here was the nub of a critical dilemma. For how to tell the difference between the force that maintains and protects the law and the force that usurps and overturns its authority? How to separate illegitimate violence from legitimate force, and how to distinguish measure from excess? Was it always the case that the legitimacy of the end justified the means, or could only the legality of the means guarantee the justice of the ends? And if it was a matter of challenging prevailing legal conventions in order to appeal to more pressing principles not enshrined in statute, in whose name was it legitimate to do so? Who or what, in other words, was the proper subject of politics? Who or what was the source of political sovereignty? In the 1930s, one after the other, Blanchot's contemporaries made their choices, putting their faith now in the consensuality and compromises of parliamentary democracy, now in the revolutionary mission of the European proletariat under the leadership of the Third International, now in the mystified nationalism and racial purity of the Volk, gathered under the tutelage of a charismatic leader, and so on. But throughout that whole turbulent period, it is striking that none of these so-called political solutions ever held any attraction whatsoever for Blanchot, who rejected all three outright, and turned instead to the only subject remaining, still separated from itself, still absent, still mired in abject humiliation, but which Blanchot fervently hoped might be restored to its past grandeur, reawakened to proper immediacy, and returned to its commanding sovereign presence, not unlike an irrepressible and sublime work of art: the nation of France itself.

During the 1920s and 1930s, Blanchot was not the only commentator to be exercised by the question of the relationship between law and violence. Writing in 1921 in the essay 'Zur Kritik der Gewalt' (Critique of Violence), read at the time with some interest, it seems, by the influential legal theorist (and later apologist of the Third Reich) Carl Schmitt, Walter Benjamin had responded to similar problems by distinguishing between two types of violence, one that laid down the law, and one that upheld it.[7] 'All violence [*Gewalt*: meaning violence *and* power]', he wrote, 'as a means is either law-making [*rechtsetzend*, i.e., it poses or constitutes the law] or law-preserving [*rechtserhaltend*, i.e., it maintains the law]'.[8] If violence or power in the second of Benjamin's two senses referred to the role of authority in preserving at least a certain form of (repressive or protective) legal order, in the first sense it was premissed on the aporetics of constitution, that paradox, embodied among others in the American constitution, by which law can only be founded by that which is illegal, as Blanchot was surely aware when he spoke for instance in 1933 of the need for spiritual — national — revolution to overturn the State, and predicted, logically enough, that any such upheaval would be excessive, violent, illegal: 'pitiless, bloody, and unjust, our last chance of salvation [*dure, sanglante, injuste, notre dernière chance de salut*]'.[9] There remained however the problem, as Benjamin was quick to point out, that the boundary between constitution and enforcement, between the posing and the imposing of law was anything but clear, either in law or in fact. Whenever the police were involved, he remarked, referring likewise to the early Weimar Republic as well as the French nineteenth century, it was always possible for the one to tip uneasily and eerily into the other 'in a kind of spooky amalgam [*einer gleichsam gespenstischen Vermischung*]'.[10] What this implied was that no law was ever wholly in accord with itself. No law could not *not* correspond, in part, to an act of illegitimate foundation, and every statute, however legal, retained the memory of the time when, still belonging to the future, it was paradoxically outside all law. Here lay both a chance and a danger. The violence inherent in all law meant, on the one hand, that it was always legitimate — in the name of the law itself — to challenge the law; but, on the other, there was no guarantee that to do so would not simply culminate in further violence. There was always the risk, then, that the force of law might be overwhelmed by the law of force, and legitimate violence become no different from its illegitimate double.

In the end, however, Benjamin argued, questions of legality and legitimacy could not be divorced from the demands of something far more pressing and immediate than the inconclusive circle of legitimate ends and justifiable means allowed: justice itself. Accordingly, he went on in his 1921 essay to distinguish further between two radically opposed aspects of law-making (*Rechtsetzung*). Here too there was a division, an alternative, a choice, between what Benjamin boldly described on the one hand as mythic violence (or power), whose object was to enact, found, and constitute law, and, on the other, what he termed divine violence (or power), whose goal was the singularity of justice in so far as it was irreducible to any given human statute. 'If mythic violence is law-making [*rechtsetzend*]', he argued, 'divine violence is law-destroying [*rechtsvernichtend*]; if the former sets boundaries, the latter boundlessly destroys them; if mythic violence brings at once guilt and retribution, divine violence only expiates; if the former threatens, the latter strikes; if the former is bloody, the latter is lethal without spilling blood.'[11] 'Mythic violence [*Die mythische Gewalt*]', Benjamin added, 'is bloody power [*Blutgewalt*] over mere life [*das bloße Leben*] for its own sake; divine violence is pure power [*reine Gewalt*] over all life for the sake of the living [*um des Lebendigen willen*, i.e. that which lives]. The first demands sacrifice; the second accepts it.'[12] These are no doubt exalted as well as chilling words, and Derrida was surely right to find their ambiguity both troubling and revealing: troubling for what they make thinkable, but

'Not In Our Name': Blanchot, Politics, the Neuter   147

revealing, too, of the challenges and temptations of political thinking in 1920s and 1930s Europe.¹³

Benjamin, however, was not alone. Blanchot too, as some of his more vehement editorials from 1936 and 1937 testify, was often given to excessive, over-heated prognostications, laden with menace and promise alike — probably no more so than when, barely a month after the precarious formation of Léon Blum's first Popular Front coalition government in June 1936, in a gesture born of the very political impasse it aimed to overcome, he dryly appealed over the heads of his faint-hearted readership to unnamed others who might be ready to embark on acts of terrorism: as a method of public safety. 'We are not among those who judge it preferable to do without a revolution or who speak hypocritically of a peaceful, spiritual revolution', Blanchot fulminated. And he went on:

> Such hopefulness is absurd and cowardly. It is necessary for there to be a revolution, because it is impossible to modify a regime that has everything in its grip and its roots everywhere, it must be killed and utterly destroyed [*on le supprime, on l'abat*]. It is necessary for this revolution to be violent because it is not possible to find the force and passion required for renewal in a people as weakened [*aveuli*: lacking willpower] as our own by employing respectable measures [*mesures décentes*], but only by administering bloody shocks [*secousses sanglantes*] and unleashing a violent storm that will bring it to its senses [*qui le bouleversera afin de l'éveiller*].¹⁴

Blanchot's philippic was no doubt rhetorical before it was practical, but it conveys accurately enough the uncompromising ferocity with which, in 1936, the writer challenged the legitimacy of the newly elected government. This was not the first time Blanchot had done so in his career as a political commentator. Nor was it to be the last. Indeed, though much else would change, it is fair to say that politics in general for Blanchot were to remain largely synonymous with precisely those sporadic yet recurrent moments of crisis, interruption, or upheaval that featured regularly in French political life in subsequent years: the Munich accords of September 1938, the armistice between Pétain and Hitler signed at Compiègne on 22 June 1940 and the illegal self-dissolution of the Third Republic eighteen days later (which Blanchot is reported to have witnessed personally), the Liberation of Paris in 1944, de Gaulle's alleged *coup d'état* of 13 May 1958, and so on. For also belonging to this strangely persistent historical sequence were the events of December 1965 — a legitimate transition for some, for others an unjustifiable *coup de force* — when

148 *Paragraph*

France prepared for the first time to elect its head of state by direct universal suffrage, under a modification to the constitution put to referendum by de Gaulle three years before, with the express purpose of weakening the legitimacy of the National Assembly in favour of the personal authority of the President. Blanchot's response, as the election campaign began, was in the form of an essay on Sade's famous pamphlet of 1795, similarly written at a time of constitutional transition that, soon after, would allow a previous first consul to identify himself, with quasi-religious hubris, with the fate of the nation: 'Français, encore un effort si vous voulez être républicains...' ('Citizens of France, Try Harder If You Wish To Be Republicans...').[15] And as he made the parallel between Bonaparte and de Gaulle explicit, Blanchot commented:

> What Sade calls a revolutionary regime is that pure moment in time when history, having been suspended, marks an epoch, the time of between-times [*ce temps de l'entre-temps*] when between the old laws and the new reigns the silence of the absence of laws, that interval which precisely corresponds to the gap in speaking [*l'entre-dire*, i.e. both speaking-between and inter-diction] when everything ceases and stops, including the eternal drive to speak, because, then, there is no longer any prohibition [*interdit*].[16]

In 1936, in order to contest the legitimacy of the state, Blanchot's rhetoric had urged a series of exemplary, cathartic acts of political violence. In 1965, the writer turned instead to something more resembling a work of literature, albeit in the unusual form of a detachable supplement contained within a larger, fictional work whose confines it nevertheless exceeded, and authored by a writer who, for some, was the embodiment of violence itself, yet who, for that very reason, had begun to figure as early as 1947, for Blanchot, as *the* writer *par excellence*.[17] This was not simply a matter of replacing a political discourse with a literary one, assuming it can be said with confidence where the one ends and the other begins. It was to testify to a radically different relationship to the law. For what revealed itself now in the explicit or implicit interregnum that was a precondition of all politics as such for Blanchot was not, as entrusted in 1936 to a determined few, the effervescent, ebullient, and immediate sovereign presence of the people.[18] No, what spoke now, in December 1965, as Blanchot remembered Sade, was something other; it was the loquacious, neutral silence of the absence of all laws, 'social, moral, natural':[19] law without laws, so to speak, law before laws, law in excess of all laws, law as a neutral suspension of all laws.

But of what, and to whom, and in whose name, did this interruption of law now speak?

'For a period', wrote Blanchot in 1949 in the voice of one of his narrators, arguably summing up the distance his own thinking had travelled during the previous decade and a half,

I lived a public life [*j'ai été un homme public*]. I found the law appealing, and loved the multitude. I was obscure in others. As a nonentity, I was sovereign. But one day I grew tired of being the stone that castigates men alone [*lapide les hommes seuls*]. To tempt the law, I called out gently to her [*la loi* is in the feminine], 'Come closer, let me see you face to face.' (I wanted, for a moment, to take her aside.) These were incautious words. What would I have done had she replied?[20]

But if the law declined to answer, this did not mean Blanchot was tempted or even allowed to do the same. On the contrary, once Blanchot began to exchange daily journalism for another kind of writing, undertaken by necessity at night, a very different exposure to the law's demands began to affirm itself. This, I suggest, is what principally is at stake in *Le Très-Haut*, and why the novel asks to be read as a sustained settling of accounts or explanation with politics or the political. Already the title of the novel provides an important, if enigmatic clue. For alongside its standard theological meaning, with which Blanchot was familiar, it was also the title, in the neuter ('Das Höchste', 'The Highest'), given by Hölderlin around 1805 to his translation of a famous fragment from Pindar (Fr. 169), attested in Herodotus and Plato, which Hölderlin, most likely taking his text from *Gorgias* 484b (where, for polemical purposes of his own, Plato cites an amended version of Pindar's text), renders as follows: 'Das Gesez [*nomos*],/Von allen der König [*basileus*], Sterblichen und/Unsterblichen; das führt eben/Darum gewaltig/Das gerechteste Recht mit allerhöchster Hand' (The Law,/Of everyone the King, mortals and/Immortals; which is just why/It mightily guides/The rightest right with the very highest hand).[21]

Also accompanying Hölderlin's translation was a commentary by the poet, which Blanchot is certain also to have known since it is cited by Heidegger in the course of a famous essay on Hölderlin's unfinished Pindaric hymn, 'Wie wenn am Feiertage...' ('As on a holiday...'), which, shortly before sending his novel to the publisher, Blanchot reviewed for *Critique* in December 1946.[22] More particularly, Heidegger in the essay had quoted the two famous opening paragraphs of Hölderlin's commentary, which are as follows:

The immediate [*Das Unmittelbare*], strictly speaking, is impossible for mortals, as it is for the immortals; a God must distinguish different worlds, according to his nature, since heavenly goodness, because of itself, must be sacred, unalloyed. Man, as a knowing creature, must also distinguish different worlds, because knowledge is only possible through opposition. For this reason, the immediate [*das Unmittelbare*] is, strictly speaking, impossible for mortals, as for immortals. Strict mediacy [*Die strenge Mittelbarkeit*], however, is the law [*das Gesez*].[23]

Interpreting these lines, Heidegger explains that only immediacy, which is not itself communicable, can give rise to that which is communicated (or mediated), in much the same way that, for Benjamin and others, that which grounds the law cannot itself be subject to it. And this is the reading Blanchot also proposes, at least up to a certain point, by drawing on Heidegger's gloss. 'What is the Sacred?', Blanchot asks, and answers: 'It is the immediate, says Heidegger, taking his lead from a prose fragment by Hölderlin, the immediate that is never communicated, but is the principle of all possibility of communicating.'[24]

The ramifications of Pindar's fragment are extensive, and reach far beyond Hölderlin's translation and the subsequent interest shown in it by Heidegger and Blanchot. In his book *Homo sacer*, for instance, Giorgio Agamben identifies in Pindar's enigmatic pronouncement an essential *topos* in Greek and later philosophical thinking regarding the fundamental relationship between law and violence: 'Pindar's fragment on the *nomos basileus*', he writes, 'contains the hidden paradigm guiding every successive definition of sovereignty: the sovereign is the point of indistinction between violence and law, the threshold on which violence passes over into law and law passes over into violence'.[25] In the ensuing discussion, Agamben points, too, to the presence of Fr. 169 in Carl Schmitt's *Der Nomos der Erde* of 1950, where Hölderlin is taken to task for mistranslating Pindar, at least according to Schmitt, in so far as Hölderlin, in rendering *nomos* as *Gesetz*, that is, in Schmittian terminology, as a derivative convention posed or posited as such [i.e. *gesetzt*] and reliant for its legitimacy on prior, constituent sovereign power, misses the proper sense of the term as an unmediated originating principle. 'Nomos in the original sense', Schmitt contends, 'is precisely the full immediacy [*Unmittelbarkeit*] of juridical power not mediated by laws [*Gesetze*]; it is a constitutive, historical event [*ein konstituierendes geschichtliches Ereignis*], an act of *legitimacy* which alone gives the legality of mere law [*des bloßen Gesetzes*] its meaning.'[26] Schmitt's purpose, then, not unlike Benjamin's in 1921, was to isolate and radically privilege the violent primacy of *nomos* as an originary, immediate and unmediated foundational decision, irreducible to any legal statute in so far as the latter was always authorized, mediated by the former. This at any rate is the forced, some might say violent, construction Schmitt puts on Hölderlin's remark, cited above, to the effect that '[s]trict mediacy, however, is the law [*Gesez*]'.[27]

One of the significant causes for the divergence between Hölderlin and Schmitt, as Agamben rightly observes, is that, in addressing the status of *nomos basileus*, Hölderlin, unlike Schmitt, was not concerned with legal theory, but with epistemology, not with sovereignty as such, but with the conditions of possibility of knowledge, and thus, paradoxically, not only with what was highest, but also what was lowest. This becomes explicit at the end of Hölderlin's commentary when the poet remarks that '"King" here means the superlative, which is only the sign for the highest ground of knowing [*den höchsten Erkenntnißgrund*], not for the highest power [*nicht für die höchste Macht*]'. But like Schmitt, Agamben at this point probes no further, and abandons Hölderlin's alternative reading of Pindar's fragment in order to develop a politological account of the state of exception or state of emergency, that strange, seemingly self-contradictory moment when constitutions are required to suspend themselves (as does de Gaulle's 1958 constitution, for instance, under its notorious Article 16, invoked from April to September 1961, which de Gaulle threatened to use again in May 1968), and which, in a Schmittian perspective at least, Agamben argues, 'is not so much a spatio-temporal suspension as a complex topological figure in which not only the exception and the rule but also the state of nature and law, outside and inside, pass through one another', and as a result of which, adds Agamben,

what happened [in the wake of the First World War] and is still happening before our eyes is that the 'juridically empty' space of the state of exception (in which law is in force in the figure — that is, etymologically, in the *fiction* — of its own dissolution, and in which everything that the sovereign deemed *de facto* necessary could happen) has transgressed its spatio-temporal boundaries and now, overflowing outside them, is starting to coincide with the normal order, in which everything again becomes possible.[28]

But what if what was precisely at stake in Hölderlin's translation from Pindar, rather than pointing, under the auspices of sovereignty, to a threshold of indistinction between violence and law, was more like an interruption of possibility, a deferral or difference that, like a caesura, voiced in the neuter, and irreducible to any opposition between immanence and transcendence, divided the origin from itself, put immediacy at a distance, ruined all prospect of foundation, and revoked the supremacy of sovereign power as such?

And what if what was at issue for Blanchot in his encounter with Hölderlin was an experience of the law far removed from the nihilistic principle of absolute, unmediated sovereignty?

Blanchot approaches 'Das Höchste' very differently to Heidegger, Schmitt or Agamben. First, in the whole of his work he quotes from it explicitly perhaps three times at most, admittedly in three strategically important contexts: the first in 1946, in the course of his discussion of Heidegger, where the barest of allusions to 'absolute mediacy [*médiatité absolue*]' allows him to complicate Heidegger's claim that 'chaos' for Hölderlin is 'the sacred' or 'holy' as such, the very essence of nature [*physis*] and Being in general; the second in 1955, in an essay on Hölderlin originally entitled 'Le Tournant [The Turning]', and incorporated later the same year in *L'Espace littéraire*, which gave the writer the opportunity of amplifying his remarks on 'Das Höchste'; and the third in 1969, in *L'Entretien infini*, in a page added to an essay on the poetry of Yves Bonnefoy first published ten years earlier.[29] Though on each occasion the reference to 'Das Höchste' arrives like a marginal afterthought, this is arguably in inverse proportion to its significance, for it would not be hard to show its implications exert a binding influence on Blanchot's reading not only of Hölderlin but of modern poetry in general, and that its lesson may be found echoing like a distant murmur through Blanchot's own fiction too, including the pages of the shadowy twin or double of Pindar's fragment: *Le Très-Haut* itself.[30]

But in what way? Everything turns on the singular character of the supreme law to which Fr. 169 alludes. What law Pindar himself had in mind when those lines were first composed is impossible to say. But from Blanchot's and even Hölderlin's perspective this is unimportant. More revealing are the names of those to whom the law applies, those mortals and immortals evoked in the second line of Pindar's fragment. This suggests that the law in question is none other than the law of dying itself, in that its necessity is laid on the ones as inescapable possibility and on the others as inescapable impossibility, for if humans are forever promised the unrelieved prospect of dying, so the gods for their part are perpetually threatened with the relentless inability to die. This apparent opposition, however, is more tortuous than it might appear. For as Fios Arietos observes, Hölderlin, unlike Pindar, introduces a line break or caesura between the mention of the ones and that of the others,[31] as though to mark the fact that, yes, the possibility of dying is what separates men from gods, but that also, at the same time, this separation is what joins them together, since in neither case is dying truly possible: for if the gods are condemned never properly to die, so too are humans, who, as Hölderlin implies, and Blanchot never tires of insisting, are equally unable to make death their own and bring it within the orbit of power, potency, or possibility. Dying, in a word, is not something one *can* do as an object of will, mastery or power, since death, as it occurs, destroys precisely these faculties. 'Mortal, immortal', Blanchot would ask in 1980: 'does this reversal have any meaning?'[32]

Nomos was all-powerful, then, according to Hölderlin's commentary, not because its authority was grounded in the omnipotence of the gods, but because it was a condition of both possibility and impossibility which, as such, deprived both gods and humans of sovereignty over it. Rather than empowering mortals or immortals, it set a limit on their condition; and even as it constituted that which was most singular to them, the relationship to dying, by that token it also remained unapproachable and ungraspable as such: an empty, but nonetheless compelling enigma or secret. As the law promulgated itself, then, it also withdrew, simultaneously inscribing and effacing itself, the one as the other, and the other as the one, in a paradoxical intertwining of the two, not unlike the relationship between blindness and vision explored by Blanchot (as Derrida has shown) in *La Folie du jour*, the implication of which was that the law, far from embodying the immediacy or plenitude of the origin, was but a singular case of the neuter: infinite detour, irreducible otherness, unspoken futurity. It could not therefore be made present in the guise of some constitutive sublunar sovereign authority, and therefore conferred no power upon those whom it addressed, gods or humans alike. As Hölderlin rightly contends, in so far as it was immediate, it was impossible, available only at a distance from itself, in indirect, oblique, or mediated fashion. It could not be named or appropriated in or for itself. It was not itself therefore properly founded nor could it found anything in its turn. Its only authority in the end was that of interruption, deferral, alterity.

From Hölderlin's perspective, and as Blanchot discovered in his turn, the law to which writing was exposed, which it obeyed just as much in the breach as it did in the observance, was no figure of sovereign power or violence. It was experienced instead as a compelling, nameless demand synonymous with an abyssal suspension of possibility. So although the law reigned supreme, what it proposed or imposed was not power as such, nor anything that corresponded to a threshold of indistinction between law and violence, to use Agamben's formulation, but an affirmative powerlessness or non-power (not to be confused with impotence) which, as Blanchot's friend Robert Antelme testified in *L'Espèce humaine*, was also a radical resistance to power.[33] It was this, perhaps, that Blanchot was able to read in Hölderlin's commentary, which echoes much of what Blanchot wrote about death and dying in *Le Très-Haut* and elsewhere. For death too is immediate, in that it escapes all possibility of mediation; its supremacy, however, can never be made present, and it can only be approached as a suspension of possibility. Sovereignty, in these circumstances, as Bataille famously observes, 'is NOTHING'.[34] It constitutes no subject — of desire, meaning, or politics — that is not already undone by the stringent limits within which it is bound.

Gods and mortals, Hölderlin went on, are under an obligation to differentiate. They come together under the law, which is itself inaccessible, only as a function of this logic of separation, the effects of which are singular in that they affect each differently and universal in that they affect all without exception. The law enjoins, then, but also disjoins, and to obey the law is to attend to both movements at once: fragile necessity *and* necessary fragility. Writing follows a similar logic, for if language imposes a measure shared by all ('One thing is sure even now', writes Hölderlin in the poem 'Brod und Wein' (Bread and Wine') that Blanchot was fond of quoting: 'at noon or just before midnight,/Whether it's early or late, always a measure [*ein Maß*] exists,/Common to all, though his own to each one is also allotted/Each of us makes for the place, reaches the place that he can'[35]), it is by effecting a separation between this person and the next, without which no communication would occur at all. What is measured, then, by language is also the immeasurable, and the task entrusted to literature in such circumstances, Blanchot puts it, was nothing short of mediating the immediate, communicating the incommunicable, testifying to the impossible. The lesson is a political as well as a poetological one, and argues in favour of effusiveness and sobriety alike, urging patience as well as impatience, and a responsiveness and responsibility both to the immediate and the impossible which cannot be posited as such, and to that which is mediate, which comprises an infinite detour — without either of these demands being confused as one, or the one subordinated to the other. And if it followed that the law was somehow supreme, this was not because all had to be sanctioned by law, but because the law, following the dictates of the neuter, always appealed to what was more originary than any letter of the law, in much the same way as that which Derrida, in reading *La Folie du jour*, calls counterlaw — in which Blanchot in his turn was able to recognize, without piety or anthropomorphism, the entanglement of the one with the other, as witnessed by the neuter, and which he formulates thus:

> Responsibility or obligation towards the Other [*Autrui*: Blanchot uses the impersonal neuter form] which does not derive from the Law, but from which the Law itself may be thought to derive, in respect of everything that makes it irreducible to legality in all its forms, through which necessarily the attempt is made to regulate it, even as it is declared to be the exception or extra-ordinary that cannot be uttered in any previously formulated language.[36]

III

There was something in the enactment of the law, then, that exceeded all laws, which was equivalent not to supreme force, violence or power, but to a neutral (or neuter) interruption of law which was also, perhaps more importantly, a law of neutral (or neuter) interruption: not the law as a guarantee of possible force, but the weakness of the impossible as the ground without ground of the law. And from 1958 onwards at least, in a series of explicitly political writings, this affirmative caesura, hiatus, and interval, this neutral suspension of power, irreducible to any form of negativity, was to receive in Blanchot's writing a decisive, uncompromising, always abyssal appellation: that of refusal. 'Refusal, here', he wrote, 'is absolute, categorical. It does not enter into discussions, nor does it argue its case.'[37] Incontrovertible and peremptory, it was anything but transgressive of any established legal norms. It was both more radical and more original; like writing, its only responsibility or responsiveness was to its own anonymous, fragile, and singularly insurmountable necessity: which always exceeds the presence, propriety, property, or properness of any name, including the one we dimly call our own.

NOTES

1 The campaign is still active, as may be seen from its website: *http://www.notinourname.net/*. The November 2002 response, together with a list of signatories on the French and the U.S. side, may be found at *www.nion.us/Publications/LeMonde2–28.pdf*.

2 On the aporia that affects the authorship of acts of constitution as such, see Jacques Derrida, *Otobiographies* (Paris, Galilée, 1984), 13–32; *Negotiations:*

Interventions and Interviews, 1971–2001, edited and translated by Elizabeth Rottenberg (Stanford, Stanford University Press, 2002), 46–54. 'Who signs', asks Derrida, 'the declarative act which founds an institution, and with what so-called proper name?' (16; 470; translation modified). An important moment in Derrida's analysis is marked by his reading of Blanchot's *La Folie du jour* which he presents as follows: 'Resorting to force [*le coup de force*] makes law [*fait droit*], founds law [*fonde le droit*], gives right [*donne droit*], *gives birth to the law* [*donne le jour à la loi*]. To give birth to the law: read *The Madness of the Day* by Blanchot' (23; 50; translation modified).

3 Maurice Blanchot, 'Qui?', *Cahiers Confrontation*, 20 (Winter 1989), 49–51 (50); 'Who?', translated by Eduardo Cadava, *Who Comes After the Subject?*, edited by Eduardo Cadava, Peter Connor and Jean-Luc Nancy (New York, Routledge, 1991), 58–60 (59); translation modified.

4 Maurice Blanchot, 'Qui?', 50; *Who Comes After the Subject?*, 60; translation modified. See Claude Morali, *Qui est moi aujourd'hui?* (Paris, Fayard, 1984). Compare Maurice Blanchot, *Le Pas au-delà* (Paris, Gallimard, 1973), 16; *The Step Not Beyond*, translated by Lycette Nelson (Albany, State University of New York Press, 1992), 7. It follows from Blanchot's formulation that *lui*, here, cannot be identified with one gender rather than another, but with the multiplicity that exceeds any single given gender. *Lui*, therefore, refers not only to him, her, or it, but always: the other.

5 See Jeffrey Mehlman, *Legacies of Anti-Semitism in France* (Minneapolis, University of Minnesota Press, 1983); *Genealogies of the Text: Literature, Psychoanalysis, and Politics in Modern France* (Cambridge, Cambridge University Press, 1995); Steven Ungar, *Scandal and Aftereffect: Blanchot and France since 1930* (Minneapolis and London, University of Minnesota Press, 1995); Philippe Mesnard, *Maurice Blanchot : le sujet de l'engagement* (Paris, L'Harmattan, 1996); Richard Wolin, *The Seduction of Unreason: the Intellectual Romance with Fascism from Nietzsche to Postmodernism* (Princeton, Princeton University Press, 2004).

6 On *Le Très-Haut* as a political novel, see Georges Préli, *La Force du dehors: extériorité, limite et non-pouvoir à partir de Maurice Blanchot* (Paris, Éditions Recherches, 1977), 93–139; and my *Bataille, Blanchot, Klossowski: Writing at the Limit* (Oxford, Oxford University Press, 2001), 181–206.

7 See Walter Benjamin, *Gesammelte Schriften*, edited by Rolf Tiedemann and Hermann Schweppenhäuser, 7 vols (Frankfurt, Suhrkamp, 1974–89), II: 1, 179–203; 'Critique of Violence', translated by Edmund Jephcott, *Selected Writings*, edited by Marcus Bullock and Michael W. Jennings, 4 vols (London, Harvard University Press, 1996–2003), I, 236–52. Benjamin's text has been discussed at length elsewhere, most pertinently in the present context by Derrida in *Force de loi* (Paris, Galilée, 1994); 'Force of Law', translated by Mary Quaintance, in *Deconstruction and the Possibility of Justice*, edited by Drucilla Cornell, Michael Rosenfeld, and David Gray Carlson (New York, Routledge, 1992). On Schmitt's career and thinking, see Gopal Balakrishnan,

The Enemy: an Intellectual Portrait of Carl Schmitt (London, Verso, 2000). On the relationship between Benjamin and Schmitt, see also Giorgio Agamben, *State of Exception*, translated by Kevin Attell (Chicago, University of Chicago Press, 2005), 52–64. It is worth noting that Benjamin in his analysis (*Gesammelte Schriften*, II: 1, 190; *Selected Writings*, I, 243–4) also anticipates one of the key objections made by Blanchot, among others, to French foreign policy, which was that neither national nor international law could be protected by contractual agreement alone, as successive governments appeared to believe.

8 Walter Benjamin, *Gesammelte Schriften*, II: 1, 190; *Selected Writings*, I, 243; translation modified.
9 Maurice Blanchot, 'La Révolution nécessaire', *Le Rempart*, 62, 22 June 1933, 2.
10 Walter Benjamin, *Gesammelte Schriften*, II: 1, 190; *Selected Writings*, I, 243. The expression gives rise to a lengthy commentary on Derrida's part in *Force de loi*, 101–3; *Deconstruction and the Possibility of Justice*, 42–3.
11 Walter Benjamin, *Gesammelte Schriften*, II: 1, 199; *Selected Writings*, I, 249–50; translation slightly modified.
12 Walter Benjamin, *Gesammelte Schriften*, II: 1, 200; *Selected Writings*, I, 50.
13 See Jacques Derrida, *Force de loi*, 122–46; *Deconstruction and the Possibility of Justice*, 51–63.
14 Maurice Blanchot, 'Le Terrorisme, méthode de salut public', *Combat*, 7, July 1936, 106.
15 Blanchot's essay was first published in late September under the title 'L'Inconvenance majeure' ['Irreducible Impropriety'] as a preface to a reprint of Sade's pamphlet in J.-J. Pauvert's *Libertés* series, edited by the polemicist (and co-signatory of the *Manifeste des 121*) Jean-François Revel. It appeared shortly after as 'Français, encore un effort...' ('Citizens of France, Try Harder...') in *La Nouvelle Revue française*, 154 (October 1965), 600–18, and was published for a third time as 'L'Insurrection, la folie d'écrire' ('Insurrection, the Madness of Writing') in *L'Entretien infini* (Paris, Gallimard, 1969), 323–42; *The Infinite Conversation*, translated by Susan Hanson (Minneapolis, University of Minnesota Press, 1993), 217–29. These changing titles do not signify indecision; they frame and reframe the text according to shifting political circumstances.
16 Maurice Blanchot, *L'Entretien infini*, 336; *The Infinite Conversation*, 226; translation modified. Shortly after, Blanchot describes the moment as 'this always impending instant of silent frenzy [*cet instant, toujours en instance, de la frénésie silencieuse*]', using an expression that recurs at the end of of *L'Instant de ma mort* (Paris, Gallimard, [1994] 2002), 18; *The Instant of My Death*, translated by Elizabeth Rottenberg (Stanford, Stanford University Press, 2000), 10–11.
17 See Maurice Blanchot, *La Part du feu* (Paris, Gallimard, 1949), 311; *The Work of Fire*, translated by Charlotte Mandell (Stanford, Stanford University Press, 1995), 321.

18 Later, in *La Communauté inavouable*, in an oblique commentary on the radical shift informing his postwar political thinking, Blanchot has recourse to this very expression ('présence du peuple') in evoking another of those fateful interruptions of history: the famous, seemingly spontaneous funeral cortège of 13 February 1962 from La Bourse du travail to Le Père Lachaise cemetery, followed by an estimated million or so unofficial mourners, protesting silently at the deaths of eight Algerian demonstrators killed by the Paris police five days earlier under the orders of Maurice Papon — save that here presence, wrote Blanchot, was not the prerogative of a select minority but of the anonymous many, belonged in fact to no present or even future time, and was witness instead to a determined 'declaration of powerlessness [*déclaration d'impuissance*]' whose paradoxical potential remained undiminished. See Maurice Blanchot, *La Communauté inavouable* (Paris, Minuit, 1983), 54–6 (54); *The Unavowable Community*, translated by Pierre Joris (New York, Station Hill Press, 1988), 31–3 (31); translation modified. The events are commemorated in a famous poem ('In Eins') by Paul Celan, who was also present that day; see Paul Celan, *Gesammelte Werke*, edited by Beda Allemann and Stefan Reichert in collaboration with Rudolf Bücher, 5 vols (Frankfurt, Suhrkamp, [1983] 1992), I, 270; *Selected Poems and Prose of Paul Celan*, translated by John Felstiner (London, W. W. Norton, 2001), 188–9.

19 Maurice Blanchot, *L'Entretien infini*, 337; *The Infinite Conversation*, 226; translation modified.

20 Maurice Blanchot, *La Folie du jour* (Paris, Gallimard, 2002), 14; 'The Madness of the Day', translated by Lydia Davis, *The Station Hill Blanchot Reader*, edited by George Quasha (Barrytown, Station Hill Press, 1998), 193; translation modified.

21 For the most complete transcription of Hölderlin's translation and commentary, see Friedrich Hölderlin, *Sämtliche Werke: Frankfurter Ausgabe*, edited by D. E. Sattler, 17 vols (Frankfurt, Stroemfeld, 1975–2001), XV (1987), 354–5; 'Hölderlin's "Pindar Fragments"', translated by Jeremy Adler, *Comparative Criticism*, 6 (Cambridge, Cambridge University Press, 1984), 43. On Pindar's original Greek text, see Hugh Lloyd-Jones, 'Pindar Fr. 169', *Harvard Studies in Classical Philology*, 76 (1972), 45–56; and on Plato's misquotation of it in *Gorgias* 484b, see Giorgio Agamben, *Homo Sacer: Sovereign Power and Bare Life*, translated by Daniel Heller-Roazen (Stanford, Stanford University Press, 1998), 30–5. For further discussion of Hölderlin's version, see Thomas Schestag, 'The Highest', translated by Georgia Albert, *The Solid Letter: Readings of Friedrich Hölderlin*, edited by Aris Fioretos (Stanford, Stanford University Press, 1999), 375–411; and Andrew Benjamin, 'Political Translations: Hölderlin's "Das Höchste"', *Translation and 'The Classic'*, edited by Alexandra Lianeri and Vanda Zajko (Oxford, Oxford University Press, forthcoming 2008).

22 See Maurice Blanchot, *La Part du feu*, 115–32; *The Work of Fire*, 111–31.

23 Friedrich Hölderlin, *Sämtliche Werke*, XV, 354; 'Hölderlin's "Pindar Fragments"', 43.
24 Maurice Blanchot, *La Part du feu*, 123; *The Work of Fire*, 120.
25 Giorgio Agamben, *Homo Sacer*, 31–2.
26 Carl Schmitt, *Der Nomos der Erde: im Völkerrecht des Jus Publicum Europaeum* (Cologne, Greven, 1950), 42.
27 See Carl Schmitt, *Der Nomos der Erde*, 42.
28 Giorgio Agamben, *Homo Sacer*, 37–8.
29 See Maurice Blanchot, *La Part du feu*, 126; *The Work of Fire*, 124; translation modified; *L'Espace littéraire* (Paris, Gallimard, 1955), 288; *The Space of Literature*, translated by Ann Smock (Lincoln and London, University of Nebraska Press, 1982), 273; *L'Entretien infini*, 53–4; *The Infinite Conversation*, 37–8.
30 There is evidence, too, of the presence of Hölderlin's other Pindar fragments in *Le Très-Haut*, as Robert Savage shows in his 'Between Heidegger and Hölderlin: The "Sacred" Speech of Maurice Blanchot', in *After Blanchot: Literature, Philosophy, Criticism*, edited by Leslie Hill, Brian Nelson, and Dimitris Vardoulakis (Newark, University of Delaware Press, 2005), 149–67.
31 See Fios Arietos, 'Introduction', *The Solid Letter: Readings of Friedrich Hölderlin*, 19. Pindar had written: 'thnatōn te kai athanatōn', 'Of mortals and immortals'.
32 Maurice Blanchot, *L'Écriture du désastre* (Paris, Gallimard, 1980), 183; *The Writing of the Disaster*, translated by Ann Smock (Lincoln and London, University of Nebraska Press, 1986), 119.
33 There is here an important debate between Blanchot and Agamben bearing on Antelme's testimony, which finds clearest expression in Agamben's superficial and ultimately dogmatic reference to Blanchot in *Remnants of Auschwitz: the Witness and the Archive*, translated by Daniel Heller-Roazen (New York, Zone Books, 1999), 134–5. I examine what is at stake here in *A Change of Epoch: Blanchot, Writing, the Fragmentary*, forthcoming.
34 See Georges Bataille, *Œuvres complètes*, 12 vols (Paris, Gallimard, 1970–88), VIII, 300. Blanchot pointedly cites these words twice over in *L'Écriture du désastre*, 142, 200; *The Writing of the Disaster*, 90, 131; as he does so, his principal concern is to disengage Bataille's NOTHING from any positive or negative dialectic, since in either case the result would be to ground sovereignty in subjective presence.
35 Friedrich Hölderlin, *Werke und Briefe*, edited by Friedrich Beißner and Jochen Schmidt, 3 vols (Frankfurt a. M., Insel Verlag, 1969), I, 115; *Poems and Fragments*, translated by Michael Hamburger (London, Routledge and Kegan Paul, 1966), 245.
36 Maurice Blanchot, *La Communauté inavouable*, 73; *The Unavowable Community*, 43; translation modified.
37 Maurice Blanchot, *L'Amitié* (Paris, Gallimard, 1971), 130; *Friendship*, translated by Elizabeth Rottenberg (Stanford, Stanford University Press, 1997), 111; translation modified.

Notes on Contributors

Christophe Bident is Maître de conférences at l'Université de Paris 7-Denis Diderot. He is the author of *Maurice Blanchot: partenaire invisible* (Champ Vallon, 1998), *Bernard-Marie Koltès, généalogies* (Farrago, 2000) and *Reconnaissances: Antelme, Blanchot, Deleuze* (Calmann-Lévy, 2003), and co-editor (with Pierre Vilar) of the volume *Maurice Blanchot: récits critiques* (Farrago, 2003), containing papers from the first international conference on Blanchot to be held in France. He has recently edited for Gallimard a volume containing all Blanchot's uncollected review articles from the *Journal des débats* between 1941 and 1944.

Timothy Clark is a specialist in the fields of modern literary theory and continental philosophy (especially the work of Martin Heidegger and Jacques Derrida), also in Romanticism (especially P.B. Shelley) and ecocriticism. He has published numerous articles in literary and philosophical journals and six monographs: *Embodying Revolution: The Figure of the Poet in Shelley* (OUP, 1989); *Derrida, Heidegger, Blanchot: Sources of Derrida's Notion and Practice of Literature* (CUP, 1992); *The Theory of Inspiration: Composition as a Crisis of Subjectivity in Romantic and Post-Romantic Writing* (MUP, 1997); *Charles Tomlinson* (Northcote House, 1999); *Martin Heidegger* (Routledge, 2001); *The Poetics of Singularity: The Counter-Culturalist Turn in Heidegger, Derrida, Blanchot and the later Gadamer* (Edinburgh UP, 2005). Timothy Clark is also co-editor of the *Oxford Literary Review*. His current research is concerned with what might be called a greening of elements of deconstruction under the provisional title of 'Green Anarchist Criticism'.

Christopher Fynsk is Professor of Comparative Literature and Modern Thought at the University of Aberdeen, where he is Director of the Centre for Modern Thought and Head of the School of Language and Literature. He is the author of *Heidegger: Thought and Historicity* (Cornell UP, 1993), *Language and Relation: ... that there is language* (Stanford UP, 1996), *Infant Figures* (Stanford UP, 2000) and *The Claim of Language: A Case for the Humanities* (University of Minnesota Press, 2004). These published volumes contain an extended engagement with the work of Blanchot.

Kevin Hart is the Edwin B. Kyle Professor of Christian Studies at the University of Virginia. He works in the Department of Religious Studies and the Department of English. He is most recently the author of *The Dark Gaze: Maurice Blanchot and the Sacred* (Chicago UP, 2004), and *Postmodernism: A Beginner's Guide* (Oneworld, 2003), co-editor (with Geoffrey Hartman) of *The Power of Contestation: Perspectives on Maurice Blanchot* (Johns Hopkins UP, 2004) and editor of *Counter-Experiences: Reading Jean-Luc Marion* (Notre Dame UP, 2007). His selected poems, *Flame Tree*, appeared with Bloodaxe Books in 2004.

Leslie Hill is Professor of French Studies at the University of Warwick and the author of *Beckett's Fiction: In Different Words* (CUP, 1990), *Marguerite Duras: Apocalyptic Desires* (Routledge, 1993), *Blanchot: Extreme Contemporary* (Routledge, 1997), *Bataille, Klossowski, Blanchot: Writing at the Limit* (OUP, 2001), and *The Cambridge Introduction to Jacques Derrida* (CUP, 2007). He is also co-editor (with Brian Nelson and Dimitris Vardoulakis) of *After Blanchot: Literature, Philosophy, Criticism* (University of Delaware Press, 2005), and is currently completing two books: *Radical Indecision: Barthes, Blanchot, Derrida and the Future of Criticism*, dealing with the neuter and the undecidable, and *A Change of Epoch: Maurice Blanchot, Writing, the Fragmentary*, which proposes a reading of fragmentary writing in Blanchot's work.

Michael Holland is a Fellow of St Hugh's College, Oxford, where he teaches French literature. He is the editor of *The Blanchot Reader* (Blackwell, 1995), and the author of numerous essays on Blanchot's work which have appeared both in journals and in collective volumes. He is currently working on a book entitled *About Time*, which will be a study of narrative and time in Blanchot's fiction.

Jean-Luc Nancy is Emeritus Professor of Philosophy at the Université Marc Bloch, Strasbourg, and the author of more than fifty books in the area of philosophy, aesthetics, and politics, many of which engage directly and indirectly with the work of Blanchot, including most notably *The Inoperative Community* (Minnesota UP, 1991), *Multiple Arts* (Stanford UP, 2006), and *Dis-Enclosure: The Deconstruction of Christianity* (Fordham UP, 2007).

Index:
Paragraph 30 (2007)

JAMES N. AGAR
Self-mourning in *Paradise*: Writing (about)
AIDS through death-bed Delirium   **30: 1**, 67–84

NEREA ARRUTI
Tracing the past: Marcelo Brodsky's
photography as memory art   **30: 1**, 101–20

NEREA ARRUTI
Trauma, Therapy and Representation: Theory
and Critical Reflection   **30: 1**, 1–8

CHRISTOPHE BIDENT
R/M, 1953   **30: 3**, 67–83

MAURICE BLANCHOT
Responses and Interventions (1946–98)   **30: 3**, 5–45

JENNY CHAMARETTE
Flesh, Folds and Texturality: Thinking Visual
Ellipsis via Merleau-Ponty, Hélène Cixous and
Robert Frank   **30: 2**, 34–49

TIMOTHY CLARK
A Green Blanchot: Impossible?   **30: 3**, 121–140

CAROLIN DUTTLINGER
New Perspectives on Walter Benjamin   **30: 2**, 98–108

CHRISTOPHER FYNSK
Blanchot in *The International Review*   **30: 3**, 104–120

KEVIN HART
From the Star to the Disaster   **30: 3**, 84–103

LESLIE HILL
'Not In Our Name': Blanchot,
Politics, the Neuter   **30: 3**, 141–159

LESLIE HILL AND MICHAEL HOLLAND
Introduction   **30: 3**, 1–2

MARIAN HOBSON
In Memoriam Malcolm McNaughtan Bowie
1943–2007 **30: 2**, 117–119

MICHAEL HOLLAND
The Time of his Life **30: 3**, 46–66

RICHARD KEARNEY
Narrating pain: The power of catharsis **30: 1**, 51–66

HECTOR KOLLIAS
Taking Sides: Jacques Rancière and Agonistic
Literature **30: 2**, 82–97

JEREMY F. LANE **30: 2**, 109–116
Deleuze in and out of this World

NIKOLAJ LÜBECKER
The Dedramatization of Violence in Claire
Denis's *I Can't Sleep* **30: 2**, 17–33

JEAN-LUC NANCY
Maurice Blanchot, 1907–2003 **30: 3**, 3–4

BOB PLANT
On Testimony, Sincerity and Truth **30: 1**, 30–50

SUSANNAH RADSTONE
Trauma Theory: Contexts, Politics, Ethics **30: 1**, 9–29

FRÉDÉRIC REGARD
Derrida Un-Cut: Cixous's Art of Hearts **30: 2**, 1–16

AUDREY SMALL
The Duty of Memory: A solidarity of voices
after the Rwandan genocide **30: 1**, 85–100

ELI SORENSEN
Postcolonial Melancholia **30: 2**, 65–81

CHRISTOPHER WATKIN
A Different Alterity: Jean-Luc Nancy's
'Singular Plural' **30: 2**, 50–64

Conference in honour of Malcolm Bowie

The Editors of *Paragraph* are pleased to give advance notice of a day conference to honour the memory of Malcolm Bowie as founding member of the Modern Critical Theory Group and of the journal. Amongst his many other achievements, Malcolm was a key figure in the development of critical theory in the UK. The conference will be held on Saturday, 2 February 2008 (10.30am–6.30pm) at the IGRS, Stewart House, London. Speakers will be:

Rachel Bowlby
Celia Britton
Owen Heathcote
Leslie Hill
Marian Hobson
Christina Howells
Ann Jefferson
Christopher Prendergast
Naomi Segal
Anne-Marie Smith
Michael Worton

For catering purposes please register in advance by emailing IGRS@sas.ac.uk. There will be a vegetarian buffet lunch and a wine reception at 6.30pm.

symplokē

editor-in-chief
Jeffrey R. Di Leo

associate editor
Ian Buchanan

advisory board
Charles Altieri
Michael Bérubé
Ronald Bogue
Matei Calinescu
Edward Casey
Stanley Corngold
Lennard Davis
Robert Con Davis
Henry Giroux
Karen Hanson
Phillip Brian Harper
Peter C. Herman
Candace Lang
Vincent B. Leitch
Paisley Livingston
Donald Marshall
Christian Moraru
Jeffrey Nealon
Marjorie Perloff
Mark Poster
Gerald Prince
Joseph Ricapito
Robert Scholes
Alan Schrift
Tobin Siebers
Hugh Silverman
John H. Smith
Paul M. Smith
James Sosnoski
Henry Sussman
Mark Taylor
S. Tötösy de Zepetnek
Joel Weinsheimer
Jeffrey Williams

submissions
Editor, symplokē
School of Arts and Sciences
University of Houston-Victoria
Victoria, TX 77901-5731
email editor@symploke.org

subscriptions
University of Nebraska Press
1111 Lincoln Mall
Lincoln, NE 68588-0630

www.symploke.org

a journal for the intermingling of literary, cultural and theoretical scholarship

symplokē is a comparative theory and literature journal. Our aim is to provide an arena for critical exchange between established and emerging voices in the field. We support new and developing notions of comparative literature, and are committed to interdisciplinary studies, intellectual pluralism, and open discussion. We are particularly interested in scholarship on the interrelations among philosophy, literature, culture criticism and intellectual history, though will consider articles on any aspect of the intermingling of discourses and disciplines.

forthcoming issues
GAMING AND THEORY ❧ DISCOURAGEMENT
CINEMA WITHOUT BORDERS ❧ ANONYMITY

past issues
FICTION'S PRESENT ❧ GLOBALISM AND THEORY
PRACTICING DELEUZE & GUATTARI
AFFILIATION ❧ THEORY TROUBLE
ANTHOLOGIES ❧ SITES OF PEDAGOGY
RHETORIC & THE HUMAN SCIENCES
COLLEGIALITY

some past & future contributors
Michael Apple on doing critical educational work
Peter Baker on deconstruction and violence
Michael Bernard-Donals on liberatory pedagogy
Ronald Bogue on minor literature
Frederick Buell on globalization and environmentalism
Matei Calinescu on modernity and modernization
Peter Caws on sophistry and postmodernity
Claire Colebrook on happiness, theoria, and everyday life
David Damrosch on world literature anthologies
Samuel R. Delany on fiction's present
Elizabeth Ellsworth on pedagogy and the holocaust museum
Brian Evenson on fiction and philosophy
Caryl Emerson on berlin, bakhtin and relativism
John Frow on terror and cultural studies
Elizabeth Grosz on the future in deleuze
Alphonso Lingis on bestiality
Cris Mazza on postfeminist literature
John Mowitt on queer resistance
David Palumbo-Liu on asian america and the imaginary
Marjorie Perloff on poetry and affiliation
Steven Shaviro on the sublime
David Shumway on disciplinary identities
John Smith on queering the will
William V. Spanos on humanism after 9/11
Allen Stoekl on the holocaust
Jeffrey Williams on the posttheory generation
Ewa Ziarek on foucault's ethics

please enter my one-year subscription (two issues) to *symplokē*
❏ Individuals: $20   ❏ Institutions: $40   Add $15 for subscriptions outside the U.S.

Name		
Address		Apt.
City	State	Zip

2000 CELJ PHOENIX AWARD FOR SIGNIFICANT EDITORIAL ACHIEVEMENT

PRODUCED AND DISTRIBUTED IN ASSOCIATION WITH THE UNIVERSITY OF NEBRASKA PRESS

JOURNALS FROM EUP

Edinburgh University Press publishes more than 30 scholarly journals a year in a range of subject areas covering the arts, humanities, social sciences and science:

SUBJECT AREAS

- African Studies
- Historical Studies
- Islamic Studies
- Linguistics
- Literary Studies
- Media Studies
- Philosophy and Religion
- Politics and Law
- Science and Medical
- Scottish Studies

Full details at **www.eup.ed.ac.uk**

- Browse content lists
- Search our complete catalogue
- Order online
- View every issue of every journal (2008)

Edinburgh University Press, 22 George Square, Edinburgh, EH8 9LF, UK
journals@eup.ed.ac.uk

EU Authorised Representative:
Easy Access System Europe Mustamäe tee 50, 10621 Tallinn, Estonia
gpsr.requests@easproject.com

Printed and bound by CPI Group (UK) Ltd, Croydon, CR0 4YY
22/03/2026
02076195-0003